ROAD BOWLING IN IRELAND

BRIAN TOAL

Compiled, written and published by Brian Toal
on behalf of the Ulster Branch of
Bol Chumann Na hEireann.

First published in 1996 by
Brian Toal, Armagh City, Ireland.

ACKNOWLEDGEMENTS

The author and publisher acknowledges with thanks the co-operation and assistance received from the following: Carol Burns, Portadown; Christy Santry, Carrigtwohill; Conal Hamill, Moy; Seamus O' Tuama, Carrigaline; Donald Gribben, Armagh; Tim O' Leary, Bandon; Paddy Haughian, Aghalee; Denis Mc Garry, Whitechurch; George Smith, Armagh; Michael McSweeny, Cork; Sean Gordon, Armagh; Harold Ford, Portadown; John Gribben, Armagh; Peadar Tunney, Westport; Paddy Smyth, Keenaghan; Aidan McVeigh, Armagh; Staff of the Irish Studies Library, Armagh City; Local History Library, Omagh, Co. Tyrone; and Central Library, Belfast.

ISBN 0 9527596 0 8.

Cover photographs by Denis McGarry, Whitechurch, Cork.

Printed in Ireland by
R. & S. Printers Ltd.,
The Diamond,
Monaghan.

The author and publisher, in association with the Ulster Branch of Bol Chumann na hEireann, acknowledges with gratitude the generosity of the undermentioned benefactor in sponsoring this book.

PHILIP WHITE TYRES LIMITED
STATION ROAD INDUSTRIAL ESTATE
LOUGHGALL ROAD,
ARMAGH
BT61 7NP
Tel: 01861 510666. Fax 01861 522529.

Philip White Tyres Limited is now established as one of the most successful wholesale and retail tyre sales specialists in Ireland.

The thriving business in Armagh City was established in 1982 by Philip White who had the vision and determination to develop a strong innovative capability that has seen the firm progress from the initial retail outlet to a company which combines this flourishing market with that of a very comprehensive wholesale trading strategy.

The rapid expansion of the business resulted in Philip White Tyres acquiring additional premises to accommodate a natural progression into the truck and commercial market to be later followed by investment in the agricultural and earthmover tyre markets.

Today Philip White Tyres are sole agents for a wide range of tyre brands as well as key distributors for a most extensive range of tyre manufacturers. Based on the principles of good service and fair prices the firm now has a planned distribution service throughout Ireland thus ensuring a prompt response to customer needs.

Philip White's association with the sport of road bowls extends beyond even that of his apprenticeship to the tyre business. A keen follower of the game for many years he has been a valued sponsor to the sport over the same period. His patronage of the 1995 All-Ireland Championships was enhanced at the end of that year with further financial backing for the specific promotion of youth involvement in the sport. The initial response to this development has been phenomenal.

The confirmation, in 1996, of Philip White Tyres as sponsor for the book, *Road Bowling in Ireland,* further demonstrates the firms profound commitment to the sport.

All proceeds deriving from the sale of this book shall go directly to Bol Chumann for the promotion and development of road bowls as a national and international sport.

Brian Toal, who was born at Tirgarve, Armagh on 1st June 1940, was a founder member of Grange road bowls club in 1958 and later became Honorary Secretary to the Northern Branch of Bol Chumann Na hEireann for the period from 1963 until 1968. He was a member of the northern delegation at a historic meeting in Bandon, Co Cork, on Easter Sunday 14th April 1963 when agreement was reached to institute the All- Ireland road bowls championships. In his professional capacity as a nurse tutor he founded *Nursing News* in 1982 and was managing editor of the quarterly publication until his retirement in 1994. During the late fifties and throughout the sixties he was road bowls correspondent for the *Armagh Observer*, the *Tyrone Democrat,* and the *Ulster Gazette.* In more recent years he occasionally contributed on the sport to the national daily newspaper, the *Irish News.* He has also written on aspects of the game for journals and official programmes and brings to this, his first such publication, a richness of personal experience gained through an enduring association with the sport.

Foreword
by Seamus O'Tuama

Recently a friend of mine remarked that bowling inhabits an almost secret world. For bowlers that sounds like a strange assertion, but it does have more than a grain of truth. It is surprising that a sport which is played in the most public of arenas – the public highway – should be seen in such a light. The benefits of publicity have been slow to emerge, but attempts to record its history have been even fewer. It may be easier to understand this reticence when one considers that bowling was deemed to be illegal well into this century. But the new air of confidence pervading Irish life and Irish sport has spilled through to road bowling too. In Cork people like Flor Crowley and Eamonn O'Carroll began to push out the frontiers with their contributions to the press over 40 years ago. In the 1960's Brian Toal continued the process in Armagh. There have been many scribes since and even a few historians, but no bowling book to date is as comprehensive as Brian Toal's *Road Bowling in Ireland.* From here on bowling will be less of a secret sport, and its contribution to the intricate tapestry of Irish sporting life can begin to be realised.

This is truly an encyclopaedia of the game of road bowling in Ireland. Readers who have little or no knowledge of the game will have a clear grasp of all the key essentials when they finish reading it. Brian Toal's easy, accessible style will make sure your journey along this literary bowling road is as enjoyable as the sport itself. All the high points in the recent history of bowling are visited. The fact that *Road Bowling in Ireland* is written by an expert makes it certain that what you will find between these covers is both informative and accurate.

One could not hope for a better qualified guide to the sport. Brian's father Michael was steeped in the tradition and played bullets (bowling) until he was in his seventies. The Toal family home was a bowling house. From his earliest years Brian would have heard of all the great scores and all the great bowlers in living memory. The Toal home, just a few metres from the Blackwatertown Road, was a Mecca for bowlers. They met there to discuss and arrange scores, and maybe even to discuss and arrange other things, once the inevitable céilí got under way.

In later years his brother Aidan would go on to lift the Ulster senior crown. In turn his niece Róisín Toal would win the senior women's championship and her brother Michael would carry the family name to even greater fame. He became the youngest All-Ireland senior champion in history when he won the title at Tassagh in 1988. He is the only player to date to win under-18 and Senior crowns back-to-back. But this is not a eulogy of famous relatives. Brian too has a distinguished pedigree in bowling. He never achieved the playing might of Aidan or Michael, but he created his own niche as an administrator and chronicler par excellence.

He founded the Grange club in 1958, and went on to become Honorary Secretary of Ból-Chumann Armagh in 1963. Together with his close friend, Henry Neary (Chairman) he helped establish the solid foundations for the successful Ulster branch. Naturally he was in Cork in 1963 at the historic meeting in Bandon which set the first official All-Ireland championships in train. He reaped his reward a few months later on the Moy Road when Ulster's Danny McParland won the first senior title. During his time as Secretary he also took on the role of correspondent for bowling in Ulster. He regularly contributed to *The Irish News, Armagh Observer, Ulster Gazette, and Tyrone Democrat.* He continued as Secretary until 1968, but the pressure of a very successful professional career forced him to vacate the hot seat. He never loosed his grip on bowling though.

In his professional career he went on to become a Nurse Tutor. Again his keen intellect and boundless energy brought benefits to his fellow professionals. He founded the *Nursing News* in 1982 and acted as its managing editor from then until 1994. He retired or maybe took a sabbatical in 1994. Since then he has been busy researching and writing *Road Bowling in Ireland.*

For the initiated *Road Bowling in Ireland* will resonate with famous names and famous scores. Legends like Hammerman Donnelly and Timmy Delaney, Red Crowley and Joe McVeigh come to life under his pen. From there you are quickly reacquainted with Mick Barry, Danny McParland, Aidan Toal, Denis Scully and a Who's Who of bowling legends. It does not end there though. He continues his exploration into contemporary bowling dominated by players like Michael Toal, Pat Butler, Bill Daly, Harry Toal Jnr. and James Buckley. And for the first time women bowlers find their rightful place in an account of bowling too. It highlights players like Gretta Hegarty-Cormican, Róisín Toal-Mackle, and emerging stars like Sharon O'Driscoll, Geraldine McCluskey, Susan Cullen, and Kathleen Cooney.

For the uninitiated this is the key to the door of the secret world. After reading *Road Bowling in Ireland* you will be able to take your place among the aficionados on any bowling road in Ireland and even in the outposts of London and Boston. You will have an intimate knowledge of all aspects of the sport from All-Ireland championships to the World Championships; from King of the Roads to An Ból-Fada. And this is no bluffer's guide, this is the authentic article, written by one of the acknowledged authorities of road bowling.

I am sure all readers will derive as much pleasure from reading it as Brian Toal patently did from researching it. His dedication and attention to detail make *Road Bowling in Ireland* essential reading for anyone interested in bowling and bowlers.

Séamus Ó Tuama.

Séamus Ó Tuama has been the Cork Examiner bowling correspondent since the late 1980's. He is a former secretary of Ból-Chumann na hÉireann. He was secretary of the International Bowlplaying Association for the 9th European Bowling Championships in Cork in 1992. He is also closely associated with King of the Roads which he helped found in 1985.

Contents

A Perspective

Bowling, Bullets, Bowl Playing or Road Bowls. The terms are synonymous to ardent followers of the sport. But to the uninitiated the variation in descriptive terminology serves to generate intrigue with a competitive game which is unique in its history, tradition, style, and proven capacity to survive social and cultural changes of passing generations.

The sport is played with a 28oz (793.8 grms) solid iron bowl the circumference of which is approximately 18 centimetres. Two contestants match their individual skills in throwing the bowl with optimum speed, controlled delivery, and intentional accuracy along a carefully considered and tactically selected play-path over a predetermined course distance of normal roadway. The winner is the player to reach the finishing line in the least number of throws or shots. Course distances vary in accordance with the nature of the contest, but nowadays are usually around four kilometres in length.

A score, or a match, between two road bowlers may be watched by anything from several dozen spectators to many thousands, depending on the importance of the event and the attraction of the particular pairing involved. And spectators find lots to enthuse about over the entire course as every single shot can have a significant bearing on the outcome, the result of which is often wagered upon for substantial amounts.

Several notable bowling courses exist in counties Armagh and Cork where the sport is most prevalent. The courses are, in effect, lengthy sections of curving, undulating public highway, but to the bowling fraternity they comprise a specific course

The solid iron bowl.

A typical bowling course — The renowned Knappagh Road near Armagh City.

The Road Bowling Scene : Attentive spectators, competitor markings, selected play path, distant road shower, rapid delivery, bowl in transit, and the Ulster style of delivery. Geraldine McCluskey, Armagh, releases the bowl during the 1992 All-Ireland Women's Senior Championship Final at Ballingeary, Co. Cork.
Photo : Denis McGarry

distance with virtually every hill and bend precisely named for easy reference when coaching instructions are being given or particular events recollected. Each course has a recognised par for the distance, and established records exist for best performances from starting line to the finish. Similar courses now exist in counties Tyrone, Limerick, Louth, Wexford, Mayo - even London - and though the emergence of the sport in these areas can be traced to experienced bowlers having settled there, it is nonetheless remarkable that a sizeable proportion of the local population have cultivated a keen interest in the sport.

In the last twenty-five years considerable success has been achieved in establishing formal organisational links, and sustained sporting relationships, with exponents of similar games in Holland and Germany. A series of International Championships has been conducted in each of these countries. Ireland had the honour of hosting the ninth European Bowling Championships in Cork City in 1992 and the first ever International Bowling festival in the north was held in Armagh City in 1994.

The sport of Road Bowls, largely because of its uniqueness, has attracted intermittent media attention and coverage from foreign, as well as national, press, radio and television. The sheer popularity of the game locally has ensured a consistent provincial newspaper focus and major sponsors are now keen to be publicly associated with the sport which has enhanced funding and prestige for the organising body. A prestigious annual sponsored award offers due recognition to those players or mentors who, over the years, are acknowledged as having made a formidable contribution to Road Bowls.

The sport has now progressed to a level which encompasses men's and women's national championship competitions, in a total of twelve different grades, spanning players under fourteen years, through intermediate and senior ranks, to veteran and even vintage years.

So, back to those terms synonymous with the name of the sport! Bullets was the descriptive term which prevailed in the north for many generations, and for that reason it is unlikely to ever totally disappear. Bowl playing was the name prevalent in the south throughout that same period and is still sometimes used. However, in 1963, when the first formal amalgamation of the two organisations occurred, and the All-Ireland championship competitions were launched, the respective press officers and newspaper correspondents tended to ease towards closer similarity in descriptive terms. Thus the name Bowls entered the sports sections in northern provincial newspapers and, not being without some ambiguity in identity, later became the more definitive and now well established term of Road Bowls. Bowling is the term currently used almost exclusively in the south and the prevailing variation in description poses no problem for the growing number of followers in any part of the country.

In this book it is intended to reflect the last half century in the game of Road Bowls and, inevitably, there will be reference to significant evolvement from earlier periods in the history of this exhilarating pastime and competitive sport.

Australian television crew recording the Ulster Road Bowls Championship Finals at Armagh on 2nd July, 1995.

Perfecting his accuracy is promising young bowler of 1995, Padraig Scanlon, Carrignavar, Co. Cork.
Photo: Denis McGarry.

Origins of the Sport

If one were to consult at random with a representative sample of the sizeable following at any particular score of Road Bowls, about the precise origin of the game in which they participate so actively and enjoy so much, few would respond with alacrity or indeed offer a considered definitive opinion. Those who do will almost certainly have availed of the excellent research undertaken more than twenty years ago by Dermot Hicks (1973) for his book *"Road Bowls in Armagh"* and Fr Raymond Murray (1976) in his follow-up publication, *"The Armagh Bullet Thrower"*.

A 'road-shower' in the distance as spectators await the shot in a 1995 championship score at Dunderrow, Co. Cork.

Monsignor Raymond Murray.
Photo : Irish News

Fr Raymond Murray came to the parish of Armagh as a young priest in 1967 and very soon afterwards developed a keen interest in the sport of Road Bowls. He was later to become President of the bowls association, the Northern Branch, An Bol Chumann Na hEireann, and continues to fulfil that office with undiminished interest and unceasing commitment. Dr Murray gained a PhD in Celtic Studies in 1993 and is presently Parish Priest in the South Derry parish of Ardtrea (Moneymore) having gone there in 1995. In July of that year he was conferred with the title Monsignor.

In the main, most followers of Road Bowls are quite content to merely maintain the tradition through nurturing the game that has always been a significant aspect of the sporting and cultural environment in which they live. They too have experienced the inculcation of that rich source - their own, and immediately preceding, generation - in perpetuating a traditional sport which has survived possibly several centuries. The fact that the game was played and enjoyed by previous generations, and that many champions of the past are revered in legend, is reason enough for them to be attracted to the sport and to uphold its tradition.

Not so with Monsignor Murray though! As a noted historian it was unlikely he would settle for anything less than a painstakingly thorough search for the origins of the sport. His extensive work on the subject is probably the most frequently quoted resource when earlier reference to the game is being sought. The Very Reverend Raymond Murray unearthed several theories on the origin and history of the sport, all of which are credible, but none of them necessarily conclusive. He was of the opinion that the sport appeared to be quite widespread in the eighteenth and nineteenth centuries being played, in some form or other, in Armagh, Derry, Cork, Down, Tyrone, Louth, Antrim, Tipperary, and at some time, in areas such as Carlow, Wexford, Cavan and Monaghan.

One theory proffered by Monsignor Murray is that the sport came to this country with Dutch soldiers when William of Orange came to Ireland in 1689. The relatively recent renewal of sporting contacts and revived bowling competition between Ireland and Holland, in Road Bowls and Moor Bowls, could lend further credence to that particular theory.

Another theory, and possibly the one most favoured by present day followers of the sport, is that the game came to Ireland through linen workers from east Yorkshire and west Lancashire in the North of England. The game was once popular in those regions and drew its main support from people employed in the mills. Monsignor Murray discovered several historical references which confirmed the game of Bullets as a traditional pastime and sport for weavers. The theory that Bullets came to Ireland with English immigrant weavers is supported by the close connections Cork and Armagh fostered through the linen trade and these two counties remain the stronghold of a growing and popular minority sport.

It is generally accepted that local history is the real basis of National history and, in that context, the numerous historical references to the sport of Bowling, Bullets, Bowl Playing Road Bowls, or indeed Long Bullets, have special relevance.

Monsignor Raymond Murray has ensured that the sport, whatever title it is given, is an enduring feature of National history.

Antecedent to Formal Organisation

The ordered, controlled and disciplined way in which Road Bowls is now administered in all areas where the game is played is the fulfilment of a tremendous sense of obligation to the leaders of the past who endeavoured to achieve such a structured management of the sport.

There had always been some form of loose organisation, north and south, through which the game endured but this was often ad hoc and haphazard. The consequences of such intermittent and unco-ordinated organisational control were not only a lack of clearly defined rules and properly constituted competitions but the frequent emergence of unaffiliated groups embarking upon unilateral organisation without being accountable to any recognised body or supreme authority.

The undesirability of such circumstances was evident to all true followers of the sport and none more so than those genuine enthusiasts who set about taking the necessary steps towards ensuring proper organisation. The desired outcome was clearly defined but the protracted process was a formidable one. Sustained efforts were made to gradually permeate the entire bowling domain with representative groups or clubs accountable to an executive body.

The men of the south were first to succeed in establishing proper organisational control. The need was greater there as the geographical region to be encompassed was so vast. The north was soon to follow though as the need was equally urgent even if the difficulties were of a lesser magnitude. That the game of Road Bowls endured, and the image of the sport continued to enhance throughout this necessary transition, is a measure of the calibre of the many fine sportsmen and leaders involved.

In Armagh the sport will forever remain indebted to men like Dan Gribben, a superb bowler and later administrator; Dan Mackle, a life long organiser and enthusiast for the sport; George McKenna, one time Chairman and persistent advocate; Henry Molloy, a committed follower and administrator; Joe Houlahan, a former Chairman and renowned bowls correspondent for local newspapers; Jim McAneney, long term and efficient Secretary to the northern administration; Joe Horan, a constant organiser, one time chairman and subsequent special award recipient; John Coulter, a thoroughly reliable organiser; Sean Moore, a stylish and competent player, and for many years a committed and popular administrator; Kevin Doyle, long term administrator and former Secretary; Dixie O'Neill, a consistent promoter and one- time-Secretary; Patsy McCoy, a practical organiser and dedicated official, and Joe Lappin, a keen advocate who contributed significantly to the positive development of the sport.

In the south it was former great bowler, Flor Crowley, Dunmanway, and later of Bandon, in county Cork, along with another superb bowl player, one time county

Flor Crowley.

Sean Moore.

Dan Mackle.

Dan Gribben.

hurler, and competent golfer, Eamon O'Carroll from Ballygarvan, and later Farran, who were to spearhead the emergence of a recognised authority with ultimate control of the sport. It was an essential development, and these two men, along with fellow Cork patrons of bowling Hugh O'Neill, Denis McSweeney, Donal Moynihan, Dermot Buckley, James McCarthy, Tom Ahern and Neally Warren had the wisdom and foresight to build upon the earlier administrative efforts of those such as Jim Cadden and Jimmy Deane in setting up what was originally named the All-Ireland Bowl Players Association but shortly afterwards reformed as An Bol Chumann Na hEireann, the efficient and effective organisation that it remains today.

These are the people, north and south who, without the formal mechanism of a structured organisation were able, through commitment and personal sacrifice, to bring Road Bowls onto a new plane which saw co-ordinated competition, amenable sponsorship, greater press coverage and increased attendances. It was such leadership that enabled many of the inter- provincial scores in the pre All-Ireland championship era to be organised with such aplomb, and completed with abounding satisfaction.

The historic meeting to form An Bol Chumann Na hEireann was held in Enniskeane, West Cork in 1954 and the positive influence of those southern pioneers promoted standards which have permeated the sport ever since. Clearly defined rules were devised and produced in booklet form to act as precise guidance to all affiliated club members and registered players in their obligation to comply with the regulations.

The initial objective of Bol-Chumann was to organise a senior championship in the south and the final of that inaugural competition in 1954 was won by Waterfall player Liam O'Keefe against Ned Barry. The north, with a lesser membership and a much smaller area to manage, succeeded in organising and completing their first championship in 1953 when the formidable Joe McVeigh came through to beat another great Armagh sportsman Johnny Mitchell.

The framework was now in place, north and south, for progressive and co-ordinated management of the sport. In the intervening years, prior to establishing the All-Ireland Championship series in 1963, the methods of organisation grew closer, objectives became synonymous, standards began to merge, and official bonds were forged. Amalgamation on an All-Ireland basis was now, not only desirable, but inevitable.

Preceding the Championship Era

The names of many great bowlers of the past are often recollected with intense pride but, regrettably, they are recorded as champions without portfolio because their glory years preceded the championship era. Many of them would, undoubtedly, now grace the roll of honour as All-Ireland champion of their time and grade had only the opportunity to contest such an event then existed.

The game had many quality players who, at their peak, would have earned such recognition. In the north the outstanding players during the era preceding the National Championships included Peter Donnelly, Dan Gribben, Jimmy Smith, Francie Starr, Jim Macklin, Joe Cullen, Jim Curran, Hugh Murtagh, Pat Coulter, Frank Donnelly, Johnny Rafferty, Paddy O'Neill, Gerald Ward, Barney Grimley, Jimmy Moore, Tommy Toal, Peter McGleenan, Eddie McKenna, Johnny Darragh, Geordie McKenna, Barney Rafferty, Joe Horan, Mosie Daly, Pat Lyttle, Pat Donnelly, Paul Feighan, Johnny McParland, Harry Donnelly, Andy Mallon, Harry Macklin, Johnny Mitchell, Bill George, Tom McGlone, Mick Toal, Paddy Kirk Mallon, Johnny Oliver, Terence Toal, Whitey Fegan, Eddie McCoy, Pat Campbell, Pat McCormack, Jackie McCarthy, James Smith, Seamus Mackle, Sean Moore, Harry Toal, Mick Reilly, Oliver O'Neill, Danny Reilly, Barney McBride, Joe McVeigh and perhaps even many more.

In the south, the glory days of bowling belonged to such redoubtable exponents as Bill Bennett, John Buck McGrath, Michael McCarthy-Quirke, Jer O'Driscoll,

Denny Murphy, Bandon, in an exhibition score at Tipperary in 1957.

Jimmy Mahon, Geordie Bennett, Denis 'Sonny' O'Leary, Mick Deasy, Dan McAulliffe, Eddie Healy, Tim McCarthy, Red Crowley, Tim Delaney, Mick O'Driscoll, Jim Hurley, Patsy Goggin, Jim O'Mahoney, Donald Forde, Eamon Sweeney, Dan Hurley, Eamon O'Carroll, Donal O'Leary, Tim Crowley, Tom Sweeney, Teadna Buckley, Paddy Murphy, 'Tiger' Aherne, Tadgh Drew, Con Keane, Tim Crowley, Flor Crowley, Donie 'Buzzer' O'Sullivan, Mick Cumain, Neilly Duggan, Dan Grady, Owen Egan, Scotty Leonard, Eugene Daly, Des O'Leary, Mickey Brien, Larry Duggan, Jack Riordan, Timmy Jack Donoghue, Lar Calnan, Jim O'Leary, Brendan Donovan, Felix Connolly, Laith Rice, Block Coleman, John Buckley, Liam O'Keefe, Seanie Allen, Jack O'Driscoll, Jackie Murphy, P J O'Mahony, Denny Murphy, Tim O'Donoghue, Mick Murphy, and many others in the decidedly competitive realm of southern bowling.

That was a period too during which many inter-provincial scores took place and though some of these were officially planned and organised within the role and responsibility of the administrative bodies which then existed, others were not, and consequently the urgent need for adequate control and discipline was further emphasised.

In the early days of Armagh and Cork contests in senior road bowls it was the much admired Peter Donnelly, Armagh who lost to the great Tim Delaney, Fairhill, in 1928 and again to another Munster idol, Red Crowley, Bandon, in 1932, both events over the Knappagh course near Armagh.

Then it was that great contest between Northern champion Joe McVeigh, Armagh, and Cork phenomenon Mick Barry over Armagh's Knappagh road on 12th September 1954. Thousands watched the event as Barry proceeded to set up a new record for the course, at the time, in scoring the finishing line with his 23rd shot. McVeigh, who had often covered the course with ease in 25 shots, was well below his usual form in taking all of 27 throws in that particular score.

The undaunted Joe McVeigh was back in inter-provincial action once again in 1955 when, on the 18th September, he played Denny Murphy, Bandon, over the Moy road near Armagh. Murphy had a 20 metre lead on the last shot and won fairly comfortably on the bowl over the line.

A score between Harry Toal, Armagh and Tom O'Neill, Cork drew a big crowd to a neutral venue at Knockbridge, Co Louth on 13th November 1955. Toal was twice in the lead but lost on the last shot by 40 metres. Success for the south continued for a time in inter-provincial scores as Joe McVeigh went down twice to Liam O'Keefe, Waterfall, in 1954 and again in 1955. But it was the irrepressible Joe McVeigh who was to record the first win over a southern opponent when he produced a faultless display of fast and accurate bowling, at Cloghroe, County Cork, in 1956, to easily beat the great Mick Barry and set up a new record for the course before more than 3,000 spectators.

In the same year Armagh's Mick Reilly gained a hard earned victory over Cork's Con Desmond, Inniscarra, but lost to Owen Healy at Westport, Co Mayo in 1959. It was the turn of the current Munster senior champion, Johnny Creedon, Clondrohid, to travel north in 1961 for a clash with the rapidly emerging, Danny McParland, Armagh, on Easter Sunday, 2nd April, in a spectacular score over the

At Blarney in 1956 for a bowling score were Mick Reilly, Armagh (left) and his mentors, Paddy McAneney and John Coulter.

Armagh players and officials relaxing at Blarney Castle before the start of two inter-provincial scores in 1956 involving Harry Toal (back left) and Mick Reilly (front centre). Also included are (back row) Francie Rafferty, Patsy McCoy, Jack Ryan and (front row) Joe Horan, Paddy McAneney and Tommy English.

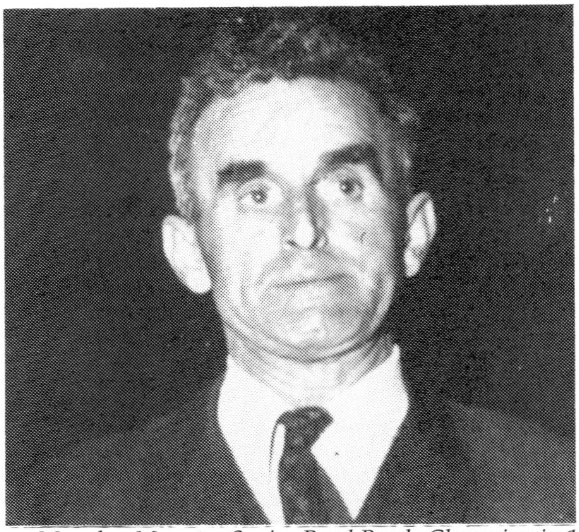

Denny Murphy, Munster Senior Road Bowls Champion in 1957.

Moy road. Creedon dropped behind initially, then almost drew level after 18 shots, but in a blistering finish McParland pulled away for a two shot win. The dynamic McParland was to add further inter-provincial wins that year over the left handed champion from Bandon, Donie Lehane whilst Armagh's Danny Reilly shared the spoils in absorbing contests with Denny Murphy, the 1957 Munster senior champion.

Those earlier, and indeed subsequent, inter-provincial scores had always intensified spectator interest in the sport and inevitably attracted the curious and the unacquainted. In the months prior to the big Barry-McVeigh clash in 1954 the *"Armagh Observer"* sent a reporter to a score of bowls to inform uninitiated readers about the nature of the sport. Here is an extract from his report:

> *A score is the technical term applied to a bowling match, a legacy of the days when a match was regularised at 20 bowls or throws from which we still have the expression - 'a score of bowls'.*
>
> *The bowl pronounced to rhyme with 'owl' - is handed to you, a 28oz perfectly round ball of crude iron, deceptively simple to throw, until you try it, and then, unless you have grown up with a bowl in your hand, you will find that smooth controlled run in, the open rapid underhand swing; the exact synchronisation of foot and arm action so essential to good bowling; you will find these exceptionally difficult to master if you have not mastered them as a boy. They look easy when performed by an expert.*
>
> *If you follow the score to the finish you will see that, though a player's supporters may shout for him and encourage him, it is his arm and his skill that must direct the bowl and his courage that must fight out a hard finish to the last trying throw of the day.*

Those bowling experts who preceded the championship era have served the sport exceptionally well with their skill, courage, and tenacious finishing.

Historic Organisational Development

It seemed rather odd that, even by 1961, when there had already been many inter-provincial scores played out between the top bowlers of the time, north and south, there had, as yet, never been a championship decider which would determine the top bowler in Ireland.

The whole issue, however, was to gain an entirely new impetus following the publication of a comprehensive article on the subject in the *"Armagh Observer"* and *"Lurgan and Portadown Examiner"* on 16th September, 1961. The article entitled, "Bowlsmen look forward to All- Ireland Games", and written by pen-name 'BT', was accorded extensive space and a prominent position on the main sports page. In it, the author reviewed the inter-provincial scores to date and then posed the pertinent question as to when, if ever, the powers that be in northern bowling will challenge the right of the Waters Cup winner - the trophy awarded to the senior champion in the south - to claim the All-Ireland Senior Road Bowling title. The writer went on to maintain he was in no doubt that Bol Chumann in Cork would welcome an All-Ireland Final between the respective champions of north and south. The premise was based on the growing informal contacts which were initiated quite some time previously.

The frank and forthright article went on to state:

> *Each year the southern association determines their senior champion through a, championship which is organised with great earnestness and efficiency. It is in this respect that the Armagh men could take a lead and give us a similar championship every year; then, and only then, will general interest be restored and player pride renewed.*
>
> *The presently constituted tournament, with all due respect to the players involved, has little relevance to true form. Some rightly ask how a competition, which has taken twelve months, and sometimes even more, to run, and mingled with dozens of poor quality challenge scores could ever provide a true champion. While some suggestions might be made that Danny McParland be nominated to meet the Cork senior champion for the overall National title it must be emphasised that this arrangement would be unacceptable. Such a final must only derive from a properly constituted championship organised for the purpose of producing a legitimate champion each year. Sooner or later this aim must be achieved. Surely the time is right for the respective champions of north and south to meet for the All-Ireland title in what would certainly prove to be the greatest attraction on the bowl-playing calendar.*
>
> *Quite recently, Michael O'Heihir, whilst giving an outline on sports coverage he envisaged would be granted fair treatment when Irish television commences this year, mentioned bowl playing as "one of the small sports with limit-*

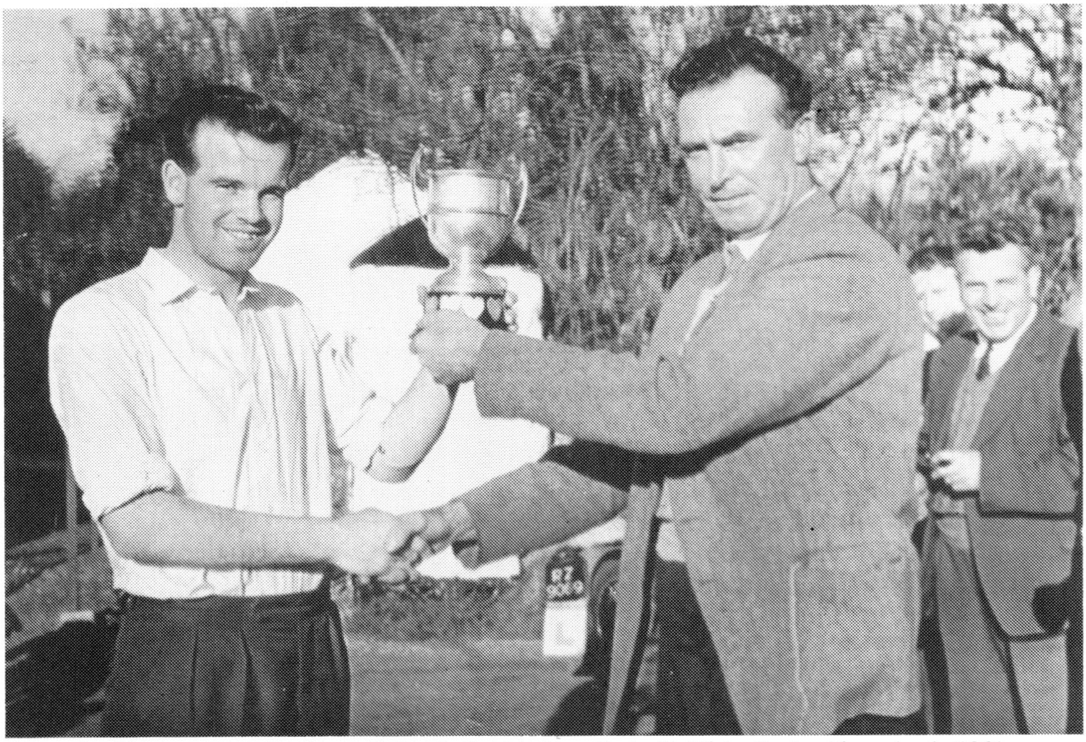

Joe Horan presents the 'Armagh Bowls Cup' to Sean Cartmill, Ulster Senior Champion in 1961.

ed spectator appeal" which would be included. It is high time that Armagh Bowls Association made a step in the right direction and organised the game on a more competitive basis. The fact that Danny McParland has achieved so much without the fillip of serious competition is a remarkable accomplishment in itself. His victories over Cork bowlers, Johnny Creedon, Denny Murphy and Donie Lehane places northern road bowls in a position never before enjoyed. To quote a prominent southern bowls reporter after McParland set up a new record for the Tinker's Cross, Bandon venue in the Lehane score last month, "... on this form he'll beat any Cork man on any road."

The article concluded with the hopeful speculation that bowling enthusiasts could envisage a Barry - McParland All-Ireland encounter should the Armagh man's present run of success continue unabated.

In little over a month after the article was published the senior championship concluded in Cork with Jackie Forde winning the Waters Cup against Dooley Lehane on 22nd October 1961 at Tinkers Cross near Bandon. In the same year up north it was Armagh city player Sean Cartmill who came through in the "Armagh Bowls Challenge Cup" when he beat Harry Toal. But yet there remained no provision for a National decider.

The campaign for change though was now unrelenting and in a follow-up article in Observer Newspapers on 11th November, 1961, the same author carried the argument further with a contribution headed, "Armagh and Cork to Unite for Bowls Championship". The article read as follows:

> *In a recent issue of this newspaper the prospect of an All-Ireland Bowling Championship was discussed at length. This development would necessitate the Armagh and Cork ruling bodies uniting to form an All-Ireland Executive Committee. This is the only solution if bowling is to become a nationally recognised sport. Counties like Mayo, Kilkenny, Limerick, Tipperary and Waterford, who take an active interest in the sport, would be given the necessary stimulus to promote bowling alongside the rest of our national games. Here in Armagh one can convincingly state that it has been the dream of all our past champions to win an All-Ireland title and indeed many would have been quite worthy of that honour. But it was not until about eight years ago that we have had any real organisation in the sport. This came in the form of an enthusiastic committee the members of which have since maintained the sport even if not necessarily attaining dynamic progress. The efforts have been pioneered by that grand exponent of the game, Joseph Horan, who by the sheer impact of his personality has managed to keep the organisation intact even though little headway has been made regarding All-Ireland competitions.*
>
> *The main northern obstacle to a uniting of the two bodies in Cork and Armagh will be the adoption of new rules which will require to be exactly the same as the existing set established and effected by An Bol Chumann in the south. It is absolutely essential that the one and same set of rules apply to the playing of all scores, north and south. Also necessary is the selection and appointment of three persons, capable of effectively representing the Northern Association on the Bol Chumann Executive Committee. A meeting of that body is due to take place early next year to discuss the admission of the northern section.*

The debate about change was by then gaining momentum and the discussion generated at club level by the whole issue added much needed impetus to the period preceding the Annual General Meeting of the Northern Association on 27th February, 1963.

At that well-attended meeting Joe Horan, Salters Grange, was unanimously re-elected Chairman; Brian Toal, Tirgarve, was unanimously elected as new incoming Secretary; Henry Neary, Knockaconey was elected new incoming Treasurer, having won the vote to replace the popular, Sean Moore, Armagh who did not seek re-election.

There were seventeen nominations for the ten places on the Executive Committee of the Northern Association and these positions were taken by those with the highest vote: Jack Ryan, St Brigids; Frank Horan, Salters Grange; Pat Lyttle, Niall's Crescent; James Shannon, Emania Terrace; Charles O'Hagan, Knockaconey; Mick Reilly, Drumarg Park; Francie Daly, Blundell's Grange; Jim Mone, Tirgarve; and Harry Toal, Castle Street.

The new association membership was now in place and momentous decisions lay ahead.

A HISTORIC MEETING

Within weeks of the new Executive Committee in Armagh having taken office they were in crucial discussions with their counterparts in the south at a specially convened meeting in Bandon, Co Cork. The occasion was that of a return match between Armagh's Danny McParland and Cork's Derry Kenny, the first such inter-provincial score to be arranged and organised through official channels since the Creedon-McParland return match failed to materialise in 1961. The much heralded meeting was aimed at reaching agreement on all matters relating to the launching and inauguration of the All-Ireland Road Bowling Championships. The onus on those present was particularly great but the commitment to reaching satisfactory conclusions was always evident on all sides.

The historic meeting took place on Easter Sunday 14th April, 1963.

This is how the *Armagh Observer* of 20th April, 1963 reported the momentous occasion:

> *The weekend just passed is one which will go down in history for the significance of a meeting between representatives of bowling organisations, north and south, aimed at amalgamating both associations and to make plans for the inauguration of an All- Ireland Championship series.*
>
> *At a reception held in the Devonshire Arms Hotel, Bandon on Easter Sunday evening, and sponsored by An Bol Chumann, the Chairman of the Association, Mr Flor Crowley, firstly speaking in Irish, welcomed the people of*

Eamon O'Carroll.

Flor Crowley.

Joe Horan.

Henry Neary.

Armagh and went on to express his admiration for the sporting qualities of their northern counterparts. He stated that in recent times inter-provincial scores had been arranged unofficially in the south and had done a great deal of harm to the game as a result. Mr Crowley went on to say how thankful his organisation was to their northern friends for the necessary assistance in rectifying the matter and he looked forward to the day when they could work as a complete unit.

Brian Toal, Armagh Secretary replied on behalf of the northern visitors thanking An Bol Chumann for the very fine reception accorded them and commending the Association for the efficient way in which the weekend events had been organised and conducted. He went on to thank individually the Chairman and Secretary of An Bol Chumann, Mr Flor Crowley and Mr Eamon O'Carroll for the way in which the Armagh proposals regarding the All-Ireland Championships had been received. Mr Toal concluded by wishing every success to the subsequent talks and expressed the hope that an amalgamation would promote a very favourable future for the sport. Messrs Eamon O'Carroll, Cork, Henry Neary, Armagh and Denis Kenny, Cork also spoke.

Following the reception the important discussions which ensued resulted in the Associations, north and south, amalgamating into one unit under the name An Bol Chumann Na hEireann.

Representative delegates from north and south were then selected and this body will be responsible for any arrangements regarding the All-Ireland Finals, and any other commitments which entail both parties. The delegates are:

South: Flor Crowley, Eamon O'Carroll, Denis McSweeney
North: Joe Horan, Brian Toal, Henry Neary

Plans were then formulated for the 1963 All-Ireland Final - the first ever - and it was agreed that a toss of a coin would decide which province would be honoured with the distinction of hosting this first All-Ireland Final. Before this decision was made it was further agreed to select a venue or road in each of Armagh and Cork on which the final would be staged should that county win the toss. The roads selected were: CORK - Dublin Hill; ARMAGH - Moy Road. Armagh won the toss of a coin and this automatically brings to the city the first ever All-Ireland Road Bowls Championship decider. It will be played on the Moy road for the Hughie Trainor Cup which has been generously donated by the well known Armagh newsagent and band leader. All that remained to be decided was the date for the event and as subsequent finals will be played on alternate years in Cork and Armagh the organising body opted for a holiday weekend on which to hold the fixture. The August weekend has been chosen for the 1963 All-Ireland Final and so this historic event will be played on Sunday, 4th August over the Moy Road, Armagh.

That was one report of what had proven to be a truly historic occasion. The All-Ireland Championship series had been inaugurated. Road Bowls or Bowl Playing had embarked upon a new and exciting era. Players and officials, supporters and spectators, had much to contemplate. Historical events in this intriguing sport were really beginning to unfold.

The First National Championship

The imminence of the All-Ireland senior road bowling championship in 1963 created tremendous interest within the sport and generated renewed impetus for local and national competitions. Speculation was rampant as to which of the top bowlers would emerge in Ulster and Munster to contest this historic All-Ireland event.

In the north it was considered to be relatively clear cut. The pundits had narrowed the field down to what was generally accepted as the top five senior players and were confident about which of them would win through. But all five, Danny McParland, Danny Reilly, Harry Toal, Mick Reilly, and, despite having announced his retirement nearly three years previously, Joe McVeigh, had their strong body of supporters, and opinions differed as to which of them was best. All of them had inter-provincial experience and each was considered capable of taking the first All-Ireland title. There were others too who warranted support. Sean Cartmill and Oliver O'Neill were always hovering close to the top bracket and Aidan Toal was beginning to emerge as a potential threat to all of them.

In the south the established senior championship had taken on much greater significance. A national title was ultimately at stake. There too, speculation was prevalent about the outcome, and with numerous potential champions in their senior ranks the competition was guaranteed to be particularly intense. The greatest exponent of the game Mick Barry from Waterfall was at the top of everyone's short list, to not only come through Munster, but also to make yet another of his own little pieces of history by winning the first ever All-Ireland senior road bowling championship. And there were others down south with that ambition too. Justifiably confident were senior contestants like Denis Donovan, Fishers Cross; John Creedon, Clondrohid; Jackie Forde; Denis O'Donovan, Bandon; Mick Murphy; Donie Lehane, Bandon; and a formidable young player yet to reach full potential, Derry Kenny from Clogheen.

The Ulster senior championships attracted twenty-three entries and amongst them was Joe McVeigh, back from what many considered to be premature retirement, and keen to participate in this glorious new era of championship bowling McVeigh, proved he was still the greatest crowd-puller in the game when a huge attendance assembled at Knappagh for his championship clash with fellow city man Danny Reilly. He won that one and then drew a tremendous crowd to the Moy road, and the biggest stake for many years, for his great score with the promising Aidan Toal, Tirgarve, who had just won the Grange Senior Tournament. Toal led to Allistragh and was level with four shots to go but McVeigh got up to win well on the last shot. Meanwhile Pat Campbell, Armagh's great forward in the All-Ireland senior football final against Kerry in 1953, had accounted for Pat McCormack in the

This 1956 'Beetle' was the mobile public address system at the 1963 All-Ireland Senior Road Bowls Final. Standing in right forefront is senior bowler, Pat Campbell, who played for Armagh in the 1953 All-Ireland Gaelic Football Final.

bowling championship but later went out to Danny McParland. The semi-final line-up saw Sean Cartmill, the 1961 Cup holder, drawn against Danny McParland with Harry Toal pitted against the revitalised Joe McVeigh. But the real drama of the championship had yet to come. Whilst McParland had a convincing win over Cartmill at Knappagh it was a disastrous finishing shot by McVeigh which handed dramatic victory to Toal. Joe McVeigh had appeared certain to qualify for the Ulster final but an inexplicably short penultimate bowl cost him the score and lost him that eagerly pursued opportunity. The great Joe McVeigh was gone from the championship and lost forever was his chance of winning an All-Ireland senior road bowling title. He had come out of retirement for this one and the crowds loved him for it. The sports pages of the local press record that the highest stakes and the biggest crowds of the entire championship were the three scores in which Armagh's Joe McVeigh featured. He made the championship what it was in its inaugural year.

It was Danny McParland and Harry Toal for the Ulster final on 21st July, 1963. The score was played at Knappagh but Toal's semi-final form deserted him as McParland coasted to victory and earned the right to take on the Munster champion for the National senior title.

That Munster championship was also producing great contests and drawing big crowds. The young Clogheen player, Derry Kenny had accounted for Mallow's Mick Murphy and Mick Barry beat Tedser Murphy in a semi-final clash. It was a Barry versus Kenny Munster final on 21st July 1963 and a big surprise was in store.

Danny McParland.

Derry Kenny, Clogheen, in the Veterans Championship some thirty years after his All-Ireland Final appearance in 1963.

Photo: Denis McGarry.

Derry Kenny confounded the pundits by becoming the youngest player ever to win the Munster senior title and, by defeating the might of Mick Barry in the process, had suddenly emerged as the new phenomenon in Road Bowls.

It was Armagh's Danny McParland and Cork's Derry Kenny for the All-Ireland senior Final to be played in Armagh on Sunday 4th August, 1963. Not the pairing most had predicted but particularly intriguing nonetheless. Ironically, the only two inter-provincial scores McParland had played that year to date were against Kenny, and the Cork man won both. The first of these was the occasion of Kenny's first visit to Armagh on Monday 18th March for a Saint Patrick's weekend fixture. It was played at Knappagh in glorious weather and though McParland was strong favourite at the outset, Kenny romped home with a shot to spare. The return match was on Easter Sunday, 14th April, 1963, over the Tinker's Cross venue at Bandon, the scene of McParland's twenty-two shot record against local bowler Donie Lehane in 1961. But again Kenny was the victor, this time by two shots, having led from start to finish.

THE FIRST ALL-IRELAND FINAL

It was billed as the greatest bowling attraction in the history of the game. The first ever All- Ireland Senior Road Bowls Final on that August public holiday weekend of 1963 was expected to draw a record crowd to the Moy road venue. The national daily newspapers the "Irish Press" and "Irish Independent" each carried a small advertisement for this special sporting occasion. Both Danny McParland and Derry Kenny were certain to have huge support, not only through the significance of the occasion, but also as a consequence of the bowling record of each. They were both highly experienced in big time bowling and the Hugh Trainor All- Ireland Cup was now their ultimate target.

At the start of the big event a mobile public address system conveyed details of rules and regulations to the vast crowd and was also used to good effect throughout the score in attempting to clear a path for each individual shot. The slow moving mass of shirt-sleeved spectators, in perfect weather conditions, provided a magnificent splash of colour with the score taking over six hours to cover the three-mile course.

McParland won the first shot and, with colourful bookmaker P G McQuaid from Dungannon shouting the odds, the atmosphere was tense and thrilling. Kenny led on the tenth and was still in front at the half-way stage but entering the last quarter McParland was back in front. It was all to play for as the massive crowd sensed a close finish. And that is what transpired. McParland took the title on the last shot with just eleven yards to spare. The first All-Ireland senior Road Bowls Champion was greeted with wild delight by his supporters.

Danny McParland was now something special and his name is indelibly in the record books of road bowling history.

When Padraig Puirseal First Learned of Bol Chumann

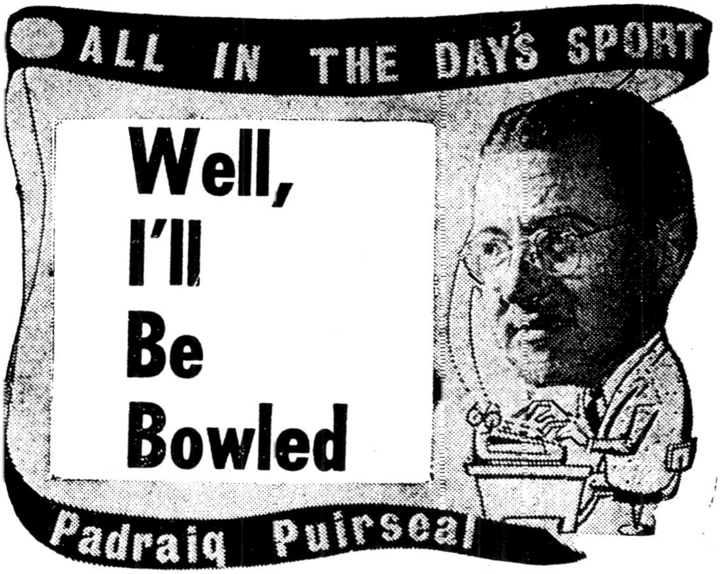

It generally requires a significant, team or individual, performance to merit prominent space on the sports pages of the Dublin based national daily newspapers. But then there is always the exception - as the humble administrative body for road bowls in the north was to find out.

With the new administration in northern bowl playing less than a year in place it was inevitable that the normative process would generate initial difficulties and these were compounded, ironically, by the rapidly developing success of the sport in the area. New vibrant clubs with inspirational leaders, strong membership, attractive tournaments, increased spectator interest, and extensive press coverage, was a developing feature of the game since the inauguration of the All-Ireland Senior Championship and the much publicised success of Danny McParland in taking the first national road bowls title.

Two of the more successful clubs at the time, Grange and Keady, were not entirely satisfied that every effort was being made to ensure proper affiliation of all clubs and consequently they issued a joint statement, and press release, having first consulted with the Executive of Bol Chumann Na hEireann in the south. The statement, issued by the respective Chairman of each club, Henry Neary, Knockaconey and John Gribben, Farmacaffley, resulted from a specially convened joint meeting and referred to the crux of club representation and responsibility at administrative level. The wording in the statement adopted a firm but nonetheless conciliatory tone in confronting the issue and urging a satisfactory resolution. The officers of the two clubs, endeavouring to resolve the matter, Grange and Keady, had successfully managed to arrange a top level meeting of the Executive of Bol Chumann Na hEireann in Armagh on Saturday, 28th March, 1964. The subsequent press release from that meeting had this to say:

> *Following a series of specially convened meetings the organisational split between Road Bowls clubs in County Armagh has been satisfactorily resolved, with representatives of Bol Chumann Na hEireann acting as mediators throughout the proceedings. On Saturday, 28th March, 1964 the Executive Committee in the south met with officers of the northern administration and after some deliberation it was agreed to refrain from any decisions until all clubs could be represented. A second meeting was then arranged for the morning of Sunday 29th March 1964 at which five members of each club were present. The business of that assembly was overseen by southern members of Bol Chumann Na hEireann including Mr Eamon O'Carroll, N.T.; Mr Hedley McCay, B.L.; Mr Patrick Kerrigan; Mr Dan O'Mahony and Mr Frank Teegan; all from Cork.*
>
> *Following more than two hours of debate largely taken up through matters of principle, it was agreed to elect members to an incoming Northern Branch, An Bol Chumann and the proceedings for this have been set in place. The resolution of the crisis has resulted in the following membership being elected to administer road bowls in the north and continue to be amalgamated with An Bol Chumann Na hEireann.*
>
> *Chairman: Henry Neary, Knockaconey; Deputy Chairman: John Gribben, Farmacaffley; Secretary: Brian Toal, Tirgarve; Treasurer: Joe Horan, Salters Grange; Registrar: Frank Daly, Grange; Committee: Jimmy Corr, Lislea, Danny Donnelly, Umgola; Francie Toal, Armagh; Danny O'Brien, Armagh; Kevin Kennedy, Drumcairne; Tom McGleenan, Mullanstown; Charles O'Hagan, Knockaconey; Vincent Kelly, Tullygoonigan.*
>
> *The President of the Association is Rev Tom Quinn, C.C., and Patrons are Hugh Trainor and Harry Irwin.*

So the entire matter had been amicably resolved. The organising body was once again enabled to focus firmly on promoting the sport, with players and spectators concentrating on enjoyment of the game devoid of any administrative distraction.

But the episode did gain the attention of the talented and popular sportswriter PADRAIG PUIRSEAL who devoted his much favoured column, "All in the Day's Sport", to the controversy and its resolution. This is how Padraig Puirseal conveyed the story to readers of the *'Irish Press'* in April, 1964.

We have managed, from time to time, to achieve "splits" in many forms of sport in Ireland, some in major sports, some in minor sports, so it is surely news, and good news at that, to hear of a "split" being healed in one of these sports and absolute unity being achieved. The news is all the more remarkable when one considers that the vast majority of sports fol-

lowers, myself included, must have been alike unaware of the fact that such a body as Bol Chumann na hEireann existed, not to say that its forces were in any way divided.

An Bol Chumann, in case you are as ignorant as myself in such matters, is the body which controls road-bowling in Ireland - Ireland as far as road-bowling is concerned being confined to parts of the counties of Cork and Armagh, with possible small portions of Waterford, Cavan and Tyrone added on for good measure.

Now the aforesaid split occurred among the boys who go bowling in the County Armagh. It seems that the Armagh City Club has claimed leadership of the entire county, but in actual fact, had no control whatever over the Grange and Keady clubs. Indeed the men of Grange and Keady combined to form a Northern Branch of An Bol Chumann which took control of all "scores" in that part of the world.

For the benefit of the uninitiated, a "score" is a match at bowling - I nearly committed the unforgivable crime of calling the game "bowls."

Well, at the Easter Weekend, the Corkmen went North for a senior challenge score on the road to The Moy, and the Executive Committee very sensibly got together with the Northern Branch and the Armagh City Club, and complete unity was achieved. Armagh City, Keady and The Grange clubs will all have equal representation in a new Northern Branch which will have complete control up there and will be responsible for the Ulster championship.

Congratulations to An Bol Chumann, for settling its differences so quickly and so amicably, and it does seem that there are a few athletic organisations, North and South, that obviously have a great deal to learn from Bol Chumann na hEireann.

The Boys of Fairhill, often revered in song by Cork ballad singer, Jimmy Crowley. Along with the great Tim Delaney in the centre front of this nineteen thirties group are (front left) Paddy O'Sullivan, Billser O'Shea, Jack Casey, Ned Spriggs, Fox O'Donovan, Tim Delaney, Paddy Healy, Mickey O'Sullivan, Jimmy Mahony, Dan O'Shea, George Farmer and Paddy Clifford. The renowned bowling tactician, Jack O'Shea, is third from left behind Jack Casey.

The Year of a Veritable Champion

The new All-Ireland Senior Champion, Danny McParland, drew a tremendous crowd to Dublin Hill, Cork, for a meeting with Bandon's Denny Murphy on 1st December, 1963. It was McParlands first time on the course and he won the score by seventy five yards. Later the same month Aidan Toal, Tirgarve, had his first win over Danny McParland in a challenge score on the Moy road and it was a foretaste of what was to come the following Spring.

In a score played on Sunday 8th March, 1964, which was acclaimed as the greatest seen for many years, Aidan Toal beat All-Ireland champion Danny McParland in the Keady Tournament after a most thrilling, pulsating and exceptionally close encounter which kept the enormous crowd seething with excitement from start to finish. It was said McParland had seldom played a better score; it was claimed Toal had never played a better one. Played over the wide open space of the Keady road, which provided ample scope for two of the fastest bowlers in the game, the score developed into the greatest tussle that followers of the sport could ever hope to see. Every single shot in this thriller, which carried the highest sidestake for any Tournament score, was accurate and powerful but the report of the score suggests at least a dozen of those shots were utterly amazing. Never once was a bowl put astray by either player and in a thrilling finish Toal won on the last shot by fifteen yards in a score which will rank among the best ever.

It was a narrow defeat for the All-Ireland champion but, as subsequent events were to confirm, a spectacular year for Danny McParland was only beginning to unfold. And yet it was Aidan Toal who generated the greater speculation in the earlier part of that particular year. He was pitched in against top southern bowler Jack Forde in an inter-provincial challenge score over the Moy road on Sunday 29th March, 1964. Forde, who was Munster senior champion in 1961 was back to his brilliant best and like most of his counterparts in southern senior bowling had his sights set on later wresting the All-Ireland title from its northern pedestal. Toal was facing his first score of such magnitude and as such was practically unknown to Munster followers but his dramatic win over Danny McParland just three weeks previously guaranteed him huge support. The result proved to be a memorable inter-provincial debut for Aidan Toal as he proceeded to dismantle an early lead by Forde and with faultless play throughout the second half of the score drew away for an amazing three shot win against a player who had been enjoying a great run of success over the preceding months. The nature of Toal's win had created an enormous flurry, particularly in the south where followers were unaware of his emerging talents, and such fascination was reflected in this report by "Boithreach", in the Cork *"Evening Echo"*, of 3rd April, 1964:

Does it not seem today that the greatest Armagh bowler of them all has just appeared on the scene? Can we any longer blind ourselves to the fact that now, if never before, our brethren of the bowl in the north have finally caught up with us, possibly surpassed us, in our generations-old struggle with them for mastery of the 28oz?

True enough, our men have been beaten by Armagh men before now, in Cork as well as in Armagh. But they have never been beaten so conclusively that we could not find some ray of hope, however meagre, to reassure us that either it shouldn't have happened at all or that it happened by some lucky accident - lucky, that is, for the Armagh side.

In our smugness and in complacent over-confidence, we have always been able to convince ourselves and each other, that we were still monarchs of the bowling roads and that we were going to continue as such seculoram.

When Danny O'Reilly beat us, we were off form. When Harry Toal beat us, he was lucky. When Danny McParland beat us , we got bad road-showing. When Joe McVeigh beat us, the road was against us. We said all those things. And we believed them.

Can we still feel smug and secure in the ancient assurance that our Cork bowlplayers still are, and likely to remain, the unbeatable kingpins of bowl-playing? Can we continue to think so with our heads buried deep in the sands of our own conceit after the humiliating and eye-opening lesson on the great Moy road at Armagh?

I must confess that I cannot continue to think so, and as I write this in the

Danny McParland unleashes a shot at Allen's Corner, on the Moy Road, during the 1964 City Tournament Score against Aidan Toal.

drawing room of a London suburb - possibly the first bowling article ever written in this vast and terrifying wilderness of ten million strangers - my Corkman's confidence, unshaken in the past, is definitely shaken now.

And it was badly shaken at 8.30 on yesterday evening when I got through by phone to Eamonn O'Carroll and Brian Toal at the Charlemont Hotel in Armagh to find out the result of the day's score. Eamonn's opening words, "we had a bad day" did not quite prepare me for the dispiriting details that were to follow when Brian Toal took over to give me a few details of the afternoons bowling.

A week ago, I said in this column that I could not see how Jack Forde could lose the score at Armagh. Other Cork bowlers might be beaten there, but not Jack Forde, who would match the best northern player for speed, for his ability to take a chance when one came his way; for everything, in fact, which should go towards winning a score at Moy or elsewhere.

It had been my belief, and not mine alone, that Jack was just the man to take on any Armagh man at Moy, and with Jack's form at its highest peak, as it had been in the last three months, I regarded him as well-nigh unbeatable on almost any road.

And he probably would have been unbeatable against any one of those Armagh bowlers whom we had seen so often, North and South, in the last dozen years. Had Jack's opponent been Danny McParland, All-Ireland champion though he is, or Harry Toal, or either of the two O'Reillys, then our ex-champion would probably have won.

Not against Aidan Toal, however, twenty years old newcomer who beat McParland three weeks ago, and possibly the greatest Armagh bowler of them all, if not at present, then in the making. No man has reached his peak at 20, and the twenty-years old player who can now beat Jack Forde by a runaway should beat any man in Ireland when he is 25!

Will there be a "next time" for Forde and Toal, and if there is, where will it be? Dublin Hill or Moy, or Knappagh? Can Toal do in Cork what he did in Armagh? Or will Cork supporters have to call upon Mick Barry, the man whom only one Armagh man has ever beaten, North or South, to retrieve the bowling honour of our county?

There was indeed a "next time" for Forde and Toal and that encounter was at Tinkers Cross, near Bandon, Co Cork on Sunday 17th May 1964 when a sun-baked crowd, estimated to be in excess of 10,000, tightly packed the narrow, winding course. In that score Forde came from behind for a last shot win after Toal had faltered on the penultimate throw. Both players found great difficulty in determining a choice of play such was the density of the crowd and each suffered a degree of crushing at the point of delivery as spectators fervently interested themselves in the contrasting styles. The *"Southern Star"* of 23rd May, 1964, devoted considerable space to the event in a comprehensive article by pen name "Raymond", in which he commented:

Aidan Toal in pensive study when competing in a bowling score at Cork in 1964.

The score itself is one that will be discussed for many a week to come. For one thing it was probably the biggest ever in the matter of crowds, which went well beyond the 10,000 mark, possibly the most extensive crowd ever seen at a score at Tinker's Cross, not even excepting the 1957 championship final between Denny Murphy and Seamus Fitzgerald.

"Raymond" concluded his review of the play with the comment: *I mean no slight to the great Joe McVeigh, nor to the brothers O'Reilly or Danny McParland when I say that I place young Aidan Toal as the coolest and steadiest bowler I have seen coming south from Armagh. Give Aidan a Corkman's swing and style, with his own wonderfully well-balanced temperament, and you would have a bowler of great worth!*

The same score drew a detailed analysis from "BARRA" in *"The Kerryman"*, newspaper of Saturday, 23rd May, 1964 in which Forde's brilliant finish was noted and an overall perspective offered:

Whit week-end 1964 would have been a disastrous one for the greater part of the bowling men of Cork City and County if Jack Forde had not finished better than he started in last Sunday's big challenge score at Tinker's Cross against youthful but steady Aidan Toal of Armagh.

I say Forde finished brilliantly, and I say so because of that great second last shot of his down to and beyond "The Pump". Before that shot was thrown the position looked anything but good for the Corkmen. Forde was in a tricky position at incomplete sight and faced with the most vital shot of the day, a shot he has missed in the past more frequently than he has got, and which four out of every five men miss most of the time. Toal was 40 very useful yards down the fall from which tip he seemed almost a certainty to go down to The Pump.

In that vital shot, more than in any other I have ever seen him throw, Jack Forde used his own judgement and insisted upon getting his own play. He flatly refused to run more right and play more left, as he was advised to do. Instead he ran more centre and played slightly left - and he went down like a cannon-ball, not only down, but so far around that Toal could hardly have beaten the tip if he had got a full run of the fastest bowl he could have thrown.

Toal made a really grand effort with his last shot, an intelligent, well judged throw around the bend and over the end line, but he was too far back and it would have taken a miracle shot from his tip to put Forde in danger.

It is not easy to assess Toal's real merit on last Sunday's score. He was a total stranger to Tinker's Cross, with its many trick shots and dangerous patches. With the vast crowds which milled all over the road during the entire score - a crowd which was hard to control, the road was never adequately cleared, so that young Toal was frequently bowling blind. This was a serious draw-back for a newcomer on the road, a mere youth with limited big-score experience and it is very likely that at least some of his mistakes were due to the fact that he had no clear view of the road ahead when he made those mistakes.

Personally I was able to form an opinion regarding young Toal's general approach to last Sunday's score. For a boy of his age - and he is little more than a boy in years - he is the steadiest and least demonstrative player I have seen for a long time. Neither good luck nor bad, long shots or short ones seem to affect him. He was almost stoical in manner and in facial expression all through last Sunday's score, and if he spoke at all, it was the bare minimum of words which was required by the emergency of the moment.

Altogether, I felt that this was as fine a specimen of sportsman as we have ever seen upon a bowling road, the type of youth who seems destined to develop into a really great man, the type of young bowler who should one day reign as champion of All- Ireland. We in Cork could do with a few more young men of Aidan Toal's type, and I say that with no expressed or implied slight upon those fine young men we already have in our Cork game.

Meanwhile the 1964 Ulster senior championship, the draws for which had been announced in early May, was commanding widespread attention. Speculation on the outcome was rife in view of Danny McParland's first round defeat in each of the Grange and Keady Senior Tournaments but on the opening day of the championship, 31st May, the All-Ireland champion was back to his devastating best and it was no less than what was required to counter a great challenge by fellow city player Danny Reilly. In a tremendous contest over the Moy road from the Milestone to Callan bridge, Reilly made a super start and kept the champion trailing for a good part of the way before losing out in the end by less than seventy metres.

On the same day at Dublin hill, the first round of the Munster senior championship saw Mick Barry outclass the 1963 Intermediate champion, Mick O'Driscoll by almost three bowls. In subsequent weeks the intrigue of the Munster senior

Sean Cartmill.
Photo: Larry Dickinson.

championship unfolded with Derry Kenny recording a 60 metre win over Donie Lehane at Templemartin and Johnny Creedon, surprisingly, going out in a two shot defeat by Mick Collins at Tinker's Cross. The man fancied by many to take the Munster title, Jack Forde, reinforced his claims with a brilliant two shot win over Mick Murphy at Waterloo.

Other first round ties in the 1964 Ulster championship saw Danny Donnelly, Umgola beat James Reilly, Armagh; Mick Reilly, Armagh oust Liam Donnelly, Allistragh; and Oliver O'Neill, Armagh, dispense with the challenge of John Gribben, Farmacaffely, all of them played at Knappagh. Two further first round scores at Knappagh resulted in Aidan Toal gaining an easy win over Armagh's Billy Quigley and a shock win for Sean Cartmill, Ballyheridan over a strongly fancied Harry Toal.

More sensational results were to come though. There had been an air of anticipation about a possible championship meeting between Danny McParland and Aidan Toal, and when they avoided each other in the draw for the second round, speculation mounted about the prospect of a provincial final pairing involving, whom were then generally accepted, the two top bowlers in Ulster. All that expectancy rapidly evaporated on 28th June, 1964 when Joe Molloy, Grangemore, who had earlier beaten Denis Nugent, Armagh in the championship, created a sensation by dictating the pace from the outset against Aidan Toal and successfully resisting a late challenge to hold out for a shock win over the Moy road.

The next sensational result was the defeat of Mick Reilly by Jim Campbell, Lisadian, in a tremendously close finish on the last throw. Jim Cullen, Ballyheridan, who came through to contest the 1995 Veterans All-Ireland Final, had been the player ousted in the first round by Campbell but the Lisadian bowler succumbed to the semi-final challenge of Joe Molloy who was a surprise final contender. And whatever about surprises on the road of play it came as a major shock to learn that Sean Cartmill, who, by all standards was having a very successful lengthy period at the top end of the game, had astonishingly withdrawn from the championship on the morning of his scheduled semi-final clash with Danny McParland.

If there ever had been any serious doubts about Danny McParland's ability to retain, at least, his Ulster senior title, they were quickly dispelled in the Ulster final on 19th July, 1964. Played over the Moy road from the Milestone to Callanbridge the strongly built Joe Molloy performed very well initially but he was confronted with a combination of speed and accuracy from the reigning champion, which produced record play for the road, in that direction, and convinced his supporters that their Armagh idol was on course for another All-Ireland title.

The Munster Senior Final had also been scheduled for 19th July but was deferred for a week owing to a clash with the Munster Football Final of 1964. The momentum of the bowling championship in the south had been exceedingly powerful, and passionately competitive with so many formidable bowlers striving to win the Hugh Trainor Cup and coveted All-Ireland title. It was clear from the outset that Mick Barry, in particular, was fiercely determined to contest the National final having smarted from a surprise defeat in the 1963 Munster senior decider and thus thwarted of the opportunity to claim the historic record of becoming the first ever official All-Ireland Road Bowling Champion. It was Denny Murphy, Bandon who was next to fall to the powerful Barry bowling at Upton but the surprise of the Munster championship, Mick Collins, in a semi-final clash with Mick Barry, produced a scintillating display to lead most of the way over the Tinker's Cross course only to lose on the final throw. It was a marvellous contest and that last shot win of 40 metres was achieved through a tremendous drive by Mick Barry on his final throw. Derry Kenny, meanwhile, was vigorously pursuing two consecutive Munster titles and did his chances no harm with a convincing win over Pat Joe O'Mahony at Dublin Hill. But it was the strongly fancied Jack Forde who was waiting for him in a semi-final encounter and Kenny's title hopes ended at Ballyvolane when he went down by a bowl of odds. Those semi-final results brought about a dream pairing for the Munster senior final. Mick Barry, whatever about the occasional defeat, was acknowledged and widely accepted, then, since and before, as the greatest bowl player of all time. His challenger for the 1964 provincial title, and tilt at the All-Ireland, was a stupendous young bowler in Jack Forde who had enjoyed a marvellous run of success and a huge following to sustain him.

That Munster final of 1964 lived up to all its promise and indeed surpassed

Aidan Toal breaking off at Callan Bridge in the City Tournament Score against Danny McParland at Moy Road, Armagh in 1964.

even the most ambitious expectations. It was a brilliant contest, declared by many to have been the greatest final seen for many years. It was one of those scores in which it seems a pity there has to be a loser but Mick Barry was the one to pull it off with a dramatic last shot win.

THE ALL-IRELAND FINAL AT DUBLIN HILL

The scene was set for a mammoth bowling attraction of which proportions there had been no precedent. Previews in the bowling press had speculated on a crowd of up to 15,000 thronging the Dublin Hill venue, not far from Cork city, to see the Waterfall maestro aim for a repeat of his incisive performance over the same course just a week earlier. The huge contingent of supporters behind Armagh's Danny McParland were mindful of the fact that he had recorded a win over Bandon's Denny Murphy at the same Dublin Hill venue and were almost boastful of his devastating show of power and accuracy in the Ulster final. The referee for the big event was the efficient and effective Dan O'Leary from Waterloo, Co Cork.

This is part of the report on the final by 'B.T.' in the *Armagh Observer* of Saturday 8th August, 1964:

> *With the finest overall performance he has ever achieved, and undoubtedly the greatest finish of his career, Armagh's Danny McParland successfully defended his All-Ireland title against the might of Munster champion, Mick Barry, Waterfall, at Dublin Hill, Cork in a final which will forever rank among the greatest and go down in history as a thrilling, pulsating and highly sporting occasion.*

This was bowl playing at its very best. Time and again when Barry, who was odds-on favourite for the score, went through for a probable lead with a terrific bowl, it was followed and beaten by McParland who had the massive crowd filled with excitement at the quality of play. As officials worked hard to clear a play path through the tightly packed crowd, Barry had a bowl accidently stopped and McParland was instructed not to continue until further efforts were made to control the crowd.

Twice during the score the spectators saw fit to stand and loudly applaud two magnificent shots and this was an experience new to many of the followers, north and south. The first of these was a fantastic loft by Mick Barry at the three-quarter stage. It was where he decided to loft the bowl over a corner which necessitated clearing a licensed premises complete with television aerial and telephone wires - and all of this no less than 65 yards away from the point of delivery! The well deserved applause was already under way as the bowl went skywards, completely cleared the building and landed 20 yards on the other side, onto the road of play, to crown the greatest exhibition of competitive lofting in the midst of a score that has ever been seen.

Sustained applause was again well deserved at a point when McParland appeared to be in trouble within two shots of the finish after Barry had put in a terrific drive around a double bend. This really looked a winning action but McParland, after studying the lay-out decided to play his bowl very wide with a strong 'pull' in the hope that it would take the bend. McParland played his bowl perfectly with a delightful 'pull' which dragged it round the bend to beat Barry's distant mark by 30 yards in one of the most amazing shots he has ever played.

The score had everything a bowls follower could ask for - excitement all the way, a closely fought contest throughout; magnificent lofting; sensational shots; excellent sportsmanship; and probably the greatest finish ever witnessed.

McParland has been noted as a great finisher. This one must be out on its own for quality. His last three shots covered an enormous amount of difficult ground and each of those was almost matched by equally fine efforts from Barry. What sheer excitement and tremendous tension encompassed the closing stages of this thrilling final.

Danny McParland has now really established himself as a great bowl player. He has just had his greatest season to date. Throughout the Ulster championship he was unbackable and unbeatable and he has now crowned that flawless campaign with this glorious fifty yard victory in such a showpiece final.

It was a great day for McParland; a great day for bowling in Armagh; a great day for bowling in Ireland.

That report unashamedly reflects northern pleasure at such a wonderful occasion and spectacular performance. It was very much Mick Barry's Munster championship and, equally, the Ulster championship belonged to Danny McParland. Between them they had generated a bowling spectacle in a historic final which elevated the sport to unprecedented stature in skill and drama.

In the early part of 1964 the bowling headlines were dominated by Jack Forde

Mick Barry pictured in the 1995 Vintage Final, more than thirty years after his first All-Ireland Senior Final appearance in 1964, and exactly forty years after winning his first Munster Senior Championship title.
Photo: Denis McGarry.

and Aidan Toal. And the semi-retired Joe McVeigh was still drawing the crowds when he and Aidan Toal had their own little battle on 12th July in the Grange senior tournament. McVeigh lost the score but his appeal to the bowling public was as intense as ever. The big surprise in the Grange tournament, which was open to all the top senior players, was the phenomenal power bowling and ultimate success of Kevin McGleenan, Ballytrodden, who, on his way to winning the Cup accounted for many renowned bowlers including Pat McCormack and Aidan Toal before astounding everybody in the final by beating the Blackwatertown road, course specialist, Sean Cartmill. The final drew a very big crowd to the Port Mor venue where Sean Cartmill, who held a twenty-one shot record for the course, and had already beaten Harry Toal, Mick Reilly, Vincent Webb, Annahagh, and Jim Hughes, Allistragh, in earlier rounds, was expected to win easily but lost out on the last shot. Kevin McGleenan, whose son Matt was a significant factor in Tyrone's gaelic football championship success in 1995, also went through to the semi-final stage of the Benburb road bowls tournament in 1968. Kevin died unexpectedly on 12th April, 1988 when only 51 years old.

A great charity exhibition score in Dunmanway was the feature event in September, 1964 and that big occasion is explored in another chapter. So too is the record breaking shot in the City Tournament also dealt with later. Danny McParland made the City Tournament his own when he beat Aidan Toal and Joe McVeigh on his way to the final on 22nd November 1964 in which he easily accounted for the challenge of Harry Toal.

It was undoubtedly the year of Danny McParland. The first issue of the *Armagh Observer* newspaper in 1965, in an exceptional departure, devoted the total space on the main sports page to a review of the bowling year and introduced the comprehensive recapitulation with the banner headline "It was McParland's Year." That, it surely was.

Competing to Win for Charity

When any of the top bowlers engage in direct competition the appeal of such an event always generates its own speculative intrigue and captivating attention. But when such a contest involves the top six bowlers in Ireland, and the competition is in aid of a special charity, then the nature of the attraction is manifestly intensified.

Road bowls followers, in common with most other sports enthusiasts, have played their role in raising funds for charity when special need arose and a response was required. Such a need was identified back in 1964 by the late Flor Crowley when he set out to personally pioneer the staging of a mammoth exhibition score involving Ireland's best in bowl players. The fund to benefit was that of St Mary's Convent Building scheme in Dunmanaway, the west Cork town where Flor was, for many years, a young teacher in the local national school.

That unique event, involving a doubles score with three sets of partners, was accorded exceptional publicity, north and south. And little wonder. The exhibition score had succeeded in bringing together in one prodigious contest the undisputed principals in the sport in Ireland. The partnerships for the doubles event encompassed the greatest pairings imaginable. Heading the list, and unashamedly acknowledged by the organisers as the pairing they wanted most, was the Armagh partnership of Danny McParland and Aidan Toal. The other four selections from the leading bowlers in the country were formidable Cork partners Mick Barry, Waterfall and Denis O'Donovan, Fisher's Cross, along with two senior players who had each been blazing a trail of individual southern success, Jack Forde and Clogheen's Derry Kenny.

Each of these players were, in themselves, a huge attraction in any event but the combination of such bowling talent, and the inherent contrast in playing styles, made this a score with tremendous drawing power and a potential for spectacular bowling.

The big exhibition charity score was scheduled for Dunmanaway, on Sunday 6th September, 1964 and the organisers geared themselves for a record attendance. The pre-score publicity was enormous. In the south the local press had been speculating on the event for weeks and in the north the *Armagh Observer* of Saturday 5th September 1964, accorded the full width of the main sports page to a huge banner headline, "Ireland's Big Six Bowlers - And Two of them are from County Armagh."

The attendance was indeed a record one. All of the players were individually introduced to the massive crowd at the start and the biggest reception was reserved for Danny McParland, the reigning All-Ireland senior champion. It was an honour for each of the players to be chosen for the mammoth exhibition score and a privilege to be associated with such an honourable event.

The Cork pairing of Forde and Kenny were most fancied to win the score. But it was Barry and O'Donovan who set the standard, with the latter player probably the best of the six on the day. Between them, this powerful partnership produced a faultless performance to set up a new record of eighteen shots for the Derinasafa road. The formidable Armagh partners, McParland and Toal were ousted to third place by the stronger finishing favourites, Forde and Kenny, who got ahead of the northerners close to the finish. All of the players were presented with special trophies in recognition of their selection and participation in the prestigious and noble event.

The winning partners, Mick Barry and Denis O'Donovan made an additional donation to the benefit fund and the entire event proved a worthy and valuable contribution to St Mary's Convent Building Scheme, Dunmanway, Co Cork.

The success of that particular charitable event provided the inspiration for a similar venture in the north to raise funds for the restoration of the Sacred Heart Convent in Armagh, which had been seriously damaged in a fire during the early morning of the 14th February 1964.

St. Mary's Convent, Dunmanway, Co. Cork.

The score was fixed for Easter Sunday, 18th April, 1965 and the same six leading bowlers had signalled their intention to take part in this, the first such major attraction to be bowled out over northern roads. But in January of that year came the news that Forde and Kenny were out of the big Easter event. Nonetheless the anticipated doubles score remained hugely attractive and was being accorded the full promotional efforts of Bol Chumann in the south with commensurate newspaper publicity. The Executive in Cork had reassured the northern organisers of their intense desire to return the compliment of full participation in such a worthy cause.

The Armagh partnership of McParland and Toal were determined from the beginning of the year to set about reversing the result of the big Dunmanway event. Preparation by each was meticulous. A narrow defeat by a mere four yards at the hands of Kevin McGleenan in the Blackwatertown tournament (now Port Mor) hardened McParlands resolve to lose no more. Toal was equally resolute. The Tirgarve man had beaten Joe McVeigh in the January final of the Keady Tournament and the ambition of each was to maintain a winning formula and consolidate a growing confidence. The form of both players over the period was awesome and McParland was holding a slight edge on Toal in direct challenges. In one such score, on Sunday 14th February 1965, Danny McParland broke the Blackwatertown course record when he covered the distance in twenty marvellous shots, going almost 90 metres over the finishing line in the process. Speculation was rife as to when, if ever, it would be beaten. Sensationally, a week later, McParland shattered his own seven day record when he scored the line in nineteen fantastic shots, and amazingly, he was followed over the finish by Toal who had also got inside his opponents week-old spectacular performance. The huge crowd of spectators were electrified by such astonishing play which provided a tremendous boost for bowling and set fans eagerly awaiting the Easter charity score and a possible subsequent Ulster championship confrontation.

The Northern Branch, An Bol Chumann embarked upon elaborate plans for the big Easter event. It was a busy period for Armagh. William Cardinal Conway had returned home to the city on Tuesday 2nd March, 1965, having received the insignia of his rank in Rome. Incidentally, some months later, following a busy schedule of episcopal engagements by the new Cardinal, it is reliably told that during an informal lesson about religious knowledge at a Cork school the teacher asked the question, "What famous person resides in Armagh?" A young boy named John Kenny promptly answered, "Danny McParland, Sir."

Evidently each individual has their own criteria for determining eminence.

Sacred Heart Convent, Armagh.

The big Easter charity score, featuring the pick of Ireland's bowl players, drew many thousands to the Moy road just outside Armagh city. Never before had a bowling match created so much interest. It was the first time that a partner or doubles score at inter- provincial level had been played in Armagh and there was the added momentum of fulfilling a worthy cause. The play was equally powerful to the occasion. Toal opened spectacularly with a 65 metre lead over O'Donovan and despite some fine bowls by Barry the Armagh pair were headed only once. The last seven shots, to the point where Barry and O'Donovan were to retire well beaten, were brilliantly executed by McParland and Toal with the margin of victory at the end increasing to three bowls of odds.

The real winner on the day though was the Sacred Heart Convent Restoration Fund. It was a huge sporting, cultural and financial success. Pupils from the convent helped to raise additional contributions during the score and the winning pair made a further donation to the overall fund. Each player was presented with a Cup to mark the occasion, and in recognition of being chosen as one of Ireland's top four bowlers. The referee for the score was Joe Horan, Armagh, and the official markers were Dan O'Mahony, Cork and Patsy McCoy, Armagh.

The most ambitious charity event undertaken by Bol Chumann Na hEireann was almost twenty-five years later when the first Dublin Road Bowling

The Super Ból Trophy.

Tournament, "Super-Bol" was played out over a defined course on the roads of the Phoenix Park in the capital city. In aid of Cerebral Palsy Ireland, and sponsored by Allied Irish Banks, the "Super-Bol" event was held on Sunday 14th May, 1989 and the varied programme included a Pro-Am Celebrity Tournament; the "Super-Bol" Road Bowling Contest featuring teams from Cork and Armagh; and an International Lofting Competition between Ireland and Germany.

The official opening was conducted by the then Minister of State at the Department of the Taoiseach, Mr Noel Treacy, T.D. who played the first shot to open the "Super-Bol" competition. The Pro-Am tournament attracted forty eight teams in seventeen separate road bowling scores. Germany won the International Lofting Competition. In the "Super-Bol", Road Bowling contest, Cork were victorious when their very strong team of Dan O'Halloran, Seamus Sexton, and Bill Daly, proved much too strong and accurate for the combined talents of the Armagh trio, Patrick Mallon, Michael Toal and Harry Toal.

But again, as in all charity events, the overall winner was the intended benefit fund. In this case Cerebral Palsy Ireland, which, in conjunction with the associated efforts of Bol Chumann Na hEireann, Allied Irish Banks, and a very energetic Organising Committee, ensured a unique sporting occasion had contributed handsomely to a very worthy charity organisation.

A special "Super-Bol" trophy was designed for the event by sculptor Vincent Browne and the deserving recipient of the fine award was the Cork Road Bowling Team.

A novel charity event, and a highly successful one at that, was a "Fun for All" bowling tournament organised on Sunday 21st August, 1983, on the Carrigrohane Straight, Cork city, in which one hundred teams, each of four participants, engaged in the fund raising activity. The late Christy Kelleher, the then Managing Director of Blarney Woollen Mills, had sponsored prizes in excess of £1,000 and the event raised more than £6,000 for Cork Polio and General After Care Association. The out outstanding success of the event was due largely to the exceptional efficiency of public relations officer Teresa Walsh, Bonnington, Montenotte, Cork, and at a special function in Christy's Hotel, Blarney the money was donated towards a 3.2 million project at Glasheen. For many years since then the "Fun for All" bowling tournament continued to raise substantial sums of money for various charities with staff from the Woollen Mills at Blarney very much to the fore in organising the events.

Through generations, in ways large and small, the traditional sport of road bowling has always been readily accessible and appropriately responsive to an identified charitable need.

A Mighty Power Reigned Supreme

It had by no means been easy for the hitherto acknowledged unrivalled force in road bowling to accept, that almost three years after the All-Ireland senior championship had begun, the distinguished bowlers of the south had not yet won a National title.

The psychological pressure, subtle and otherwise, on Munster's senior bowlers to regain supremacy and restore personal and provincial pride was a meaningful and motivating factor with the 1965 senior championship pending. The confidence of northern followers was never more prevalent. They had just experienced a glorious period of unprecedented dominance and their dual champion was surpassing even the most aspiring expectations of his followers. Other senior players were running Danny McParland close in tournament scores and it soon became apparent that legitimate challengers for senior honours were emerging. The late Kevin McGleenan, Ballytrodden, having beaten Joe McVeigh, in the Monaghan Road Tournament in January 1965 by two shots, followed this up in the same month with a narrow four yard win over McParland in the Blackwatertown Tournament. In the top grade final of the Keady Tournament Aidan Toal had a comfortable win over Joe McVeigh and the McParland-Toal duels over subsequent months produced astonishing performances in excitement and quality. All this new found self belief and established credence had local tournaments abounding with success. The lesser grades in the Keady finals saw Gerry McGleenan, Ballytrodden, beat Francie Daly, Grange, and the versatile Jim McGrail who excelled in many sports, overcame the challenge of Tassagh's Francie Corr. The new St Patrick's Club, embracing, Granemore, Madden, and Keady, attracted a colossal entry for a Tournament launch which brought veterans Mick Leer, Lagan, and Basil Shields, Tassagh into opposition on the opening day.

The first score in that Tournament, in 1965, featured Joe Mee, Keady, against Patrick Leer, Carnagh, and the Keady man successfully played his way through each subsequent round of the entire field to eventually win the final over the late Jim Toal, Granemore, and Patsy Kilroy, Keady. During that Tournament, the late Eamon Gamble, Farmacaffley, broke the record for the Chapel Road, Keady, when he passed the Christian Brothers Gates in nineteen shots from Bluehill to beat Sean Shortt, the first Keady man to play and beat Joe McVeigh, and whose son Joe is a current formidable bowler and all round sportsman. The previous record of twenty shots for the course was held by Basil Shields.

The outcome of the big Easter charity score at Armagh, 1965, did nothing for southern confidence and indeed future aspirations but their conviction was regained in part on Easter Monday when Mick Madden, Blarney, a young player who was then making a big name for himself down south, had a relatively easy win over John Gribben, Farmacaffley, on the Keady road. The selection of John Gribben for the challenge, from more than a dozen options, had been something of a surprise and his preparations received a dent on Sunday 4th April on the Monaghan road when Jim Campbell, Lisadian, gave a masterly display to cover the course in a record breaking seventeen shots and leave the Farmacaffley man trailing hopelessly. Campbell's record was broken later that year by the extremely promising Patsy McKenna, Knappagh, who eclipsed Navan's Peter McCreesh with brilliant bowling in the Monaghan Tournament. Yet another Armagh discovery with a surprising burst of speed, and one of the youngest players to emerge in 1965, was Gerald McKee who swept through the early stages of the City Tournament on the Loughgall road with consummate ease. McKee was later to win the All-Ireland Junior title in 1969 at Grenagh against Paddy O'Donoghue, Cork, and maintained his progress to take the All-Ireland Intermediate title in the 1971 final at Cloghroe over Mick Sexton, Cork. Gerald's sons, Seamus and Brian look sufficiently promising to be destined for future championship honours.

The Ulster Senior championship, having demonstrated in the preceding two years the exacting standard required to succeed, attracted only the top players for the 1965 competition. The preliminary rounds, with championship interest fully emphasised by large crowds, resulted in the very fast Michael Hughes, Madden, going out to reigning champion Danny McParland, over the Keady road, and Joe Molloy, Grangemore, outclassing, Jim Campbell, Lisadian at Knappagh. And for the second year in succession the anticipated championship clash of Danny McParland and Aidan Toal failed to materialise when the latter was sensationally beaten by relative veteran Harry Toal who constantly held the lead in a score of poor standard at Knappagh. Harry Toal went on to contest the Ulster Final having beaten Gerry McGleenan, Ballytrodden, a newcomer to senior ranks, by a close margin on the last shot. McGleenan, with a bowl of great speed, had earlier disposed of the challenge by Armagh's Billy Quigley, in a two shot win at Keady road.

In the other half of the draw Oliver O'Neill, Armagh came through to the semi-final with a win over Joe Molloy and thus earned a clash with the holder who had earlier ended the championship hopes of Kevin McGleenan. That semi-final pairing promised much following the June finals of the Monaghan Road Tournament in which Oliver O'Neill, before a large and enthusiastic crowd, pressed the champion all the way to often take the lead before eventually losing out on the final throw after a score of superb bowling. The lesser grades in that Tournament final were won by Danny O'Brien, Armagh and Patsy McKenna, Knappagh. As anticipated, O'Neill and McParland produced the most exciting contest in the 1965 Ulster Championship. It showed the champion at his best and he required all his skill to finally oust O'Neill over the finishing stretch after the challenger had led through the first quarter and was level going into the last.

In the Ulster senior final Danny McParland collected his third consecutive championship title with a two shot win over Harry Toal, who at one stage headed for a bowl lead but a mistake set him back and he lost out from that to the finish.

The contestants in the 1965 Munster senior championship each bore the knowl-

Oliver O'Neill.
Photo: Larry Dickinson.

edge it had to be the year in which bowling honour and prestige was restored to the province. There would be a heavy onus on the ultimate champion but such responsibility was no deterrent to participants in the fiercely contested championship. Out went Liam Daly at Upton, beaten by Mick Collins, whilst Dooley O'Mahony fell by a bowl of odds to Denis O'Donovan, Fishers Cross, at Ballinadee. The shock of the championship was the defeat of 1963 All-Ireland finalist Derry Kenny by John O'Donoghue, who in his first year as a senior bowler, also beat Mick Murphy to make it through to the semi-finals. Jack Forde had a massive three shot win over Christy Keating but he, in turn, went out to superb play by Donie Lehane in the quarter- finals. Mick Barry, the man so many southerners were relying upon to break McParland's dominance, had beaten Johnny Creedon, and then, in a brilliant score at Tinker's Cross, ousted his partner of the doubles charity score in Armagh at Easter, Denis O'Donovan, before qualifying for the semi-finals with a win over Pat

O'Mahony. The remaining semi-final place was filled by Bandon's Denis O'Donovan who beat fellow Bandon player Denny Murphy.

Mick Barry continued on target for the title with a semi-final win over John O'Donoghue when he went almost a full bowl up on the first shot and protected that lead to the finish. Joining him in the final was Denis O'Donovan who got the better of Donie Lehane. The 1965 Munster senior final at Dunmanway drew a huge crowd and they were rewarded with an excellent score. Again Mick Barry showed the grit and determination of a skilful bowler, hungry for success, when he got away to a glorious start which immediately put him into a full shot lead. It was becoming a familiar opening scenario for Barry and despite the best challenging efforts by Denis O'Donovan throughout the final that terrific first bowl by the Waterfall expert subsequently determined the margin of victory in the end. Mick Barry was Munster champion once more and, more significantly, that yearning opportunity to avenge his All-Ireland defeat in 1964 was, at last, a palpable reality.

The All-Ireland senior road bowls final of 1965 had all the necessary ingredients for the showpiece of the year. Danny McParland, by then a phenomenon in senior bowling was going all out for his third successive National title. And just about everybody associated with the sport in Ireland sensed the resolute dedication of the great Mick Barry as he approached a championship final with one ultimate aim firmly and constantly in focus. Interest extended even beyond Ireland as a number of Dutch tourists, who co-incidentally played a variation of the sport in Holland and had joined spectators at the Munster final, cycled to Armagh during the intervening

Mick Barry delivers a shot in the 1965 All-Ireland Senior Final at Keady Road, Armagh.

week to see and film the much awaited and highly publicised All-Ireland encounter on Sunday, 1st August, 1965.

The Keady Road course on the edge of Armagh City, the most suitable road at that time for such a star attraction, drew an unprecedented crowd to a road bowls event at a northern venue. The outcome of that memorable contest is best summarised in this part of an account by pen- name B.T. in the *Armagh Observer* of 7th August, 1965.

> *Mick Barry, with one of the finest performances of his long bowling career, won his first All-Ireland senior bowls title on Sunday when beating the reigning champion Danny McParland with almost three shots to spare after leading from start to finish.*
>
> *Barry was in magnificent form showing fantastic speed and unerring accuracy which had McParland in trouble from the first throw. The champion never really hit it off and was beaten for speed almost the entire way. This was certainly not McParland's best form and though he had anything but a happy first quarter it was obvious that some of his acknowledged speed was absent throughout the score just as it had been at Clonakilty a few weeks earlier. Barry, on the other hand, has seldom been faster and with total accuracy over the first half he gradually drew ahead of the title holder. He had a dream start with three great bowls which left McParland trailing and though the reigning champion never dropped more than a shot behind up to the last quarter he could never really get on close terms and, frankly, at no stage looked like a winner.*

Danny McParland, Armagh, drives a shot between the lines of spectators in the 1965 All-Ireland Final.

> *Mick Barry was in devastating form and during the first half of the score there is not a bowler in Ireland who could have held his own with that wonderful performance. It is no secret that Barry, widely regarded as the best bowler of all time, had set his sights on this National title at the outset of the Munster senior championship and each performance throughout that highly competitive series confirmed his determination to win through. On Sunday last he was unbeatable with a perfect combination of speed and accuracy which consumed the road before him and saw him finish with three of the longest shots he has ever played. Immediately afterwards, Barry declared it was his best score in 27 years of bowling.*

That spontaneous comment at the end of the score in 1965 still holds relevant for the famous Cork bowler. In an interview almost twenty-five years later Mick Barry cited that particular All-Ireland win over Danny McParland as his most cherished victory, and after a quarter century of reflection his pleasure was obviously undiminished with the comment, "I was inspired that day and there was no way he could have beaten me."

The bowling record of Mick Barry in the years since that memorable win in 1965 has evidenced numerous victories some of which could be considered to have superseded his particular abiding memory. But at that stage he had not yet equalled Danny McParland's two consecutive National titles and so a further ambition was about to be launched.

In the Ulster Senior championship of 1966, in which all scores were played at Knappagh, Jim Hughes, Allistragh, got the better of Jim Campbell, Lisadian, but lost out in the next round to Armagh's Danny Reilly who ran up a very convincing win. A first round defeat ensued for Joe Molloy, Grangemore, when he went down to Aidan Toal, Tirgarve, who in turn beat a much fancied city player Oliver O'Neill to go through to a semi-final clash with Danny Reilly. Another formidable bowler to go out in the first round was Tommy Quinn, Drumcairne, who was beaten only seventy yards by Danny McParland before the holder, chasing his fourth consecutive Ulster title, went on to end the championship hopes of John Gribben, Farmacaffley who actually led the champion within four shots of the finish.

The evergreen bowler and relative veteran of the twelve contestants, Harry Toal, Armagh went through to the semi finals with a win over the late James Reilly and then faced a daunting engagement with reigning champion, McParland. The tantalising prospect of a hitherto thwarted Ulster Final clash of Aidan Toal and Danny McParland was soon to become a reality. In a strong finish during which he produced six tremendous shots towards the end Aidan Toal beat Danny Reilly for a final place and confirmation of the line-up for the championship decider was soon to follow with Danny McParland's full shot win over Harry Toal.

The pairing offered the prospect of the greatest Ulster senior championship encounter of all time. They had never before met in direct confrontation in any championship round and to do so in the final was a riveting reality. Followers of the sport needed no reminding of the most recent clash of Aidan Toal and Danny McParland on Sunday 12th September 1965 when a mere two yards divided the pair after an exciting tension filled finish to a Keady Road Tournament score which produced some extraordinary shots. Toal had come from behind to take the lead for the final shot and appeared certain of victory until McParland unleashed one of the longest shots ever played on the Keady road. He crossed the finishing line by forty yards to leave the leader with a daunting task. Amid a tense silence Toal made his effort and with his strongest and finest bowl of the day crossed the mark by only two yards for a finish rarely equalled in excitement.

What greater ingredients could be desired for an Ulster Senior Championship Final. This is a brief section of a report on the outcome:

> *Danny McParland has qualified for his fourth consecutive All-Ireland Bowls Final with a brilliant performance in retaining his Ulster title despite a strong challenge from Aidan Toal in a tense, sometimes thrilling, and always entertaining senior final which drew the biggest crowd to Knappagh for many years. McParland saved his best form for the final and got well over the line in twenty-four shots with Toal requiring his twenty-fifth to beat the mark. A useful lead by Toal was squandered at Stuart's Bridge when a slow bowl mistake put him a shot*

Mick Barry, Cork, contracts every muscle to ensure victory in the 1965 All-Ireland Final at Keady Road, Armagh.

down. McParland, back to his best in speed and accuracy, was giving no ground and he took the title in style with Toal, despite that costly error, attaining a personal best for the course.

Meanwhile the Munster Senior Championship of 1966 had been generating its own special aura. Derry Kenny acknowledged as the bowling stylist of the age, won a good score against Jack Forde and went on to record a further victory over that great sportsman Mick Murphy in a fine score at Ballygarvan. Mick Barry, whom they all had to beat if a Munster title was to come their way, had a relatively easy passage against John Creedon and followed this up with an impressive result over Dooley O'Mahony at Grenagh to clinch a semi-final place.

John O'Donohue, who had beaten Denny Murphy at an earlier stage subsequently lost out at Grenagh, to Jim Geasley who had beaten Pat Joe O'Mahony in the opening round. Geasley had previously won the Junior and Intermediate championships and was then through to the senior semi-finals for the first time. Denis O'Donovan completed the four semi-final places and was faced with bowling Mick Barry at Clancool whilst Jim Geasley confronted Derry Kenny at Ballyvolane.

There was naturally much speculation about the prospect of a Barry-Kenny final, considered by most as a bowling showpiece of the season, and that is exactly how the line up transpired. The two top senior bowlers in the province, Barry the accepted master; Kenny the most improved senior in the game and readily acknowledged threat to the champion's supremacy. They were both into the Munster final. That senior final at Togher, on 14th August, 1966, a score of huge attraction but less than perfect bowling, saw Kenny lead on two occasions before giving way in the second half to the power of Barry who dominated the finish for a one shot win to gain three consecutive Munster senior titles.

The contest for All-Ireland senior honours was once again between the two undisputed supremos in the sport, Barry and McParland, and the impelling urge to succeed was no less intense in this their third successive confrontation in the National decider. Barry's provincial win was less impressive than McParland's but the southern champion had been beaten before in the All-Ireland on home ground and was in no mood to experience that indignation once again.

The All-Ireland Final of 1966, on Sunday 28th August, was played at Kilpatrick, near Bandon in County Cork and the wide open space of this particular road made it the ideal venue for staging such a score. But the start of the contest was unduly delayed in chaotic conditions as strenuous efforts were made to control the vast crowd such was the density of the unprecedented spectator attendance.

This is how 'B.T.' reflected on the event in the *Armagh Observer* of 3rd September, 1966.

In a closely contested and thoroughly exciting All-Ireland senior final, Mick Barry earned a full shot win over Danny McParland, before the biggest crowd ever seen at a bowling match. McParland went into the lead with a brilliant fourth shot and held the advantage for the greater part of the Kilpatrick road. It was only over the last quarter, with terrific bowling, that Barry began to edge out in front. After a rather subdued Munster final performance Barry was back to his very best in this contest and a daring loft on his twelfth shot succeeded in putting him back on level terms from which point he really exerted pressure to the finish.

The highlight of the score from McParlands point of view was that magnificent effort on his fourth shot which covered tremendous ground and shot him into the lead for the first time. It was down the long hill where the dense crowd stretched out for well over half a mile and was to be McParland's best shot of the day. On the eleventh shot the Armagh man held a lead of nearly 20 metres, being a very significant advantage at a sharp right hand bend. It was at this stage Barry made his daring loft which amazed even his own supporters. From a relatively hopeless position he actually regained the lead with that courageous effort and with his best bowling reserved for the final quarter was on his way to yet another major victory.

The indomitable Mick Barry had, by then, remained unbeaten anywhere in Ireland for more than two years and had equalled Danny McParland's enviable record of two All-Ireland titles in a row. Would he relent? Not likely! There was a new personal record to be pursued and the 1967 championship awaited the onslaught.

That too was to be a Mick Barry dominated Munster senior championship. The reigning champion was again into the provincial decider, having beaten John Creedon in a semi-final score and the Waterfall phenomenon was by then contesting his ninth Munster final, six of them in succession. Of those previous eight he had lost only two and these were to Seamus Allen in 1958 and Derry Kenny in 1963. The men who knew what it was like to lose a Munster final against Mick Barry were Tedser Murphy, Tommy Forde, Denis O'Donovan, (Fisher's Cross), Jack Forde, Denis O'Donovan, (Bandon) and Derry Kenny. The unenviable task of avoiding that list of defeated finalists, and gaining his own coveted title, fell to the Kilkenny born bowler with lots of power, John O'Donoghue, who had beaten Tedser Murphy, the 1966 Intermediate champion, in the semi-final at Togher.

The Munster senior final at Kilpatrick on 23rd July 1967 was considered by many keen observers to have been the finest of them all. But despite the unrelenting pressure and unwavering bowling power of the challenger, John O'Donoghue, it was Mick Barry who held out for yet another glorious win and the ever growing prospect of three in a row National titles.

The Ulster senior championship that year was a less demanding one. Many potential seniors were deterred by the manifestly exacting standards and daunting nature of championship competition. The entry list was further depleted by the surprise, self imposed, resting of Danny McParland and in the end it was Aidan Toal who made it to the final after a semi-final win against Danny Reilly. He was joined in the final by cousin Harry Toal who had belied his veteran status with a great display against Oliver O'Neill in which he went very close to the finishing line at Knappagh in twenty-four shots. But Harry's renewed impetus was not sustained for the final, on Sunday 16th July 1967, when the Knappagh course proved a testing experience for both contestants. Aidan was expected to come through easily and he

Aidan Toal delivers from his mark in the 1967 All-Ireland Final. The referee is Joe Horan.
Photo : Belfast Telegraph

did so with a bowl to spare but was none too impressive in the doing. Despite that, he was having his best period in the game. In the only senior inter-provincial score played in Armagh during 1966 he beat Derry Kenny, who was on his first northern visit since the 1963 All-Ireland final, in a thrilling score over the Keady road on Sunday 16th October. Toal led from start to finish and it was to mark his first win over a Cork opponent for almost two and a half years. The Tirgarve player's restored confidence was carried into 1967 when he and Patsy McKenna, Knappagh, won a doubles score against Danny McParland, and promising city junior Gerald McKee, in a historic event at Newtownhamilton, south Armagh on Sunday 19th March. Toal's run continued in the City Tournament on Sunday 7th May 1967 when he beat McParland by two shots over the Loughgall road. Later that month he lost a return score to Derry Kenny who gained his revenge by a two shot margin at Ballyclough, Limerick, on Sunday 21st May. Toal later gained some local compensation by picking up the top grade award in the Macardles Ale tournament which was confined to northern players and not to be confused with the interprovincial Macardles series.

However in the 1967 All-Ireland senior final Toal was facing his most difficult bowling assignment. He could hardly be other than mindful of the fact that he had lost heavily to Barry at Limerick in June 1966 and knew it would take a supreme

Crowded lines of tense spectators as Aidan Toal bowls at Knappagh in the 1967 All-Ireland Senior Final.
Photo: Belfast Telegraph.

Fachtna O'Donovan, Limerick, bowling at the Blackwatertown (Port Mor) Road, Armagh in 1966.

effort to thwart the reigning champion's attempt at a record breaking three successive All-Ireland senior road bowling titles.

The All-Ireland senior final at Knappagh on Sunday 6th August, 1967 attracted a huge crowd the enthusiasm of which was manifest throughout the entire event. This is part of a comprehensive report on that great final by Malachy Digby in the *Armagh Observer* of 12th August 1967.

> *The task of facing an All-Ireland senior bowls final is at all times a trying experience and when confronted by a player the calibre of Mick Barry it must be doubly so. Yet to his credit Aidan Toal, on Sunday last, faced up to the task admirably, and over the first half of the course must have had his illustrious opponent beginning to wonder just what he was going to have to do to win; for despite bringing all his expertise and ability to bear on the contest he found, at this stage, the Armagh man only ten yards behind him. This was one of Toal's finest scores to this point for it was here that Barry, through two sets of circumstances, had wonderfully good fortune in not going a bowl down. Had Toal gone a shot in front at this stage, as his play had entitled him to do, Barry might not have continued with the same confidence and the northern champion might just have had the boost to inspire him with the renewed ability to overcome this great opponent. That this was the vital turning point is undisputed. Both players were in the Condy Corner, the halfway point, in twelve shots. After two more it was Barry who began to dominate the exchanges and he continued to stretch his lead over the last quarter. In the end Barry was well over the line in twenty-three shots whilst Toal topped his mark on the twenty-fifth to lose by less than two bowls of odds.*

That personal record of three successive All-Ireland senior road bowling titles, so difficult to accomplish and even more elusive to equal, is a fitting achievement through which the mighty power of Mick Barry, who has reigned supreme throughout a durable bowling career, will long be remembered. The respectful admiration extended to this wonderful bowl player is exemplified in this section of the 1967 final report by Malachy Digby, and provides, for this particular chapter, an apt conclusion.

> *Fantastic, unbelievable, invincible; these are some of the adjectives freely tossed around in a floundering attempt to describe the phenomenon that is Mick Barry. But all of them are simply inadequate. One can only stand in awe and silently appreciate the artistry of this great bowl player for Mick Barry is an artist, an actor, who draws forth applause from even the most unwilling spectators, for the seemingly impossible is made to look easy by this, surely, the greatest player ever to take a bowl in his hand. Some players may possess one or two of the qualities that go towards making greatness, be it speed, or accuracy, or both. But Mick Barry has these qualities to the maximum, allied to well nigh perfect judgement and temperament. He strides the bowling world like a colossus, virtually unbeatable, and will continue so, given lasting health, for many years to come.*

A Memory Sustained Through Youthful Endeavour

The inter provincial bowling programme scheduled for the Easter weekend of 1967 was equally attractive to any other that had gone before. Perhaps even more so as the fixtures arranged for Grenagh, Co Cork over the holiday period promised two particularly inviting junior and senior scores. The ambitious challenge taken up by two Armagh bowlers reflected evolvement of the sport in the north and demonstrated an unbridled enthusiasm for competing at the highest level.

It had been a thoroughly successful developmental period in the sport, particularly since the new Northern Branch Executive of Bol Chumann had experienced a stable few years of consolidated effort at organising and promoting the game. A flourishing junior championship had been inaugurated in 1966 to enable competition on a parallel with the previously established tournament in the south which involved the qualifying champions from Cork, Limerick and Waterford. It was Limerick based Garda Fachtna O'Donovan, who came through Munster that year having won the Limerick junior title before going on to beat the West Cork and South Cork champions. He had his closest score on Sunday 21st August, 1966, on his way to the All-Ireland Junior Final when he got over the finishing line with just yards to spare against Tom Ennis of Bandon at Templemartin. In the north it was Sean Cullen, Lisadian, who won the inaugural Ulster Junior championship having beaten Joe Horan, Salters Grange, Jim Cullen, Ballyheridan, Sean Oliver, Aughanore, Patsy McKenna, Knappagh, and in the final, the late Brendan Digby, Armagh City. The first ever All-Ireland Junior title was the honour beckoning Limerick's Fachtna O'Donovan and Armagh's Sean Cullen, at Grenagh, ten miles from Cork on Saturday 27th August, 1966. And that special honour went to the fast, forceful and confident O'Donovan who won by a two shot margin over Cullen, who, on the day, lacked sufficient speed to narrow the contest.

Despite that defeat it had been a great year for a large and talented group of junior players in the north. In a review of the sporting year at the end of 1966, bowling correspondent Malachy Digby named seven emerging junior bowlers for whom he predicted future championship honours: Gerald McKee, Patsy McKenna, Brendan Digby, Sean Cullen, Al Mallon, Stephen Donnelly and Sean Oliver. Six of these players subsequently won Ulster and All-Ireland championship honours at varying levels in the sport.

There were several other encouraging and progressive features about the bowling game in 1966. Apart from Festival scores, which are reflected upon in another chapter, there was yet another close contest between Donie Lehane, Bandon and Danny McParland, Armagh, at Ballinadee on Easter Monday, 11th April which was played throughout in continuous rain, exacerbated by frequent heavier cloud bursts, which twice delayed the score. Lehane won through on the final throw. A month later a very big crowd on the Moy road, Armagh, saw Danny McParland, gain a twenty-five yard win over Aidan Toal on Sunday 15th May, 1966, in a well publicised challenge score. Toal was handled and coached in that particular event by two of the most experienced men in the game at the time, Joe McVeigh, an expert bowler, and McVeigh's own handler, Henry Molloy. All records for the Newtown road were broken by Mick Leer, Lagan, on 11th September, 1966 when he beat Larry Feighan, Corran, in St Patricks Tournament, Keady and went on to win the final over Edmund Nugent, Darkley, to add to his 1964 victory in the same Tournament. One of the most exciting juniors to emerge in 1966, Al Mallon, Kilmore, recorded a convincing win at Blackwatertown (now Port Mor) over newly crowned All-Ireland Junior champion, Fachtna O'Donovan, on Sunday 2nd October that year. It was a tremendous sporting and social occasion hosted by Grange club Chairman, Henry Neary, and complimented by a large and enthusiastic visiting contingent led by Jim Cummings, Chairman of the Ballyclough Bowling Club in Limerick. The only senior interprovincial score to be played in Armagh in 1966 saw Aidan Toal lead all the way over Derry Kenny, on Sunday 16th October, at the Keady road.

In all it was a reflective period about which Henry Neary, Chairman of the Northern Branch, An Bol Chumann Na hEireann had much to be proud as players and officials in the north contemplated the bowling year ahead. The inter-provincial scores scheduled for the 1967 Easter weekend in March echoed that pride and confidence. The programme billing included Patsy McKenna, a brilliant young junior discovery who was due to take on Cork's Larry Murphy. The senior encounter represented a third meeting for Aidan Toal and Derry Kenny. The first of these saw Kenny win by 50 yards at the Miles, near Clonakilty, in July 1966, and the second was that shot win by Toal over the Keady road the following October. It was an attractive programme. The Armagh Democrat newspaper of Thursday 23rd March 1967 devoted a full page preview to the big Easter bowling contests with advertising space taken up by local business people in support of the event. Everything was set for a mass exodus of northern road bowls followers at Easter - or so it seemed.

On the morning of Wednesday 22nd March, 1967, three days before Easter, the Chairman and Secretary of the Northern Branch, An Bol Chumann, both nurses, met briefly as one was coming off duty and the other was going on. There was a natural projection towards the weekend bowling programme and a short conversation ensued about the final arrangements. That same day, in mid afternoon, the Secretary took an urgent telephone message at his place of work from a staff reporter with Democrat newspapers. The journalist, the late Sean Hughes, had arrived at the scene of a road traffic accident near Caledon, Co Tyrone, involving a saloon car and an oil tanker. The driver of the car, Henry Neary, was dead. It was stunning news. A shattering blow personally, and the consequence of his tragic loss was to be sorely felt by so many. Two days later Henry Neary, aged 40 years, who had guided northern bowling through four crucial years, was laid to rest in St Patrick's Cemetery, Armagh, mourned by bowls followers from every part of Ireland where the game was played. In the sombre days that followed the Secretary arranged an emergency meeting of the Northern Branch, An Bol Chumann, after which a statement was issued, signed by each Club Secretary who was present at the specially convened assembly. The statement opened and concluded with specific expressions of sympathy and the central import read as follows:

> *The officers and members of all clubs affiliated to the Northern Branch, An Bol Chumann Na hEireann deeply regret the sudden death, in tragic circumstances, of our late Chairman, Henry Neary, who was greatly respected by everyone and held in such high esteem by all his sporting colleagues. Chairman of our parent association since its inception, his loss to An Bol Chumann is incalculable. His infinite popularity as our leader down through the years has been apparent. He was the first elected Chairman under the present constitution and his unopposed return ever since is affirmation of his conscientious and unswerving approach to the onerous position he daily filled with honour. We fully appreciate the tremendous work Henry Neary has done for the sport, much of which was conducted behind the scenes and often extended beyond the call of duty as Chairman. He was largely responsible for the initiation of the successful All- Ireland championship series and freely devoted immense time and energy towards achieving this aim. We are pleased and proud that he did so and will always remember him for his untiring efforts towards the success of the sport.*
>
> *We pledge ourselves to perpetuate the memory of Henry Neary with a worthy memorial trophy which will grace one of our major competitions.*

Henry Neary.

Signed: Brian Toal, Grange Club; Malachy Digby, Tassagh Club; Sean Moore, Armagh City Club; John Gribben, Keady Road Club; Dick Burke, Newtownhamilton Club; Sean Cullen, Knappagh Club; Joe Molloy, St Patrick's Club, Keady.

The high esteem in which the late Henry Neary was held by his counterparts in Cork is aptly testified in this laudatory tribute by "Boithreach", in the *Cork Evening Echo* of 31st March, 1967.

Most unhappy bowling news of the last week and for a long time past was the news of the tragic death of Mr Henry Neary of Armagh. One of the founder members of the Armagh Branch of an Bol-Chumann, and chairman of that branch for a number of years past, Henry Neary was probably the best known and most widely popular bowling executive in Armagh. He was certainly one of the Armagh men best known to us in Cork, one of those men upon whom we depended to ensure that bowling affairs in Armagh and those in Cork were run on closely parallel lines.

Henry Neary was a quiet man, a pleasant and very amiable companion, a man of few words. But with all that he was a man of determination, a man of unwavering loyalty, a man whose quiet manner and unobtrusive demeanour hid a very powerful and very firm character. Henry stood for what was right, no matter who was wrong, and no argument, no pressure could change him once he was convinced where the right lay and where the wrong. The man was steady as he was straight. In our years of intimate dealings with him we never once found him any where but on the side of that which was straight and just and honourable.

For us in Cork bowl playing circles our first direct contact with Henry Neary was at a Cork-Armagh executive meeting in Bandon a good number of years ago. Henry was one of a strong Armagh representation at that meeting, but very early on most of us were able to decide where the power behind the Armagh throne existed. It was characteristic of the man that he spoke but seldom and said but little when he did speak; yet the sincerity of the man was so apparent and the sound logic of his suggestions so clear-cut that he had an extra-ordinary capacity of swaying a meeting without appearing to do so.

For our own part we can only say that we will endeavour to cleave as closely as may be to the Neary doctrine of North-South relations. In life his word and worth meant much to us. In death his memory will always mean just as much.

A significant sector of the bowling developments in hand by the late Chairman at the time of his death was the planned inauguration of a Juvenile championship for players under 16 years. It was with the minimum delay that the Northern Branch, An Bol Chumann accelerated these arrangements. Henry Neary's keen interest in promoting the involvement of young players was always evident and a decision was very quickly taken to grace the Under-16 championship with an award to be named, "The Henry Neary Memorial Trophy."

That inaugural Juvenile championship in 1967 attracted entries from sixteen of the best under age players in the game and comprised Conor Gribben, Terry McGerrigan, Donal Toal, Joe Murphy, Pat O'Hagan, Sean Grew, Kenneth McComb, Martin Rowland, Niall McKee, Kevin Hughes, Adrian Mallon, Sean Webb, Philip Hughes, Pat Lennon, John Grimley and Stephen Mackle.

The consequent Ulster Juvenile final was between Adrian Mallon, Tullygoonigan, and Kevin Hughes, Madden. A very large attendance confirmed the widespread interest in the new competition. The first winner of the Henry Neary Memorial Trophy was to be Adrian Mallon, and perhaps fittingly so, for he then resided less than a mile from the home of the late chairman whom the Ulster Under 16 championship commemorates.

The Munster Juvenile final that year was contested by Denis Santry, Clonakilty, and a young north Cork bowler Gene Hogan. It was young Santry, less than 15 years old at the time, who won through in an exciting score to quality for the National final.

In the first ever All-Ireland Juvenile final, played over the Cathedral road in Armagh on Sunday, 6th August, 1967, the northern representative Adrian Mallon, with a little extra in speed, came from behind to pip the very accurate southern champion, Denis Santry on the final shot. It was a fine inaugural score for the National juvenile title, with little distance separating the pair at any stage of the game. A terrific last shot by Mallon gained him the title as Santry, despite a valiant final effort, fell short of the mark. It was a great win for the northern champion but a perplexing realisation for the young Clonakilty player who, despite the experience of losing on the final shot when the advantage was in his favour, accepted defeat with a maturity and courtesy which belied his tender years. Such was the nature of his coping with this defeat that the Secretary to the Northern Branch, An Bol Chumann, in his extensive report to convention in February, 1968, published in Armagh Democrat and *Armagh Observer* newspapers, commented, "If Adrian Mallon showed how to win a major final, the young man who demonstrated to us all how to accept defeat was Denis Santry, his opponent in that final. This young player was the loser of the year and if these are the bowling men of the future the prospects for the game are assured."

Included too in the report was the conviction that the inauguration, and subsequent proven success, of the Under 16 championship was one of the most encouraging highlights of the year. "These young sportsmen have served up, north and south, some of the most entertaining bowling of the year and their overall contribution to the sport is something about which they can feel justifiably proud."

Also acknowledged in that detailed report was the wealth of work so admirably endured by the late Chairman Henry Neary, and how the Association members had, more than ever, pooled their resources, to fulfil a declared obligation to perpetuate his memory.

Twenty five years later in 1992, the original trophy was renewed by the former Secretary who served during the reign of Henry Neary as Chairman of the Northern Branch, An Bol Chumann Na hEireann.

Adrian Mallon on the day he won the All-Ireland Under 16 Final at Armagh in 1967.

Accepting the new Henry Neary Cup in 1992 from Brian Toal, who was Secretary during the reign of the late former Chairman, is John Gribben (second right), then Chairman of the Northern Branch An Bol Chumann Na hEireann. In the centre is Paddy Comiskey, then Treasurer, and on right is Aidan McVeigh, then Secretary. On extreme left is Adrian Mallon who was first winner of the original trophy in 1967.
Photo: Michael Campbell.

This is how the Belfast national daily newspaper, *The Irish News*, reported the occasion with accompanying photographs, on Tuesday 16 June 1992.

> *The Henry Neary Cup which is competed for in under age Championship Road Bowling in County Armagh has been renewed after twenty-five years of keen competition for the original trophy.*
>
> *The new cup will continue to be awarded to the Under-16 Ulster Road Bowls Champion and serves to perpetuate the memory of the former Chairman of the Bowling association who guided the progress of the game in the north throughout the early sixties.*
>
> *Henry Neary, from Knockaconey, Armagh had played a significant role in the formation of the Northern Branch of the All-Ireland Road Bowls Association and was inspirational in negotiating the terms for the All-Ireland Senior Championship series which began in 1963. He had been Chairman of the Association for a number of years up until his untimely death at Easter of 1967 and was the principal executive of a strong northern representation at a historic meeting in Bandon, Co Cork four years earlier at which details for the All-Ireland Road Bowling Championships were finalised.*
>
> *At the time of his death Henry Neary had plans well advanced for the inaugural Under- 16 Championship and it was played that year in his honour. Fittingly, the under age championship was won on its first running in 1967 by Adrian Mallon from the same parish area as the late Chairman. Since then the under age bowlers have competed annually for the trophy with Michael Rock from Newtownhamilton becoming the twenty- fifth winner of the title last year.*
>
> *This year's championship for the new Henry Neary Cup and the Ulster Under-16 title will be played out in the next few weeks with the winner participating in the All-Ireland series in Armagh at the beginning of August.*
>
> *Previous winners of the Henry Neary Under-16 Championship have been:-*
>
> *Adrian Mallon (1967); Thomas Moore (1968); John Cromie (1969); Patrick Comiskey (1970 & 1971); Harry Toal (1972); Malachy Comiskey (1973 & 1974); Liam Boylan (1975); Kieran Toal (1976); Martin Boylan (1977 & 1978); Philip Rafferty (1979); Francis Kiernan (1980); Dermot Grimley (1981); Dominic Donnelly (1982); Brian Kiernan (1983); Michael Toal (1984); Patrick McCreesh (1985); Brian Kinchin (1986); Liam Gribben (1987); Stephen Druse (1988); Michael Rafferty (1989); Mark McKeown (1990); Michael Rock (1991).*

The new Henry Neary Cup for the Under-16 Ulster Championship has since been won by:- Paul Rafferty (1992 & 1993); Austin McKeown (1994); Philip McKeever (1995).

The enduring competition for the Henry Neary Cup, through the honest endeavour of these under age enthusiasts, is a fitting and lasting memory to a late Chairman who valued so greatly the participation of younger players as a basis for the continued success of the sport.

Road Bowls at Popular Festivals

The revitalized interest and renewed impetus generated by publicity which followed the instigation of the All-Ireland championship series had the desired consequence of road bowls becoming a feature at some of the major Festivals around the country.

The interest by various Festival Committees first emerged in 1965 and any request for participation by top bowl players in towns and cities outside the recognised bowling domain was a welcome evolution to which the association was keen to make a positive response. Any exposure of the sport to a wider audience has got to be welcomed but there can be impediments to such exhibition scores as participation in some festivals tended to confirm. With road bowls being traditionally played where the game is properly marshalled, and the nature of a score adequately understood by the attendance, it is a radical departure for exhibition scores to be contested before large crowds of uninitiated spectators many of whom are unaware of the personal responsibility and basic safety precautions to be fulfilled at such an event. There are very few sports in which the contestants and spectators share the same playing area. And whilst large crowds at any score of road bowls can and do create problems these tend to be exacerbated at Festival events where there is a more intense curiosity on the part of the spectator coupled with a lesser awareness of the obligation to provide adequate space for the player, and the need to ensure personal safety.

However numerous very successful exhibition scores have been played at major Festivals and undoubtedly these will continue to be an attractive feature at such events for many years to come.

One of the first of these exhibition scores to be sponsored by a Festival Committee was on Sunday 6th June 1965 when the organisers of Kilkenny Beer Festival hosted a score of road bowls as an added attraction to the week long programme of sporting and cultural activities. It was Whit weekend and the score was arranged for the very picturesque village of Innistioge, some twelve miles from the city of Kilkenny. The organisers, through the good offices of Bol Chumann had secured the participation of two leading senior bowlers, Danny McParland, All-Ireland champion in 1963 and '64, and formidable opposition in Donie Lehane, who had recorded wins over Mick Barry, John Creedon, and Jack Forde. The players and spectators were welcomed at the start by the then parish priest of Innistioge, Rev Fr Noonan and the score, refereed by Hedley McCay, set off, accompanied by a huge crowd, the vast majority of whom were seeing the game for the first time. Lehane won the first shot with a great opening drive and the lead exchanged several times in an exciting score before McParland, with the faster bowl, got into a full shot lead which be held to the finish.

The Festival of West Cork in Clonakilty went a stage further when the organisers also introduced a "long shot" competition in 1964 and the following year decided to make it an All- Ireland event with one particular day reserved for northern bowlers. The first throw in the long shot competition was made by radio and television personality Al Byrne on Sunday 4th July 1965 and throughout the following week players of senior rank performed their efforts. The northern bowlers were allotted Sunday 11th July to coincide with a Festival road bowling score between Donie Lehane and Danny McParland. But that was where their participation in the long shot competition ended. Such was the extent of the crowd at the road bowling score, estimated to be in excess of 12,000 during the peak, that it took more than eight hours to cover the two and a half mile course. The score drew the biggest crowd of any event at the Festival and, for the most part, these were spectators well acquainted with the intricacies of the sport. After all, this was the home of the mighty Michael McCarthy-Quirke who, as early as 1922, was a spectacular bowler of rare quality. But the protracted playing time, resulting in a late evening finish, prevented the northern challenge in the long shot competition from taking place. However, shots in plenty there were between Lehane and McParland as poor play extended both of them well beyond the course record in a score of high excitement and a close tension-filled finish. In the end Lehane gained revenge for the Kilkenny defeat when he won by the narrow margin of fifteen yards.

It was the turn of Limerick city in 1966 to stage a major bowling fixture as part of the Festival of Sport programme and the organisers there succeeded in attracting reigning All-Ireland senior champion Mick Barry and Armagh's Aidan Toal who was enjoying his best ever season in senior bowling. The Festival of Sport committee were fortunate to have the services of a very active Bol Chumann affiliated club within their sphere and this greatly enhanced the efficiency of initial preparations and the practical management of the event. The Ballyclough Bowling Club along with the personal efforts of Chairman Jim Cummings and Secretary Fachtna O'Donovan ensured superb organisation of the event which was sponsored by the clothing firm Danus Ltd. The pre score publicity included the distribution of action pictures and posters related to the Barry-Toal clash and huge banners, spaced at 100 yard intervals, marked the course which drew very favourable comment from all sides as being one of the best and fairest in Ireland with its sweeping curves and smooth surface. Again, as in most Festival scores the event attracted a huge attendance most of whom were having their first introduction to the sport. At the start, the players were introduced to the then Minister for Health, the late Donagh O'Malley, who played a first shot to officially open the score. At the halfway stage, the Festival Queen, Miss Rita Keane, escorted by Order of Malta personnel, was introduced to the players.

The score itself on Sunday 5th June, 1966, resulted in another great win for Mick Barry who had remained unbeaten for the preceding two years. Aidan Toal made a disastrous start from which he never recovered, in contrast to Barry who opened superbly with a dream shot which assured him of a big lead over the first quarter and subsequently, a comfortable two shot victory.

The 1966 Festival of West Cork in Clonakilty secured a very attractive senior exhibition score for that year's programme when Derry Kenny and Aidan Toal each accepted invitations to compete in a Guinness sponsored event at the Miles. It was the first meeting of Toal and Kenny. The Clogheen player was, at that stage, already through to the Munster senior championship semi-finals and was rated Mick Barry's greatest danger. Kenny subsequently came close to toppling Barry in that year's final but despite leading on two separate occasions over the Togher course he lost out during the final quarter. In the Festival score, on Sunday, 10th July, 1966, Aidan Toal, produced his best ever performance at a Cork venue but despite such stupendous form it was not sufficient to fend off the brilliant Derry Kenny, who won by 50 yards in a score which thrilled thousands of spectators. Both players cut four shots off the winning total for the corresponding score the previous year.

The successful resolution to a protracted dispute was marked with the eventual completion, in April 1967, of a long delayed resumption to a score between Donie Lehane and Danny McParland which the latter ultimately won by three shots. The incident distinctly underlined the necessity for official control and management of scores at neutral venues. More importantly it emphasised the total determination of Bol Chumann Na hEireann to exercise its absolute authority in securing a fair and firm resolution to this or any other such similar matter.

The Ballyclough Club in Limerick staged a mini version of the Festival of Sport on Sunday 21st May, 1967 when the magnificent junior player, Al Mallon, Kilmore, Co Armagh, produced the best performance of his career to that point by leading from start to finish to record a second win over Limerick based Fachtna O'Donovan, the 1966 All-Ireland Junior Champion. In the senior event that day, Derry Kenny beat Aidan Toal by two shots to gain ample compensation for his defeat by the Armagh man over the Keady road on 16th October 1966.

The first occasion of Festival bowling in the north was April 1968 when a road bowls score formed part of an attractive programme for Armagh Civic Week. The score was sponsored by Danus Ltd and their involvement with the event was confirmed when an executive of the firm Noel O'Donovan met Irwin Wilson, Chairman of Armagh Civic Week Committee, when both men were on a business trip to London. The pairing for the big event was intended to be the 1967 All-Ireland Junior Champion Patsy McKenna, Knappagh, and Cork's dynamic new discovery, eighteen year old Denis Scully but much to the disappointment of the organisers the latter was ruled out through injury just as 8,000 brochures for Armagh Civic Week had gone on distribution. The new pairing saw McKenna take on Al Mallon, the popular Kilmore player who had already recorded two big wins over the champion. It proved to be an inspired substitution. When Danus representative Brian Sterritt played the first shot to officially open the road bowls event for Armagh Civic Week it was greeted with great enthusiasm. But it was mild when compared with what followed. McKenna and Mallon provided one of the hardest fought and closely contested scores for a very long time to thrill a huge crowd with brilliant bowling over the entire course at Armagh. McKenna had set a blistering pace with perfect bowling but Mallon, with a coolness that was almost unreal, followed him relentlessly.

The late Donagh O'Malley, then Minister for Sport in the Republic of Ireland, throws the first bowl in a score between Mick Barry, Cork and Aidan Toal, Armagh, at the 1966 Festival of Sport in Limerick. Included (from left) are Dan O'Leary, referee); Eamon O'Carroll; Jim Cummings; Mick Barry; Donagh O'Malley, Aidan Toal; Noel O'Donovan, sponsor and Fachtna O'Donovan, Secretary of the promoting club.
Photo: Sean Cooke, Limerick.

Spectators at a bowling score on Cathedral Road, Armagh.

The finish was tense, close and exciting when Al Mallon beat Patsy McKenna's final effort with a tremendous finishing shot to collect the Danus Cup and gain the honour of winning the first Festival score in the north. Referee Joe Horan stated after the event that he had never officiated at a score between two greater sportsmen. A fine tribute at the conclusion of an exhibition score which advertised everything that is good about the sport of road bowls.

A disused aerodrome at Ardboe in County Tyrone was the unusual venue for a Festival score on Sunday 17th May, 1970. The Festival was organised by a Committee led by Fr Pat Smith and road bowls was a prominent feature on the programme. An inspection of local roads led to the aerodrome being chosen for a doubles score between Armagh city bowlers Danny McParland and Harry Toal and rural exponents Aidan Toal and Al Mallon. The score proved to be a thriller which the city men won on the last shot. The game also featured at Downpatrick Festival in County Down in the late seventies and early eighties when Paddy McEvoy, a prominent member of the organising committee introduced the sport to that particular region. In more recent years major scores have been a regular and prominent feature at Festivals in Bantry and Kilkenny.

But any rumination on bowling participation in popular Festivals over the years will inevitably reveal numerous compelling reasons for selecting the Dundalk Maytime Festival of 1968 as the greatest of them all. The pre-festival publicity was exceptional and road bowls reaped the benefit of considerable media exposure facilitated through press conferences, radio broadcasts, festival newspapers, thousands of circulars, and greatly enhanced local and national newspaper coverage. The chief organiser for the road bowling event was Alf Dwyer, one of the leading festival officials, and the intention to make the innovation a wonderful attraction at Dundalk Maytime Festival was underlined with the designation of Road Bowling as the major sporting event on the peak day of the ten-day festival. The organisers had secured the sponsorship of Dundalk Wholesale Bottling Co Ltd, for the bowling event which carried a big prize fund and offered to the participants specially designed trophies. Elaborate plans were put in place for a most indicative sporting, and social occasion in which road bowling complemented the overall festival purpose and in the process gained in stature as a cultural ingredient.

The score , on Sunday 19th May, 1968, may have been billed as a festival exhibition match but was nonetheless highly competitive and featured what was then unquestionably the two best northern bowlers against the greatest possible pairing in the south. Danny McParland was an ex-All-Ireland senior champion and his partner Aidan Toal was the current Ulster senior champion. The daunting southern partnership comprised Mick Barry, the current All-Ireland senior champion and Derry Kenny ex Munster senior champion. The scene was set for a bowling spectacular over four kilometres of an ideally suited course from Knockbridge Cross to Louth village. The referee was Dan O'Leary, Blarney and the official marker was the late Edward Finn, Armagh. The players were introduced at the start to Festival Queen Ann McNamara as thousands of spectators, most of them at a bowling score for the first time, struggled to get a glimpse of the opening shots.

This is how the *Ulster Gazette* of Thursday, 23rd May, 1968 reported the score.

If ever there was any doubt Danny McParland and Aidan Toal are the greatest bowling combination in the country it must surely have been dispelled for ever at Dundalk Maytime Festival when these two brilliant exponents produced a superb display of fast, accurate and opportunist play that must undoubtedly have been one of their best ever performances.

In giving this sparkling exhibition they not only beat the strongest possible opposition, but coasted, almost effortlessly to a clear win that saw them approach the finishing line with a fantastic lead of close on three shots. That Mick Barry and Derry Kenny, the two leading senior players in the South, could never once get into the lead after the first shot, is evidence of the splendid performance by the Armagh men. It was their superior speed, accuracy and consistency, that held for them an early lead throughout the first half and eventually demoralised a Cork pair who, long before the finish, must have realised that against such devastating opposition they had simply no chance of victory. A complete understanding between McParland and Toal set the seal on what proved to be the greatest team effort that Armagh bowling has ever experienced. A truly magnificent second shot by Toal that wiped out an early deficit and set Armagh into the lead was an early indication that the Southern pair were in for a lesson. It was then the turn of McParland on the seventh shot to prove how jeopardy can be alleviated, when he played a brilliant drive to secure a useful Armagh lead just at a point when it seemed seriously threatened. And that was how it continued right to the finish with one brilliant shot after another and most of the really big efforts coming in the second half.

It was certainly sweet victory for Armagh but for the big Northern contingent, who followed their two idols with unwavering loyalty, the star of the day was Aidan Toal, who had his greatest ever outing. His tremendous speed, unsurpassed accuracy and overall confidence surprised even his most ardent supporters and when on more than one occasion he covered tremendous ground with unbelievable drives, sometimes covering as many as three bends, he strode away from the might of Mick Barry to the echo of the most enthusiastic vocal support ever heard at a neutral venue. This was a day Toal will long remember. Never once during the two and a half mile score did he falter even the slightest and it has certainly been a long time since Toal or any other player enjoyed such magnificent form. His delivery of the second shot quickly dispelled all fears of his suspect fitness and on every subsequent shot he delivered with perfection and pin-point accuracy.

McParland, with a misjudged opening shot, had the Northern following momentarily worried but when it again came the ex-champion's turn on the third, he set them at ease with a drive more like what we have come to expect from him. His really outstanding shot of the score was on the seventh when he carefully and expertly pulled his bowl well round a wide bend to reinstate the Armagh lead on the only one occasion on which it was threatened.

> *It was the clever adaptation to the course by the Armagh pair that did most towards obtaining such length to their shots and it was a fitting reward for the numerous training and practice scores that both men had undertaken during the past few weeks. The benefit of such training must now be obvious, for it was Toal's greatest ever score and one of McParland's most consistent displays for a very long time. Between them they set a pace that no pair in Ireland could equal and while Barry and Kenny could, and in fact should, have been a lot closer at the finish, they had rarely any hope of victory.*
>
> *Barry was his usual self with plenty of speed, but an occasional scattered bowl. Over the Knockbridge Road there was no room for inaccuracy, and in that respect he failed more than once. It was in the same respect that Kenny faltered, for despite the obvious effort this great sportsman put into every shot, he was sadly lacking in the brilliance of his recent successful visit to Armagh.*

It is performances such as that just described, played out before a new and appreciative gallery of spectators, which demonstrates the true nature of road bowling and provides an insight to the capacity of the game to prevail as a National and International sport.

The Challenge for National Honours

The supreme honour for any present day bowler, be it in road bowling, lofting or moors bowling, is to win a European championship medal in a team or individual event. At National level the ultimate achievement is to win an All-Ireland title in road bowling and that personal distinction is earnestly pursued each competitive year by avid bowlers in more than a dozen categories of championship bowling.

The challenge for national honours in championship and other prestigious competitions has been an unrelenting feature of the annual road bowling programme and the fervour with which such fame is greeted amply demonstrates the level of enthusiasm attaching that achievement.

The All-Ireland championship programme was augmented in 1966 with the introduction of the Junior championship to complement the existing competitions in Juvenile and Senior grades. Since then there has been fierce competition in these and several additional grades as players, over the years, have striven for that elusive National title.

The Junior championship of 1967 was particularly competitive. The much underrated Christy Coleman, Cork was the eventual winner of the Munster junior championship having surmounted many difficult challenges in his bid for provincial honours not least the title win over Willie Leahy at Waterloo. In the north it was Patsy McKenna who took the Ulster junior title that year after beating Liam Donnelly, James Reilly and Stephen Donnelly before recording a semi-final win over Al Mallon and subsequently producing a great display of accurate and powerful bowling to overcome Billy Quigley in the final. The All-Ireland Junior final of 1967 was extremely closely contested. Christy Coleman played the score of his life in Armagh on Saturday 5th August when he placed every bowl to perfection and just missed the finishing line by twelve inches on his final throw. Only Patsy McKenna at his very best could have stayed with him, and he did, with outstanding bowling in which he scorched over the finishing line for a last shot win. There were scenes of wild enthusiasm and jubilation as northern supporters greeted their first winner of a Junior All-Ireland title.

The spin-off from such success was evident with the formation of new clubs and additional local Tournaments. In January of 1968 a Tournament was launched by a new club in Benburb, Co Tyrone which was eventually won by Paul Mills, Portadown, over Noel Collins, Moy and Francie McKenna, Aughatarra.

A major attraction in the early part of 1968 was the prestigious Macardles National Tournament, the final of which was played in Armagh on Easter Sunday, 14th April. The southern qualifier for the national final was Derry Kenny, the 1963 All-Ireland finalist, who broke all existing records at Macroon on 7th April, 1968 in a scintillating performance that readily accounted for a very impressive Johnny Holland who had only recently been promoted to senior ranks. A week earlier

Derry Kenny had never been seen to bowl better such was the quality of his play in a doubles score at Drimoleague when he and his partner, Denis Scully, had a rare winning margin of four shots over Mick Barry and John Creedon. The 28 year old Clogheen bowler was undoubtedly facing the Macardles National final in superb form and with supreme confidence.

The northern challenger for the trophy was Harry Toal. He had accounted for Mickey Hughes, Madden in a semi-final contest and then surprisingly ousted Aidan Toal who had earlier beaten recently promoted senior player Patsy McKenna. Harry Toal, at 39 years old, was back in a National final some fifteen years following his first inter-provincial score and more than twenty years after he initially entered senior competitive bowling.

But it was the brilliant Derry Kenny who carried off the major prize with a superb display of fast and accurate bowling before a huge crowd at renowned Knappagh, near Armagh. It was a truly magnificent performance from a player in tremendous form and pundits everywhere were predicting All-Ireland senior championship honours for a most stylish player of astonishing ability. It remains one of the enigmatic anomalies of bowl playing that Derry Kenny never did win that All-Ireland senior title. Toal played a great score that day to cross the finishing line in twenty four shots. But he had met a man in devastating form whose bowling took him very close to the line in twenty-two tremendous throws.

There were eight designated senior players for the 1968 Ulster championship but in the final analysis it was between two of them, John Gribben, Farmacaffley,

Derry Kenny, Cork, is presented with the MacArdle's Shield by Des Broadberry in 1968.

and Danny McParland, Armagh, who was back with renewed vigour following a self imposed absence the previous year. It was a very determined McParland who dealt a heavy defeat to Gribben in the Ulster decider at Knappagh and the form of the ex-champion augured well for his chances of winning another National senior title.

The 1968 senior campaign in the south resulted in John Creedon, Clondrohid, and Mick Barry, Waterfall, coming through to contest the Munster final. It was the first Munster final to be played at Nadd in the north-east Cork region and Creedon emerged with a fully deserved win in a year during which he was bowling better than at any period since he last won the provincial title in 1960.

The All-Ireland senior final that year, on Sunday 1st September, was also played at Nadd and it provided John Creedon with a home venue advantage of gaining revenge over former rival Danny McParland who had recorded a clear win over the Clondrohid player at Armagh in 1961. It was an All-Ireland final McParland will have no wish to recall. Only once in the lead - and that on the first shot - the former National title holder never looked like winning as the consistent Creedon, with few errors apart from his opening throw, continually added to his lead to win by three bowls of odds. Creedon had well and truly levelled up matters after a seven year wait to assert his bowling prowess over his former victor.

In the Juvenile championship of 1968 a fine group of young northern players set out in pursuit of the Henry Neary Cup, each one of them quite capable of emulating the feat of Adrian Mallon the previous year. The honest endeavour and surprisingly high standard of bowling by the Under-16 players had really caught the imagination of followers as large crowds followed the championship through each exciting round. It was Thomas Moore, Grangemore who took the Ulster title and the marvellous quality of Juvenile bowling was never more strikingly displayed than in that superb provincial championship final in which he got clear just before the finishing line to secure a narrow victory over a very game Sean Webb, Annahagh. The new Munster Juvenile champion was Michael O'Donovan, the south west Cork representative who romped home with almost three shots to spare over Denis Crowley of Copeen. One of the best young stylists in the game this young Clonakilty player, a brother of Fachtna O'Donovan, the 1966 All-Ireland Junior champion, had set a high standard throughout the provincial championship.

The All-Ireland Juvenile final, at Grenagh, Co Cork on Saturday 31st August 1968 had a sensational ending. It was a thrilling score, one of truly magnificent bowling by Thomas Moore and Michael O'Donovan which did great credit to each of them. But for Moore, he will prefer to forget the finish. With literally nothing to beat he unaccountably failed to cross the mark of O'Donovan's final throw with possibly his shortest effort of the entire championship. It was a cruel way to lose a national final and for young O'Donovan it was redemption beyond his most imaginative belief.

The Junior championship of 1968 was not without surprises either. In fact few, if any, would have predicted Malachy McCreesh, Navan, and Neil Brannigan, Aughanore to contest the Ulster final. But contest it they did despite the challenge of many potential senior bowlers in the ranks and it was McCreesh who further confounded the critics when he took the provincial title with a runaway win. His opposition in the All-Ireland final at Grenagh, on the same day as the Juvenile decider, was Cork city bowler Mervyn McGregor, a strong player with abundant speed who had beaten the south west Cork champion Fachtna O'Callaghan, at Templemartin to win the Munster title. If McGregor had speed McCreesh certainly had support for he was encouraged throughout the score by a huge following which brought the best out of their champion to soar into a lead of almost two shots. But a serious mistake entering the last quarter lost him considerable ground, and a deal of confidence, as he slipped further back to enable McGregor gain control and hold on to win the title.

It was a bad championship year for northern bowlers, stripped of all titles held the previous year, and their gloom was compounded later in the season when the youthful Denis Scully took the Charlemont Hotel Cup at Knappagh on Sunday 27th October against Danny McParland who had not shaken off the indifferent form so evident in his bid for All-Ireland honours at Nadd two months previously.

One big feature of satisfaction in northern bowling in 1968 was the huge success of the inaugural Harp Lager Tournament promoted by the Grange club. The Harp Juvenile Tournament final was won by the fifteen years old Sean Webb, Annahagh, who proved too strong for young Grange player Joseph Murphy. In the Harp Overall final Danny McParland, winner of the top grade, and conceding two bowls of odds to the leniently graded Mick Reilly, Armagh, was narrowly beaten on the final throw by the master of the spin, with second grade winner Eamon Mallon, Lislea, just back in third place.

It was a consolation year too for John Gribben, Farmacaffley, who achieved his

John Lavery, representing the sponsors, presents the Harp Trophy to Jim Mone (centre), Chairman of Grange Road Bowls Club in 1968. David Molloy (left) was Club Treasurer.

first big tournament win by taking the Knappagh Tournament Cup in a great score against Harry Toal, Armagh. Gribben maintained his winning form into 1969 when he came through to the northern final of that year's Macardles National Tournament by beating Aidan Toal in a quarter final and then followed this up with a thrilling semi-final victory over Madden's Michael Hughes. A week later, on Sunday 16th February, 1969, the Madden player positively advertised Gribben's form by beating Danny McParland in the Madden Tournament and it was with promising prospects that he faced the Ulster senior champion in the Macardles final. However McParland maintained the unbeatable form he had shown in qualifying scores against Harry Toal and Billy Quigley, and in the end Gribben went down by a bowl of odds.

It was Denis Scully, the bowling expertise of whom is expounded in another chapter, who came through the southern section of Macardles National Tournament and he made no mistake in the final at Armagh on Sunday 16th March, 1969, with a convincing win over Danny McParland to return the trophy southbound having been won by Cork's Derry Kenny the previous year.

The most significant bowling development of 1969 was the inauguration of an Intermediate championship to bring to four the number of grades for which a National title was at stake. The best score of the Ulster Intermediate championship in that inaugural year was the clash on Sunday 15th June between Patsy McKenna, the 1967 All-Ireland Junior champion, and the in-form John Gribben; a thrilling contest of eighteen shots over the Cathedral road and it was McKenna who got through narrowly on the final throw. He went on to win his way into the provincial final on 20th July but Michael Hughes, the Madden player who had shown so much promise in tournament scores, produced superb play to take his first Ulster title in any grade. The Munster Intermediate champion of 1969 was Pat O'Sullivan, Macroom. He had beaten Liam Madden, Aherla, on 24th August at Nadd by nearly a bowl of odds and

John Lavery, sponsor, throws the first shot to open the 1968 Harp Lager Tournament at Blackwatertown Road, Armagh. Pictured, left of centre (holding a bowl), is Patsy McKenna, the 1967 All-Ireland Junior Champion.

being an outstanding Intermediate player for years, and one perfectly capable of passing up into senior ranks, was inevitably on the verge of doing so. That prospect was confirmed in the All-Ireland Intermediate final at Ballinadee on 31st August, 1969 when Pat O'Sullivan held off a gallant challenge by Michael Hughes who came close to causing a major upset by clinging tenaciously to a relatively slender margin for most of the way. It was a last shot finish, but fairly predictable outcome nonetheless, as Pat O'Sullivan became the first winner of the All-Ireland Intermediate championship series.

In the Juvenile championship of 1969, the powerfully built and strong bowling, Thomas Moore nearly did it again. He was just pipped in the Ulster final on 20th July by John Cromie, Port Mor, who had surprisingly ousted favourites Sean Webb and Conor Gribben. The player who won the Munster Juvenile final, and went on to win the National title, was later disqualified when it was discovered there had not been strict adherence to the entry age criteria. The subsequently designated Munster title holder was provincial finalist Eamon Bowen, widely regarded then as the bowling juvenile of the year. That reinstated All Ireland final of 1969 was played in Armagh on Easter Sunday, 29th March 1970. It went to the last shot between Cromie and Bowen with the latter named winning a belated National title on a magnificent final throw.

The Junior championship, since its inception in 1966, had been providing a marvellously competitive realm for a significant group of competent bowlers. It did more than that for Armagh city player Gerald McKee. In a year of consistently tremendous form this exciting young player, with a superbly effective delivery and speed to match, bowled his way through a field of twenty-seven talented entries to reach the 1960 Ulster Junior championship final. Into the final too was the holder Malachy McCreesh who confirmed his championship form of the previous year by beating all opposition. Until the final that is. The youthful new phenomenon, Gerald McKee had beaten Eamon Mallon, Billy Quigley, Brendan Digby and was about to add Malachy McCreesh to his list of vanquished when on 20th July, 1969 he served notice of more to come with a great provincial win earned through bowling of the highest order.

The final stages of the 1969 Munster Junior championship saw the Cork city champion Paddy O'Donoghue, Whites Cross, get the better of north Cork champion Pat Corkery, Donoughmore, before taking on and beating that years London champion Donie Harrington by the fore bowl at Nadd.

That All-Ireland Junior final at Grenagh, on Saturday 30th August 1969, was acclaimed, then and since, as one of the best ever seen. The bowling by both men was impeccable and it was McKee's brilliant opening four shots which set him up for a bowl lead over O'Donoghue which he never looked like shedding. McKee held it to the last and in winning his first National title had broken a long losing sequence for northern bowlers.

The destiny of the Ulster senior championship title of 1969 inevitably rested between Danny McParland and Aidan Toal. There were few Senior entries with the new Intermediate championship offering a more appropriate challenge to those with top grade potential. It was a final in which Toal produced excellent bowling. Played over the Cathedral road, Armagh on Sunday 25th May, he unleashed ten faultless shots from the start at Ballycrummy to run up a two bowl lead over his old rival Danny McParland and held it to the finish for a dividing margin that was extremely rare in either direction for these two top northern bowlers. As in 1967, Toal was again faced with the might of Mick Barry in his renewed quest for All-Ireland senior championship honours. Barry had been bowling as good as ever. On Sunday 13th July 1969 he surprisingly outclassed Derry Kenny and a week later, in the Munster final at Waterloo, faced Denis Scully, considered by many then to be the only player in Ireland actually capable of beating Barry. But on that occasion he didn't. Barry was again in devastating form and it was said then if his bowling is as good in Armagh as in Waterloo he will win yet another All-Ireland senior title. It was and he did. But Barry didn't need to be at his best over the Cathedral road on Sunday 3rd August, 1969 as Aidan Toal failed to reproduce anything like his Ulster final form on the same road. Had he done so he could well have won his first National title. He was in trouble at a very early stage when his second and third shots from the start at Ballycrummy were less than adequate and consequently Mick Barry was into a substantial early lead from which he went on to eventually win by three bowls of odds. It was Barry's fourth All-Ireland senior title, and by no means his last, complemented by three additional Munster senior titles achieved during the nine year championship period prior to the official inauguration of the All-Ireland series.

The lean year for northern victories was unalleviated at Ballyclough, Limerick on 5th October, 1969 when partners John Creedon and Denis Scully had a decisive two shot win in a doubles score over Danny McParland and Aidan Toal. However the Armagh pair did gain compensation within a month when they regained their best form and played extremely well as a team at Port Mor to come from behind to win the Charlemont Hotel Cup, on 1st November 1969, in a score which saw Scully at his most skilful.

The dominance of southern bowlers was to continue through 1970. The only National trophy won by Armagh that year was the win by Sean Cullen, Lisadian in the Macardles final at Easter. The Tournament had been redesignated for Junior players and it was east Cork bowler Pat Geasley who qualified for the final at Armagh on 29th March, 1970. Cullen had not been fancied even to win the northern section but he beat Al Mallon, Kilmore in that final and his win over Geasley, unexpected as it was, caused great scenes of jubilation when he topped his opponents final throw by a mere twenty metres.

The National championship finals of 1970 were to provide little jubilation for northern bowlers by way of title destinations. There was an all Grimley final to the Ulster Junior championship when Colm and Nial came through tough opposition from twenty-six entries. Colm, who was bowling from he was thirteen and at twenty-one had earned his first trophy, a Macardles Tournament win on 2nd July 1967, was at last gaining the profile his lively delivery, fast bowl, and accurate play had merited. Colm had also won the Clonfeacle Tournament in June 1970, and, enjoy-

Colm Grimley.
Photo: Larry Dickinson.

ing his best year in the game, beat brother Nial on the 9th August in the provincial junior decider. The last four in the Munster Junior championship comprised Pat Corkery, Paddy O'Leary, Pat Coleman and Pat Murphy. It was Murphy who came through at Togher against O'Leary for the All-Ireland final at Armagh on 23rd August 1970 over the Cathedral road. But despite the promise shown by Armagh's Colm Grimley in that and the preceding years he fell well below his own standard in a poor final where the less than powerful Pat Murphy did enough to win comfortably by a bowl of odds.

Surging through the Juvenile ranks in 1970 was newcomer Patrick Comiskey, Tyra, who ended the championship hopes of Sammy Gillespie, Armagh, Gerald Rafferty, Madden and Conor Gribben, Farmacaffley before taking on and beating Pat Mallon, Todd's Corner in the Ulster Juvenile Final on 9th August at Armagh. Three weeks later Comiskey came up against a very powerful All-Ireland final opponent in Jim O'Driscoll, Cork, who ran up an early two shot lead in their score at Ballyshonin. The Armagh bowler fought back steadily over the remainder of the course but found the leeway too great as the strong bowling O'Driscoll held on grimly to a diminishing but nonetheless sufficient margin to earn himself the National juvenile title.

The second year of the All-Ireland Intermediate championship saw Mike Sexton, Salvy Murphy, Liam Madden, Johnny Holland and Ned Dilworth contest the closing stages of the 1970 Munster title campaign and in the end it was ciotog player Liam Madden who came through to the National decider on 23rd August at Armagh following a provincial win over Ned Dilworth at Berrings. In a very talented Ulster Intermediate grouping which included Gerald McKee, John Gribben, Patsy McKenna, Oliver O'Neill, Michael Hughes and Harry Toal it was the latter who surprisingly emerged over more fancied opposition to take the Ulster title. Harry Toal had been impressive in his semi-final win over John Gribben and confirmed his form in the Ulster Intermediate final on 9th August, 1970, when he disposed of a strong challenge by Madden's Mickey Hughes.

The All-Ireland Intermediate final of 1970 played over the Cathedral road, Armagh had presented Harry Toal with renewed hope of recording his first win over a Munster bowler. Toal had been bowling for more than twenty-five years and it was a measure of his durability that he could so often surprise lauded opponents who were deemed to have more exciting championship potential. But in Cork's Liam Madden, who had lost two successive Munster Intermediate finals in 1968 and 1969, Toal had a strong opponent who was unlikely to accommodate his fervent desire for a National title. Toal played superbly in the initial stages and, against the

John Gribben, left, and Gerald McKee, both Ulster Intermediate Bowlers in 1970.

odds, held his opponent to a marginal lead for a considerable distance but the challenge ultimately proved too great. Over the final quarter he gradually dropped back to eventually go down by just over a bowl of odds against his more youthful and strong finishing competitor. Liam Madden of Aherla, Co Cork was the 1970 All-Ireland Intermediate champion and worthy of the title.

It was the Intermediate champion of the preceding year who was to contest the 1970 Munster senior championship final. In one of his few years as a senior bowler, Pat O'Sullivan, Macroom, who had beaten Michael Hughes, Madden, in the 1969 All-Ireland Intermediate final at Ballinadee, came through to win a place in the Munster senior final of 1970 with a semi-final victory on 19th July over Denis O'Donovan at Drinagh. A week earlier, at Tinker's Cross, another player of Intermediate rank a year previous, Liam Daly, lost his chance of a senior final spot when he went down to the irrepressible Mick Barry who was into his twelfth Munster senior final of which he had already won eight. This, not surprisingly, was to be his ninth provincial senior title. Played at Cloghroe on Monday 3rd August 1970 the score was watched by many Dutch and German visitors who were in Cork for the International bowling events played over the same weekend at venues near Upton and Bandon. The bowling teams from Holland and Germany had little opportunity to see Mick Barry in action at the International competitions as he saved his energy and power for the Munster senior final. That store of resources proved too much for Pat O'Sullivan and indeed was preserved into the All- Ireland senior final when four weeks later at Ballyshonin, Mick Barry ensured the issue was in the balance for only the shortest possible period when he bowled his best to overcome the strong challenge of Danny McParland and finish in great style to add to his growing total of National titles.

The stark reality of inter-provincial bowling in 1970 was that of a solitary Ulster win by Sean Cullen, Lisadian in the Macardles National Final and the dispiriting fact was further emphasised near the year end when Danny McParland lost to Christy Keating in a poor score at Knappagh on 4th October. The previous day Patrick Comiskey had renewed rivalry with All-Ireland Juvenile champion Jim O'Driscoll for the Charlemont Hotel Cup. That too resulted in a Munster win as the brilliant play of this fine young juvenile bowler stretched out to take advantage of a poor start by Comiskey and stay ahead for a fully justified win. But Patrick Comiskey, despite two important defeats, had shown sufficient confidence, determination and dedication to convince his followers that championship success was not too distant. He powered through the 1971 Juvenile championship with wins over Paul McQuaid, Armagh, Malachy McIlvenna, Madden, Stephen McKenna, Lisadian, and a new and powerful young discovery, Harry Toal, Armagh to take the Ulster Juvenile title for the second year in succession and to try again for the National honour that slipped his grasp the previous year at Ballyshonin. It was at Ballyshonin near Blarney that the Munster Juvenile final was being played out on 25th July 1971. The west Cork champion Christy Mullins had beaten the mid Cork representative, John Crowley at Dunmanway and the other semi-final, at Mallow, saw Cork city bowler Jim Twomey oust the north-east Cork champion Jim Slattery.

It was the Waterloo youngster Jim Twomey who came through to the All-Ireland Juvenile final at Armagh on Sunday 1st August 1971 at Cathedral road against the equally young but relatively experienced Patrick Comiskey. And that experience won for Comiskey his eagerly sought National title for he had to recover from serious arrears following three brilliant opening shots by the fast bowling Twomey, before edging out in front to subsequently stay there and gain ample compensation for losing out in the same final the previous year.

The year had already begun more promisingly for northern bowlers when Paul Gillespie, Armagh, who had beaten Al Mallon in the qualifying final, won the Macardles National trophy at Cathedral road on Easter Sunday 11th April 1971 against the strongly fancied Jerry O'Dwyer, Johnstown who had qualified in Munster with a win over Declan O'Donovan at Templemartin. Having won the first shot in the Macardles final, Gillespie was always in command with greater speed and better accuracy but O'Dwyer advertised his regular form more precisely with a convincing win at Limerick on 11th July 1971 when the same two players met in a renewed challenge.

The senior championship of 1971 saw Danny McParland come through for the Ulster title yet again, his seventh at that stage, when he recorded a full shot win in a three-way contest over Harry Toal and his cousin Aidan Toal on 4th July at Blackwatertown. And it was almost with monotonous regularity that Mick Barry was doing likewise in Munster. In one semi-final for provincial senior honours, Christy Keating got the better of Liam Madden on Saturday 3rd July 1971 at Togher but in the other it was Mick Barry who beat John Creedon and, almost inevitably, he strode through the final at Ballyshonin winning out in the postponed conclusion on Tuesday 27th July, bowling as well as he ever did, to gain his tenth Munster senior title.

The All-Ireland senior final that year was played at Eglish in County Tyrone. The same road had been the venue for a challenge score on Easter Monday 12th April 1971 between Cork's Christy Keating and Armagh's Danny McParland, the outcome of which was a northern win though that result was reversed three months later in a repeat challenge played at Limerick. The Tyrone venue was selected for the challenge score to help promote the efforts of players and club officials in the region and even at that stage the Ford cross road in Eglish was being mooted as the likely venue for the National senior final. That was later confirmed as the official venue for the 1971 showpiece and the Ulster champion went into that All-Ireland senior final on 1st August with tremendous recent form to his credit. He had shattered the course record at Tassagh and three weeks later, on Sunday 23rd May, 1971, almost repeated the amazing feat in winning the top grade final of the Tournament against Aidan Toal in a score of excellent quality performance. The All-Ireland final exploit was little different. McParland had bowled faultlessly for three-quarters of the course and the few errors after that were offset by supreme efforts that matched anything Mick Barry had to offer. Barry, who was untypically erratic, had virtually gifted a bowl of odds to his opponent with a major blunder on the third throw and as a result lost his first shot lead to an extent that he was never to regain fore bowl.

It was a McParland dominated final which the Armagh man won by well in excess of a bowl of odds to collect his third National senior title following a void of almost seven years.

The ever popular Junior championship continued to attract a huge entry of quality bowlers and 1971 was no different. In the Munster region Dermot O'Sullivan earned a place in the final with a win over Cork city player Nelius Aherne, at Enniskeane, and the second semi-final resulted in a win for Seamus Sexton, North Cork, over North-east champion John Doyle at Donoughmore. It was the safe playing Seamus Sexton who won the final at Ballyshonin on 22nd August to take him into the National decider at the same venue a week later. His opponent in the All-Ireland Junior final was the very fast bowling Brendan Digby, Armagh who had beaten the 1971 Macardles National Tournament winner, Paul Gillespie, before ousting Pearse McBride, Ballyheridan, and Pat Lappin, Keady, on his way to the Ulster final on 25th July 1971 in which he beat Larry Corr, Rocks, to earn a title for which he had always been a worthy contender. But in Seamus Sexton, Nadd, who was later to become a senior player of considerable ability, he found an opponent in superb form. The All-Ireland final on the forenoon of Sunday 29th August, 1971 saw the far superior Sexton literally consume the distant stretches of the Ballyshonin road as he bowled incessantly on a par with senior standard. The contrast was pronounced when Digby failed to adapt to the course and it was a decisive margin which separated them in the end.

It was of little surprise to astute followers of the sport that Gerald McKee, Armagh would take an Intermediate title in 1971 following his thoroughly impressive Junior championship success in 1969 when he burst onto the bowling scene with the potential for a National senior champion at an early age. In the Ulster Intermediate final at Armagh on Sunday 18th July he produced top class bowling to win by a bowl of odds over Colm Grimley, the Junior championship finalist of the previous year. In the Munster Intermediate-championship of 1971 Johnny Holland, Drinagh beat Mick O'Driscoll at Tinker's Cross and then recorded a semi- final win over Donie Madden at the same venue. Despite being a previous winner of the Munster Intermediate title in 1967 he went out in the 1971 final at Ballyshonin on 15th August to Mick Sexton who had earlier beaten the 1970 All-Ireland Junior champion Pat Murphy at Ballinadee, and then John Joe Kenny, a brother of senior bowler Derry, in the semi-final at Templemartin. There was a tremendous crowd at Ballyshonin on 29th August, 1971, for the All-Ireland Intermediate final and they were not disappointed. It was a marvellous contest in which both men excelled. But it was the fiercely determined McKee who strove to utilise efficiently and effectively every camber of the course as he edged in front of Sexton's powerful challenge to cross the finishing line with a mere 25 metres in hand. The Armagh find of that particular era, Gerald McKee, had won his second National title and fully justified the confident predictions surrounding the quality of his play.

One of the more significant developments of 1971 was the inauguration of a National championship for players under eighteen years. His Lordship Most Rev. Dr Lucy, Bishop of Cork donated a trophy, 'Corn an Easboig', for the All-Ireland competition and the Ulster representative in the first year of contention was Brendan McIlvenna, Madden who had beaten Sammy Gillespie, Armagh in a semi-final contest. He followed this up on Sunday 22nd August with a fairly easy provincial final win over the current Juvenile champion, sixteen year old Patrick Comiskey before a big crowd at Cathedral road. The semi-final pairings in the Munster Under 18 championship involved Mick Roche, who had beaten William Staunton at Fermoy, and Donal O'Leary who came through against Sean O'Sullivan at Grenagh. They were joined in the other semi-final by Jim O'Driscoll, following a win over Kevin Ruby at Donoughmore and Jim Keohane who accounted for Pat O'Sullivan at Drinagh. The semi-final results saw Donal O'Leary go through at Donoughmore on 8th August and his provincial final opponent was determined on the same day at Tinkers Cross when Jim O'Driscoll also qualified. The Under 18 final at Ballyshonin on Saturday 21st August 1971, did equitable favour to the quality and prestige of the overall competition such was the standard of play and level of excitement. It resulted in Jim O'Driscoll, the Juvenile champion of the preceding year, storming through for another class win. The same road, not far from Blarney, was the venue for the All-Ireland Under 18 final a week later but the Ulster champion, Brendan McIlvenna, was never able to cope with the intricacies of the unfamiliar course as the very powerful and classy bowling of Jim O'Driscoll earned him a second National tile in as many years and the distinction of being the first winner of the Bishop Lucy Cup.

The period around the All-Ireland finals in August 1971 was saddened by the death of Patron to Bol Chumann Na hEireann, Very Rev. Fr Michael O'Driscoll who was parish priest of Caheragh, and, since the inception of the Association in 1954, had been something of guide, leader, advisor and counsellor to the whole bowling fraternity.

The completion of the various championship competitions in 1971 had marked the conclusion of a successful ten year period in which the opportunity for gaining National bowling honours had expanded considerably from that of exclusively senior grade to encompass four additional categories each of which, not only generated its own particular competitive spirit and sense of accomplishment, but also provided the natural path of progression to the ultimate level of ability and performance.

A Record Enshrined in Stone

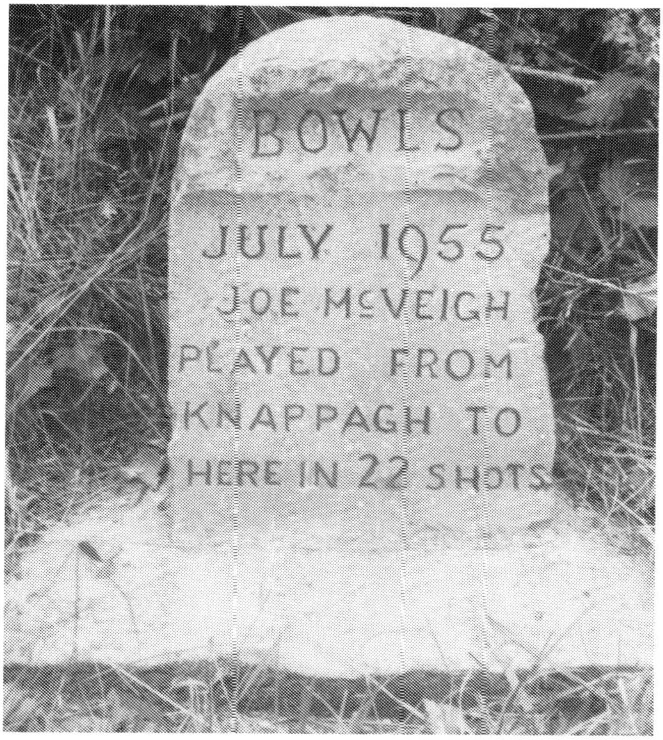

A small neatly cut stone sits snugly in the hedgerow on the side of a hill, along the Cathedral Road, just 2.4 kilometres outside Armagh City. The inscription on it reads:

Bowls. July 1955. Joe McVeigh played from Knappagh to here in 22 shots.

To passing traffic the stone may be of little significance and for the most part probably goes unnoticed. But to followers of Road Bowls it serves as a fitting monument to a record breaking performance by one of the greatest senior bowlers in the history of the sport.

Joe McVeigh, Armagh's bowling idol for many years, produced numerous superb performances throughout his playing career. But he excelled on Sunday 28th August, 1955, when he covered the famed Knappagh course in a magnificent twenty-two shots. The distance over the course from the starting line at the "Angles" to the finishing line at "Starr's Pump" is approximately 4 kilometres. Joe McVeigh's twenty-two shots, in a score against Armagh's Harry Toal, took him to a point some 160 metres beyond the finishing line at which location the little monument to this unbeaten record presently rests.

It was a truly magnificent accomplishment and one which is readily placed in perspective when viewed in the context of course performances by celebrated players over the years.

In the pre 1955 era the course had been done in twenty-four shots by top northern players, Gerald Ward, Ned Molloy, Pat Lyttle and Pat Coulter. In the big interprovincial score, in 1954, Cork's Mick Barry took twenty-three throws in his acclaimed win over Joe McVeigh. Another southern senior champion at the time, Liam O'Keefe, Waterfall, took twenty-four shots over the same course in 1954 and 1955.

Armagh's Mick Reilly once did the Knappagh course in twenty-three and crossed the line in twenty-four shots on four other occasions.

In winning the Armagh Cup for the second time, in 1955, just two months after his record breaking performance, Joe McVeigh got to the line again in a very credible twenty-three shots over the Knappagh road.

Joe McVeigh.

Danny Reilly, another top class northern bowler, and one noted for his precise accuracy, was very much on course for the record in the Armagh Cup against Danny McParland on 12th February 1961. At the halfway point Reilly had played eleven great shots but missed the elusive record by needing twelve more to cross the finishing line in a sensational two shot win.

Most followers at the time believed that if the record was to go then Danny McParland was the likely successor. And he went precariously close to it. In the Winter Senior Tournament at Knappagh, on 13th January , 1963, McParland crossed the finishing line in twenty-two shots, with his opponent Tommy Quinn, Armagh, coming in on a remarkable twenty-three bowls. Danny McParland was over the finishing line in twenty-two but still some sixty metres short of Joe McVeigh's twenty-two shot distance in 1955.

The most renowned starting point in the long history of Northern Road Bowling.

Approaching the Condy Corner, a recognised halfway mark on the famed Knappagh Course near Armagh.

In another inter-provincial score on 18th March, 1963, Derry Kenny, Cork, took twenty-six shots in a one bowl win over Danny McParland. And Mick Barry, back again at Knappagh in August 1967, covered the course in twenty-three in the All-Ireland Final against Aidan Toal. That very impressive performance was surpassed by Derry Kenny on Sunday, 14th April, 1968, when he went seventy metres better than Barry's All-Ireland final achievement by getting very close to the finishing line in twenty-two shots in the Macardles National Tournament Final against Harry Toal. In the same year the brilliant young Cork player, Denis Scully just failed to score the line in twenty-four shots in the final for the Charlemont Hotel Cup on Sunday, 27th October, 1968, against Danny McParland.

Some thirteen years later, on Sunday 5th July 1981, the reigning All-Ireland Senior champion, Gerry Boylan, Lislea, went tantalisingly close to breaking the long standing record. In the Ulster Senior championship semi-final, in which his opponent Aidan Toal had just missed the finishing line in twenty-three shots, Gerry Boylan was on target for the elusive goal almost throughout the entire score. He crossed the line in twenty-two marvellous drives but fell short of the precise record distance by some fifty metres.

The remarkable twenty-two shot performance by Joe McVeigh in 1955 has been an enduring one. So too has the memory of a most distinguished bowler been equally durable. The discreet little monument in an Armagh hedgerow fittingly represents a supreme bowling achievement which is cherished as affectionately as the memory of the great bowler who accomplished that extraordinary feat.

Adversity in Sport from Political Conflict

The sporting, cultural and social life of Ireland suffered an insipid and protracted reverse during the prolonged period of serious conflict which prevailed throughout the twenty-five years from 1969 to 1994. Since then the complete cessation of hostilities has created a realistic sense of optimism and hope as the resilience and forbearance of the people is complemented by a fervent desire to retrieve a quality of life commensurate with justice and peace.

Despite endeavours throughout that troubled period to maintain a semblance of living normality, through beneficial diversion generated by sporting and cultural activities, it was inevitable that many aspects of life would be seriously affected. The extent of such detriment can begin to be appreciated by a reinforced recognition that a relatively small geographical region like Northern Ireland suffered a death toll of 3,173 people with many thousands more, injured and maimed. Consider the families and friends of those dead and injured, whatever the circumstances, and the magnitude of bereavement and suffering becomes more apparent.

Viewed in that context the ensuing disruption to sporting activities is of little consequence. And yet the ameliorating effect of community sport was a conscious factor in the continuing efforts to maintain the All-Ireland road bowling championships just as other sporting and cultural organisations were endeavouring to attain the benefits of active promotion and sustained participation. The period throughout the seventies had been the most difficult in many ways and was a decade in which more than 2,000 people were killed, the worst year by far being 1972 in which over 470 people died.

It was also a period of years during which road bowling officials, players and followers were most reluctant to travel north and for a seven year stretch any championship finals then fulfilled were played in the south. It was a period too in which the violence had a direct impact on road bowling members. Eamon Gamble who won the top grade of St Patrick's Tournament, Keady, in November 1967 and more than two years earlier, in March 1965, broke the bowling record for the Chapel road also in Keady, died on 8th March 1972, aged 27 years, following an explosion and fire in Keady, Co Armagh. Pat Molloy, aged 48 years, who played in local tournaments and was a keen follower at all the big scores, also died in a bomb attack at Aughanlig, not far from his home, on 19th February, 1974. Four months later, on 15th June, Patrick Cunningham, aged 26 years, who rarely missed a score of bowls within reasonable travelling distance, was shot dead quite close to his home at Benburb in County Tyrone. John McGleenan, aged 45 years, whose family were keen followers of the sport, died in a bomb attack on his own business premises in Armagh on 22nd August 1975. Seamus Mallon, aged 31 years, a strong bowler who always competed in the local tournaments, died on 30th December, 1975 four days after sustaining injuries in a bomb attack at Ardress, a few miles from his home. Seamus was a son of Andy Mallon, a recipient of a Hall of Fame award in road bowls, and a brother of Adrian Mallon, who won the first All-Ireland Juvenile championship title in 1967. A keen spectator at the sport for many years, Mick Sweeney, aged 73 years, died in a bomb attack in Armagh city on 9th April 1976 and just over a month later, on 15th May, three followers and active participants in road bowls died in a bomb attack at Charlemont in County Armagh. Vincent Clancy, aged 54 years, was a regular spectator at the big scores on the Moy road. Bob McCullagh, aged 41 years had played in the Macklin Cup and Grange Tournaments throughout the sixties. Sean O'Hagan, the youngest to die in that attack, aged 22 years, was a keen bowler, ardent sports follower, and a brilliant young footballer with St Colmcille's Gaelic Football Club in Grange. Another keen road bowls follower, Fred McLaughlin, aged 49 years, who had played in Grange and Blackwatertown tournaments, died on 31st May 1976, following a gun attack at Charlemont, Co Armagh two weeks earlier. These were not the only people associated with the sport who died during that dreadful period nor were such fatalities amongst the bowling fraternity confined to the seventies. One of those to die in later years was Barney Lavery, aged 67 years, a bowling veteran who broke the course record in the opening round of the Benburb tournament in January 1968. Barney died twenty years later, quite close to his home, whilst driving past an exploding bomb at Benburb, Co Tyrone on 23rd November, 1988.

There is an impelling and enduring obligation upon us, in any recollection or portrayal of that particular twenty-five year period in the history of Ireland, be it in sport or any other feature of life, to duly acknowledge the inherent trauma and to earnestly bear in mind all those people who died as a result of the conflict.

It was in the midst of such a sombre reality that the road bowling championships of the seventies were played out. Not all of them were fulfilled and some of those successfully completed had deviated considerably from the established dates for National finals. But the fact that so many were concluded is a tribute to the commitment by the officers of the organising body throughout that difficult period.

The early part of 1972 saw the culmination of Macardles National Tournament in which the northern final was contested by Al Mallon, Kilmore, and the late Malachy Mallon, Creighan. It was Al who came through with a particularly impressive win when he covered the Cathedral road from Bally crummy in nineteen shots - and that before the realignment had clipped one or more shots off the first kilometre of the course. In the southern qualifier, Pat Murphy, Cork, the 1970 All-Ireland Junior champion, won a three way final at Waterloo over John Kenny and Seamus Sexton. The National final was played on 11th June, 1972, over the Blackwatertown road and it was Al Mallon who capitalised on initial errors by Pat Murphy to maintain an advantage throughout most of the score and win by a shot or bowl of odds at the finish.

In the Ulster Junior championship of 1972, Johnny Mills, Carrickaness, recorded a semi-final win over John Hughes, Madden, with a performance considered to

In the forefront of these spectators at a road bowls score in 1966 are two of the innocent victims who later died in the conflict. Patrick Cunningham is second from right, and Sean O'Hagan is the young boy, ninth from right, leaning forward at the front.

be the best seen in the competition that year. Paul Gillespie, Armagh, beat Noel Collins, Moy, in the other semi-final and produced a great performance in the final but it was Mills who played the score of his life to gain the Ulster title. In Munster, Donie Fehilly had a semi-final win against Declan O'Donovan at Templemartin but was then required to take on the London champion Paul Mullane at Tinker's Cross before he qualified for the provincial junior final against Neilly O'Donoghue, of Cork city, who had beaten the East Cork champion, Billy Boy O'Driscoll at Ballygarvan. In the Munster final at Waterloo on 30th July, Neilly O'Donoghue, a player who relished a venue with wide open space, came through to the All-Ireland Junior final against Armagh's Johnny Mills. The Ulster champion carried tremendous form into that contest over the Cathedral road on Sunday 6th August, but he met a formidable opponent in O'Donoghue. The lead interchanged frequently from the start at Ballycrummy but the more powerful O'Donoghue gained the upper hand in the latter half and though Mills narrowed the gap near the finish, the Cork player took the title by almost a bowl of odds.

The 1972 Intermediate championship produced some excellent encounters and it was a very talented group of bowlers who contested the provincial quarter finals in Munster. At Ballyvolane, Nelius Aherne, toppled John Kenny, whilst Seamus Sexton, Junior champion in 1971, was embarking on another National title pursuit with the defeat of Senan Horgan, at Donoughmore. Also striving for a second National championship title at a higher grade was the 1970 Junior champion Pat Murphy, who ended the Intermediate hopes of John Healy at Dublin Hill. It was a virtual line up of champions in those quarter finals as Liam Madden, the 1970 Intermediate champion was also involved but he went out to the superior bowling of Mick O'Driscoll, at Waterfall. Those results determined exciting semi-final pairings which were played at separate venues on 23rd July and saw Seamus Sexton beat Pat Murphy at Waterfall and Mick O'Driscoll win over Nelius Aherne at Dublin Hill. The Munster Intermediate final could hardly have been more intriguing such was the bowling credentials of each contestant. Sexton had all the appearance of a bowler destined to win through each of the ascending grades on his way to the very top, and O'Driscoll, noted for his skill on the bends, was also renowned for delivering a low, fast and straight bowl almost every time. It was the credence of O'Driscoll that ultimately dominated on the day when he got the better of a consistent but outmanoeuvred Sexton in an exciting final on 30th July at Waterfall, the same road on which the latter player had produced such great bowling only a week earlier. And so Mick O'Driscoll was on course for a little bit of family history. His younger brother Jim had won the 1970 All-Ireland Juvenile title and the following year went on to win the All- Ireland Under 18 championship. The pressure was then on Mick to take the National title in Intermediate grade and despite being scheduled for an away venue in Co Armagh he was favoured by most pundits to do so. But there was another family in pursuit of a unique record that year too. The consistent Harry Toal (senior) who had surprisingly outclassed Colm Grimley, at Knappagh, to win the Ulster Intermediate title for the second time, was to be O'Driscoll's opponent in the All-Ireland final at Blackwatertown on Saturday 5th August, 1972. And powering through the Juvenile ranks that same year, having given due notice of his potential the previous season, was Harry Toal (junior), son of the near veteran bowler and highly rated contender for the Under 16 National title. A fascinating prospect; father and son road bowling champions of Ireland in the same year! Even the great Bill Bennett and his son George hadn't achieved that and they had equalled or even surpassed most things in bowling accomplishment. The Intermediate final was the first to be played and on entering the final quarter it became evident that the O'Driscoll record was up. Bowling more consistently and coping steadily with the intermittent play by Toal it was O'Driscoll who eased to the front and extended his lead to eventually win by two bowls of odds. Gone was the first leg of the envisaged Toal double and confirmed was a three in a row championship run for the O'Driscoll family.

Northern wins were proving rather elusive in 1972 but hopes were high at an early stage in the Under 18 championship when Sammy Gillespie, Armagh, was in record breaking form over the Cathedral road when he went from Ballycrummy to almost the Lime Kiln in twelve unbelievable shots with the perplexed Neilus McVeigh, son of the great Joe, less than a shot behind him. He didn't win the Ulster championship though. That honour went to relative newcomer Paul McQuaid, Armagh, who had beaten Conor Gribben in a semi-final and then surprisingly beat the strongly fancied Patrick Comiskey in the final, on 30th July, over the Cathedral road in Armagh. It had been a second successive defeat for Comiskey in the Ulster Under 18 championship final. He lost the previous year to Brendan McIlvenna, but on again reaching the final in 1972, following a great semi-final score against Stephen McKenna, Lisadian, he seemed on target to make amends for that particular disappointment. However, a spectacular last shot by Paul McQuaid put paid to

Patrick Comiskey.
Photo: Larry Dickinson.

Comiskey's championship hopes once again when a five metre lead was reversed to a seventy metre deficit over the line.

The final stages of the Munster Under 18 championship of 1972 was being contested by some of the best young bowlers in the south. John Crowley, Churchtown South, had gained a final place at the expense of City champion Andrew Twomey and he was challenged in the provincial decider by Dan O'Regan, Rylane, who had beaten Noel Casey, Mallow, in a good score at Drinagh. It was the North Cork champion Dan O'Regan who won the Munster title at Dublin Hill and the All-Ireland final took him to Armagh to face the challenge of local man Paul McQuaid. The play was erratic from both bowlers in that unpredictable tussle at Cathedral road on Sunday 6th August but overall the better bowling came from McQuaid and he emerged a fairly comfortable winner over the last quarter to win his first National title and gain for the north the only championship victory that year.

The first Dunmanway bowler to take part in an All-Ireland bowling final was Juvenile player John Carroll who won the Munster title over the exact same course on which he would bowl for the National award. His opponent in that National final of 1972 at Dublin Hill was a young man many considered to be the best Juvenile player to come out of Armagh, Harry Toal, (junior), who had played a faultless Ulster final against the relentlessly pursuing Oliver Gribben, Farmacaffley, to win convincingly through vastly superior speed. The All-Ireland Juvenile final was uneventful for most of the way. Carroll won the first shot and was a bowl up at halfway but Toal gradually crept back and gained the lead entering the final quarter. Going to the last it was a closely tied score but then turmoil erupted in a hotly disputed finish in which bitter disagreement ensued over the interpretation and consequent decision in relation to a wall and adjacently painted line near where each bowl had struck. As it transpired young John Carroll was declared the winner, and 1972 All-Ireland Juvenile champion. Protests continued and an official objection was lodged but no alteration in the result was the outcome of an emergency meeting of the Executive that evening. The All-Ireland senior final scheduled for the next day became a casualty of the dispute. It should have featured what was then still considered to be the biggest bowling attraction in any season - a National senior final between Mick Barry and Danny McParland. The "nearest thing to being unbeatable" was how Barry's performance against Derry Kenny had been described as he absorbed the road at Dublin Hill in the Munster final that year. And supreme speed coupled with two tremendous finishing shots was the determining factor in McParland's 1972 Ulster final win over the 1971 Intermediate champion, Gerald McKee, who was within metres of his opponent at the three- quarter stage, but eventually succumbed to that finishing burst of powerful bowling. Regrettably that All-Ireland senior final scheduled for Dublin Hill, was never played and the 1972 records indicate a walkover granted to Mick Barry as he had presented himself at the start to fulfil the fixture. Subsequent results in championship fixtures decreed that Barry and McParland were never again to meet in a National final. It was a lamentable way in which the curtain should come down on a series of bowling contests spanning more than eight years. They had so often thrilled thousands with the supreme skill and stirring spectacle that only Mick Barry and Danny McParland could ever generate. A marvellous era of senior championship bowling had almost concluded.

The repercussions of that discordant episode in bowling organisation had an additional adverse effect on an already difficult management period for the sport. Even though the respective bodies north and south continued to promote the provincial championships there was no All- Ireland final played at any venue in 1973. Nonetheless strenuous efforts were being made to resolve the crisis. At a meeting in Naas, Co Kildare on 26th August, 1973, presided over by the late Senator Pat Kerrigan, the then Lord Mayor of Cork, representatives of the Executive body, north and south, debated the contentious issues and emerged with prospects for the future a great deal less dismal. In the end it was good news that was conveyed to the delegates at the annual Convention of Bol Chumann Na hEireann in Cork, on

Sunday 9th December 1973, when Paddy Comiskey, the then Secretary to the Northern Branch of Bol Chumann, confirmed that the 1973 All-Ireland finals would in fact be played over the St Patricks weekend and Easter period of 1974. The outstanding Senior and Juvenile National finals were to be played at Castleblaney, Co Monaghan, and the Intermediate, Under 18 and Junior All- Ireland deciders at Grenagh, Ballyshonin and Midleton respectively.

The delayed 1973 All-Ireland Juvenile final was between Malachy Comiskey, Portadown, who had beaten Gerry Mallon at Armagh on 25th November, and the brilliant young Jim O'Driscoll, Cork, a top class bowler whom it was claimed even few Junior bowlers could beat despite his young age. That assertion was realised by Tim O'Halloran, Templemartin in the Munster Juvenile final at Ballincollig. Malachy Comiskey soon knew too what they were talking about. A young man totally supreme in his own category and, as he proved that same year, equally superior in a higher grade, his mastery of the northern challenge was so complete and awe inspiring. Jim O'Driscoll, handled the road at Castleblayney to perfection and he had the inherent skill and power simply waiting to be expertly utilised. It was his first All-Ireland title but he didn't have long to wait for another. The big consolation for Malachy Comiskey that year was that, even in defeat, he was part of an unfolding history of family achievement in that he had won the Henry Neary Cup, twice held by his brother Patrick in the consecutive years of 1970 and 1971. Malachy had won it at his first attempt in 1973 and went on to emulate his brother by taking the Ulster Juvenile title and trophy again in 1974 for a unique family double that will be difficulty to surpass or even equal.

The deferred 1973 All-Ireland senior final was unavoidably delayed further still. It had been a very interesting Munster championship that year. It was the year in which Seamus Sexton, who had beaten Dermot O'Sullivan at Ballincollig was utilising to the fullest his particular style of almost effortless bowling. And that was seen to greatest effect at Beeing on 7th October 1973 when he created the flurry of the season with a dramatic win over Mick Barry in the senior championship. But that win only brought him to the semi-final to be confronted by the undisputed ascendancy of Denis Scully whose brilliance against Sexton in that event at Grenagh on 4th November, was to confirm him as favourite for the All-Ireland title. Scully's Munster final opponent was John Kenny who, in his first year competing as a senior bowler, had beaten Christy Keating in a splendid score at Waterloo on 28th October just when it seemed the City man might well win his first senior title. Keating had earlier produced the best overall score of his career at Carrigtwohill when he recorded a very comprehensive win over Derry Kenny, a classy and stylish bowler of magnificent natural ability. The Munster senior final at Fermoy on 18th November 1973 saw the supremacy of Denis Scully once again ingrained through a display of powerful bowling to which John Kenny could not adequately respond. Northern followers were thrilled at the prospect of seeing Scully's perfectionist bowling over the Castleblaney course but alas an injury which required hospitalisation dashed their hopes. It was the buoyant Harry Toal who awaited the daunting task. He had a runaway win over Aidan Toal in the Ulster senior final at Knappagh on 18th November

All eyes are on the solid iron bowl as it hurtles along the road at tremendous speed during this championship encounter.

Photo: Harold Ford, Portadown.

1973, and that much delayed All-Ireland final was eventually played at Ballyshonin, Co Cork on Saturday 12th October 1974 with Denis Scully the victor by a comfortable margin after one of the finest displays of bowling ever seen. It was this superb Cork bowlers first All-Ireland senior title and amazingly, for a player of such incredible ability, it was to be his only one.

In respect of all the bowlers engaged in this protracted competition it was difficult to see how championship form could have retained much relevance with such a period of time having elapsed between the provincial and National finals. But it was important that the players involved had the opportunity to compete for National honours and indeed for continuity in the championship series to be maintained. The long lay off was unlikely to have affected Liam Daly very much for he swept through the 1973 Munster Intermediate championship after having already been out of the game for a number of months. He beat Neilly O'Donoghue, the 1972 All-Ireland Junior champion, and then Declan O'Donovan, before winning the provincial title over Donie Coveney at Barrell Cross. In the All-Ireland final of 1973 he was opposed by Al Mallon, Kilmore who had beaten the late Brendan Digby, Armagh, in the Ulster championship final and in that delayed National decider at Grenagh, on Sunday 14th April 1974, Liam Daly maintained his form to gain the Intermediate title.

The emergence of a very powerful bowler in the formidable physique of Gerry Boylan, Lislea, was confirmed in the 1973 Junior championship when he produced the occasional long distance shot to oust Pat Mallon for the Ulster title. The margin in the Munster Junior final was a good deal less. Joe Twohig of Mid Cork had just beaten James O'Driscoll, Drinagh, a strong and stylish bowler of exceptional class who always contested his scores with a silent determination that was admirable in its practice. That semi-final win at Enniskeane over such a polished performer had Twohig well fancied going in against Cork player John Butler who amassed big odds at the finish in his semi-final score against Mick Murphy, Donoughmore, at the Ballincollig venue. There will be few provincial finals with as close a finish, or indeed as dramatic, as that of the 1973 Junior contest at Waterfall. Butler's last shot appeared to be unassailable but somehow Twohig got to it and beat the mark by a mere few metres to win everything but most of all the Munster Junior title. He faced no such challenge on the final throw at Midleton on Saturday 13th April, 1974 when he won the delayed All-Ireland final over Gerry Boylan, whose intermittent performance was insufficient to ward off the more consistent bowling of Joe Twohig which earned him his first National title.

A late rally by Stephen McKenna, Lisadian, in the Ulster final of the 1973 Under 18 championship, just failed to curb the established lead of Oliver Gribben, Farmacaffley, who held on to win the title over the Cathedral road on 18th November and he too had to wait until Easter of 1974 to determine the destiny of the National title. That final was played at Ballyshonin on Sunday 14th April 1974 when Jim O'Driscoll who had beaten Ted Hegarty, Lyre, in the Munster final at Crookstown, achieved a magnificent double by adding the All- Ireland Under 18 title to that he had already won in the Juvenile (Under 16) grade. It had been a marvellous bowling year for the brilliant young Jim O'Driscoll and in 1974 he was honoured with selection for the Youths International in Germany in which he took third Individual placing.

The bowling year of 1974 was a hectic one as the fourth International event at the end of May dominated a programme which was already congested through completing the National finals of the previous year along with the current provincial and All-Ireland championships. Many scores were completed within a severely contracted period.

In the Ulster senior championships the semi-finals and final were concluded over one weekend. Aidan Toal had beaten Danny McParland on Friday 9th August 1974 and the following day Harry Toal beat Al Mallon to go into a final twenty four hours later. It obviously did him no harm for, remarkably, at 44 years of age, Harry Toal had retained his Ulster senior title. But age was hardly an issue when it was learned his opponent in the All-Ireland final would be more than ten years his senior. The Munster senior championship had been won, yet again, by 55 years old Mick Barry who had beaten John Creedon at Oldcourt, near Skibereen, then John Kenny at Dublin Hill, and his brother Derry Denny at the same venue in the semi-final on Thursday 8th August 1974, before giving a superlative showing ten days later against the 1973 Intermediate champion Liam Daly, Shannonvale in the provincial senior final at Ballincollig. The disparity in performance level between this phenomenal bowler and his fellow players seemed to be as pronounced as ever and it was more in hope than confidence that Harry Toal attempted to achieve something the best senior bowlers in the south couldn't do in the same season. That All-Ireland senior final at Ballyshonin on Sunday 25th August, 1974 was, in the end, relatively

Armagh City and two Cathedrals.

Photo: Northern Ireland Tourist Board.

easy for Barry who commanded the score throughout to win his seventh All-Ireland title since 1963. And he hadn't finished yet!

The Intermediate championship, as that years Munster senior finalist Liam Daly had just proven, is the competition that ultimately prepares developing bowlers for taking on the best at the top grade in the sport. And remarkably it was the 1973 Munster finalist Donie Coveney who came through again to win the provincial Intermediate title the following year. He had beaten Declan O'Donovan at Kilbrittain and the 1970 Intermediate champion Liam Madden at Ballincollig before taking on and beating Neilly O'Donoghue in the final at Ballygarvan. O'Donoghue, the 1972 Junior champion, had the unenviable experience of losing two successive provincial finals when he also lost the 1975 contest to Donie O'Leary at Ballincollig. The Ulster Intermediate championship of 1974 saw Sean Doran go out to Brendan Digby, and Larry Lyttle bow to the power of Gerald McKee whilst the powerfully strong Gerry Boylan lost out to the impressively fast Marty Kelly. But the most impressive performance throughout the championship was that of John Gribben who surprisingly ousted Patsy McKenna before recording an exciting semi-final win over Marty Kelly and then confirming the consistency of his new found power and accuracy with a great provincial win over Gerald McKee who had reverted to Intermediate grade after a brief spell in senior ranks. McKee had been All-Ireland Junior champion in 1969 and took the Intermediate National title in 1971. It was a measure of John Gribben's performance that he had beaten a player of such class. But the challenge for National honours proved too great. At Carrigtwohill, on Saturday 24th August, 1974 it was Donie Coveney who dominated to win his first All-Ireland title.

The Junior championship of 1974 had a huge entry and its little wonder the standard can be so high such is the keen competition that prevails in the particular grade. In the Ulster Junior championship, Pat Mallon created a new course record when he went from Rountrees to Ballycrummy, on the Cathedral road, Armagh, in twelve magnificent shots to be followed over the line in one more by Dermot O'Connor. The protracted play-offs resulted in this particular All-Ireland final not being played until Sunday 13th October, 1974. In the Ulster Junior semi finals at Armagh on 6th October Donal Gribben, Farmacaffley beat Sean Webb, Annahagh and the surprise of the championship, Stephen Donnelly, Armagh, got the better of the record breaking Pat Mallon. Even then, Donnelly was lightly considered as potential champion but he confounded all the critics by taking the title and challenging for National honours within days at Ballyshonin. The Armagh man's opponent in the All-Ireland Junior final was one Jack Dan O'Donovan from Drinagh who had beaten John Moynihan at Crookstown in a great semi- final score before following up with a last shot win over City player Teddy O'Neill in the Munster final at Innishannon. The All-Ireland Junior final at Ballyshonin proved to be yet another of Stephen Donnelly's championship surprises when a combination of great speed and rare consistency saw him through against an equally fast but less steady Jack Dan O'Donovan who lacked nothing in courage or indeed numerical support.

In the Under 18 Ulster championship of 1974, Harry Toal, (junior) was bowling in full justification of all the positive predictions about his future prospects. Even at that age he was delivering an extremely fast bowl and was being deemed the natural successor to Danny McParland at the top of the senior ranks. He had beaten Malachy Comiskey and Liam Boylan with consummate ease before continuing to impress with a spectacular Ulster final win over another fast and accurate bowler Oliver Gribben who had raised great hopes of his own ambitions with fine performances against Gerry Mallon and Kevin McCoy. The Munster championship in the Under 18 grade had been particularly exciting due mainly to the emergence of two of the best bowlers in that category for many years. One of them was Jim O'Driscoll who had already proven his worth the previous year and was back in the final again with the same splendid bowling ability that caught the imagination of followers in the preceding season. Coming through to meet him in the provincial final was a young man rapidly building up a strong following of admirers and consistently producing the results to match their enthusiasm. Bill Daly of Leap, the Under 18 West Cork champion had overpowered the North Cork representative Pat Joe O'Driscoll before reaching the final with a great win over the mid Cork bowler Tim O'Halloran. The quality of Daly's performances was sufficient to warrant a description by that astute assessor of bowling ability, the late Flor Crowley as being "one of the nicest I have seen in years". But the experience of championship bowling was on the side of O'Driscoll and it was he who confirmed his superiority by retaining the title he had won a year before to become Munster Under 18 champion for 1974. In the All-Ireland final at Carrigtwohill on Saturday 24th August, 1974, Jim O'Driscoll, the undisputed supreme under-age bowler in Munster, was opposed by the best young prospect in Ulster, a rotund but powerfully strong Harry Toal (junior) and it was that power and phenomenal speed which carried the day to gain the Armagh youngster his first National title.

The popular Juvenile championship which never fails to intrigue spectators with the skill, commitment and coping ability of players under sixteen years was no less appealing in 1974 than hitherto. Bowling his way through the Juvenile ranks in Ulster for the second year running was Malachy Comiskey, Portadown, who beat Malachy Donnelly, Drumcairne on his way to the provincial final in which he ousted a promising young Gerald Quigley, Armagh. The Munster Juvenile title of 1974 had gone to Andy O'Callaghan, Dromohane, who just got through in the last shot of a very fine score against a great young bowler in John Hurley from Drinagh. But the experience of Comiskey's participation in the National final the previous year was particularly evident in the 1974 All-Ireland Juvenile final at Ballyshonin on Sunday 25th August when he averted any pressure from a huge early deficit to calmly regain lost ground and subsequently take the lead for a fine win over a consistent O'Callaghan who bowled steadily and impressively throughout the score.

The 1975 bowling season was not without its difficulties either. Only two of the scheduled five All-Ireland finals were actually played that year. But it was a significant year for several more positive reasons. For one thing Bill Daly, Leap, had measured up fully to his earlier promise. He had retained his West Cork regional title in a last shot victory following a marvellous score against Skibereen's Seamus

The Road Bowling Generations — Brian Daly, Glanmire, in the playing style of his father Bill (right) in the 1994 Petra Youth Finals at Macroom. In the centre is Mick Barry who won his first Munster Senior Road Bowls title in 1955.

Photo: Denis McGarry.

McCarthy at Castletownshend and then in a truly superb performance at the Miles he beat Tim O'Halloran to gain the 1975 Munster Under 18 title which had eluded him at Crookstown the previous year. His form was such that he was evidently destined for the National title as well. In Ulster it was Stephen Toal, Armagh, who had taken the Under 18 championship title with victories over Malachy Comiskey, Paul Gribben, Malachy Donnelly and Eamon McCoy. But in the All-Ireland final at Ballyshonin, Co Cork on 24th August, 1975, it was Bill Daly who maintained his brilliant form to overcome a game Stephen Toal and convincingly win his first National title. It was a marvellous climax to a great season for Bill Daly which had the unmistakable declaration of future triumph in the ascending categories of road bowling.

The 1975 season was notable too for the continued bowling success of John Gribben, Farmacaffley, who had followed up on his great Intermediate run the previous year with authoritative displays throughout the senior championship. He had beaten Aidan Toal and Danny McParland, the latter being a great score in which he unleashed six tremendous shots from the start at Knappagh to go a full bowl ahead and eventually stretch out for a two shot win. John Gribben was a worthy Ulster senior champion for 1975 but in the All-Ireland final was faced with the almost inevitable and thoroughly daunting task of taking on Mick Barry at the Cork venue of Ballyshonin. The Cork maestro had not been all that impressive in his Munster final win over Pat O'Sullivan, Macroom, at the Miles on Sunday 10th August, 1975, but he was in pursuit of his eighth All-Ireland senior title and no less motivated than the Armagh man seeking his first. But for John Gribben the form sheet was ominous. Donie Coveney, who had beaten Gribben in the 1974 Intermediate final, lost his senior championship score at Ballyshonin to Pat O'Sullivan who in turn was beaten in the senior final by Mick Barry. In the All-Ireland final on Sunday 24th August 1975 John Gribben bowled his best with some superb shots but it fell short of what was required to overpower the might of Mick Barry who regained his inspired form to record another performance of magnificent bowling the standard of which only he could achieve. Barry claimed he always had the feel of how he would perform on any given day. And he had said just before the score against John Gribben, "I'll be in good form today." He was, and he won by two shots. But it was to be his last All- Ireland senior final appearance. He hadn't given up then, nor has he done so since, as his recent performances in the Vintage championship adequately testify. But he never did win another Munster senior title and his departure from the National scene had to be viewed as the passing of a magnificent era which had brought thrills and enjoyment to many thousands over a period of years in which the sport of road bowls commanded enhanced media attention as a consequence of his spectacular feats. Mick Barry was fifty-six years of age when he won his last All-Ireland senior title. He had, by then won no less than thirteen Munster senior championship titles and, since 1963, had won eight of the thirteen All-Ireland senior finals. A phenomenal record for an extraordinary bowl player of which there has been no parallel in any era of the long sporting history that belongs to bowling. The great Mick Barry has been, and remains, unequalled in the sport.

The Redeeming Aspects of a Dismal Period

The latter half of the seventies proved to be equally difficult in the logistics of organising and completing the championships in road bowls and, in many ways, the period posed additional problems which required patient perseverance and conciliatory management.

Three of the scheduled five All-Ireland finals for 1975 remained uncontested that year even though the respective provincial championships had been satisfactorily concluded with declared champions in each category. There were several reasons for the complication. One of the northern contestants had been injured in a bomb explosion and was unable to compete. The remaining unfulfilled contests had more to do with a growing resentment of the requirement to travel annually to Cork for the National finals even though it was appreciated as being a temporary arrangement until the serious risks created by the conflict were a great deal less pronounced. There had been an increasing weariness with the prolongation of the arrangement. But misunderstandings on both sides had exacerbated the problem. Obviously the southern bowlers had good reason for their extreme reluctance to travel north at that time with the safety of players and supporters being of prime consideration. And yet it was the feeling of northern bowlers that the playing of All-Ireland finals in their territory would derive positive consequences which they were keen to generate. The predicament deepened when press speculation in Munster, following the abortive fixtures in 1975, began to question the wisdom of continuing with the All-Ireland series of road bowling championships. It was a dismal period for the sport in the north. For almost six years the Armagh newspapers carried little or no coverage of road bowls with mere fixtures and results forming the basis of the weekly scanty reference to the sport. There just didn't seem to be the will to adequately utilise the media space available and the consequences of inadequate publicity soon became evident during that period.

A major diversion from northern road bowls in 1977 was the all too infrequent appearance of Armagh county team in the All-Ireland senior gaelic football final. It was in 1953, all of twenty four years earlier, that Armagh county first reached the All-Ireland senior final and the renewed impetus of that new era in the seventies was a welcome diversion for young and old alike throughout the entire province. The temporary cost to road bowls in terms of enthusiasm was more than adequately offset by the refreshing distraction from concerns about the political conflict, even if Armagh did lose to Dublin in that memorable football event.

But the period throughout the seventies was not all dismal for road bowls followers and indeed had many redeeming aspects to it. In 1973 the Aughatarra club, near Benburb, attracted more than two hundred entries for a local Tournament that year. It was in the same year that Sean Doran, the tremendously fast bowler and renowned boxing coach, created a major stir with three successive wins on the

Cathedral road, Armagh, against Aidan Toal, Danny McParland and Oliver O'Neill. And in 1974 the Tiev Tara club in Armagh city was formed with the inaugural tournament attracting a huge entry. It was that year too in which the Ardfield club in Cork was founded and on the first anniversary of their inauguration they hosted the 1975 senior championship score between Dermot O'Sullivan and John Kenny. But the more significant positive aspect of the period was the urgency with which the powers-that-be set about resolving the 1975 crisis and this was achieved through a thorough clarification and subsequent total agreement at a meeting in Naas on Saturday 20th September 1975 between northern and southern representatives of the Executive of Bol Chumann Na hEireann. The tone of conciliation had been admirably set three weeks earlier by Dan O'Leary, father of Munster champion brothers Jerry and Donal who had been awarded, according to rule, the All- Ireland titles in Juvenile and Intermediate respectively. In an exceedingly sporting gesture Dan O'Leary promptly announced a willingness to have the scores re-fixed if agreement on a date and venue was reached through the approval of Bol Chumann. The outstanding finals were indeed subsequently re-scheduled in conjunction with the 1976 All-Ireland contests at Ballyshonin, Co Cork.

Jerry O'Leary, Waterloo, had been Munster Juvenile champion for 1975 after a marvellous final at Crookstown on 15th August that year against Jerry Dinan, Donoughmore, a son of Jack Dinan, the great bowler of the fifties. They were each young bowlers of exceptional talent for Juvenile grade and following O'Leary's win he was being freely tipped as a player with a great future. The Ulster Juvenile champion for 1975 was Liam Boylan, Lislea who had beaten his brother Martin in the final, a circumstance about which Donie and Liam Madden would know something following the Munster Intermediate final of 1968. The Boylans had beaten John Donnelly, Tray, and Ciaran Toal, Armagh in the semi-finals and it was Liam who faced Jerry O'Leary in that re-fixed All-Ireland Juvenile final at Ballyshonin in August 1976. This time Jerry won it on the road of play, the way he always wanted to, and was a worthy champion on the day when he capped an excellent performance with a great win on the last shot. His older brother Donal, who had won the Munster Intermediate final of 1975 with record bowling at Ballincollig on Saturday 16th August, in a one shot win over Neilly O'Donaghue, also became All-Ireland champion for that year by virtue of a justifiable walkover when the refixed National final engagement could not be fulfilled by the Ulster champion.

It is a sad reality of passing time that some twenty years later, on 14th November 1995, Jerry O'Leary tragically died in a road traffic accident near Mitchelstown in his native Co Cork. It was on that same evening the members of Bol Chumann Na hEireann were conducting their annual convention and when the sad news was conveyed to delegates all business was suspended as the attendance stood in silent tribute to a great bowl player and true gentleman of the sport. In the words of Christy Santry, bowling correspondent for the *Southern Star*, he was "one of the finest sportsmen ever to play the game", and that same writer, in the newspaper issue of 2nd December 1995, paid outstanding tribute to the exceptional qualities of Jerry O'Leary. A guard of honour by bowling colleagues included former

Jerry O'Leary, Cork, All-Ireland Under 16 Champion for 1975, who tragically died in a road traffic accident in 1995.

Billy Quigley.
Photo: Larry Dickinson.

senior players Mick Barry and Denis Scully, and as the flag of Bol Chumann Na hEireann was folded, the Chairman of the sporting organisation, Jerry Desmond, delivered a poignant graveside oration extolling the acknowledged virtues of the young man whose bowling career had spanned more than two decades in the sport.

In that mid seventies era of postponed fixtures there remained only the Junior All-Ireland final of 1975 to be concluded in a contest which saw Ulster champion Sean Webb, Annahagh, oppose Munster champion Billy Hurley who was also the London regional junior champion that year. Webb had beaten Billy Quigley, Armagh, in the provincial final with a powerful display in which he gained an early lead and went a shot up before dropping back to level terms after which he steadied to win fairly easily. The Munster Junior championship of 1975 was less clear cut. Billy Hurley had come through the London region with a final win over Jim Deasy. He then faced the mid Cork champion John Murphy, Templemartin, in a quarter final score at Ballineen and qualified for the semi finals with a last shot win. In one semi-final John O'Mahony, Cobh, the east Cork champion, lost by a shot at Crookstown to the west Cork representative, Percy Deane from Dunmanway. In the other it was Billy Hurley who had a convincing win over the south west champion from Clogagh, David Walsh in a rather one sided score at Kilbrittain. The Munster junior final at Ballinadee on 17th August 1975 was something special. It was a Dunmanway duel in every sense as Hurley was a native of the west Cork town and had a strong London following to urge on his title ambitions. The demanding Ballinadee road required plenty of power and each of them had it in abundance. The score attracted many thousands to the venue to record perhaps the biggest crowd at any bowling event that year. And their anticipation of a cracking contest was duly confirmed. The lead exchanged several times with some spectacular bowling from both men. The outcome was in doubt all the way until a rather scattered bowl by Deane, close to the finish, provided Hurley with the opportunity and inspiration to finish it off and he did so with a relatively safe final throw. Billy Hurley did more than merely retain his form into the following year for that long delayed All-Ireland junior final against Ulster champion Sean Webb. He not only won that in style at Ballyshonin on 28th August 1976, but, remarkably, achieved a magnificent double by taking the All-Ireland Intermediate title as well on the same weekend. It was a great year for Billy Hurley and all his London followers. It was a great year too for bowling administration. Yet another discordant episode had been amicably surmounted. The outstanding All-Ireland finals had, in so far as possible, been successfully completed and the unity of the organising body was again fully consolidated.

And so to the 1976 championships. They too had something special to offer. Willie Collins of Clashmore, Co Waterford created his own bit of history by winning the All-Ireland Juvenile title that year and thus becoming the first bowler outside of Cork or Armagh to gain National honours in any grade of the sport. His opponent in the final was Ciaran Toal, Armagh, who had beaten Frank Donnelly and the rapidly improving Martin Boylan, before surprising Jarlath Devlin in the provincial final. Toal had been bowling with great speed and was just beaten in the provincial Under 18 final the same year. But despite being strongly fancied to win the National title, and indeed leading that score for most of the way, he finished in less impressive style and Collins came through to win on the last shot. Without being strongly fancied in any of his championship outings Willie Collins had continued to defy the odds right through to the final encounter and on becoming the first Waterford player to win an All-Ireland title in road bowls had boldly countered the balance against that probability.

In the Under 18 championship, Ciaran Toal, the defeated Juvenile finalist, had also been a surprise packet in the higher grade, particularly in his semi-final win over Paul Gribben, But his final opponent, Liam Boylan, had been equally impressive in the qualifying score against Gerald Quigley, and in a real battle of speed it was Boylan who utilised it best to take the Ulster Under 18 title. The Munster championship in the same grade had been even more impressive in speed and quality. John Hurley of Drinagh had a one shot win over Dan Kenneally, Churchtown South, and with consistently good bowling ousted Pat Fleming, Ring, in a fine score at Ahiohill, before taking the provincial title with a notable win over Andy O'Callaghan at Crossbarry. A great National final was anticipated. Liam Boylan, Armagh, a fast bowler amongst a family of particularly strong players and John Hurley a prominent player of proven ability and, to go with it, a record of being an exceptional sportsman in keeping with the recognised sporting demeanour of his

The spectators move forward for the next shot at a score on Cathedral Road, Armagh.

large contingent of Drinagh followers. It was played at Ballyshonin on Sunday 28th August 1976 and produced everything expected by the spectators. Fast and true bowling almost all the way; a keenly contested score throughout; a narrow margin separating the players in a rapidly exchanging lead; and one of the closest and best finishes in any major contest that year. The outcome and destination of the All-Ireland Under 18 title went down to the last shot and it was Hurley who pulled it off with Boylan very narrowly beaten on that final throw.

The Junior championship of 1976 was typically competitive. A surprise result in the Munster section was the defeat of Bill Daly, the spectacular Under 18 National champion of the previous year. But the facts explained the reason. It had been an absolute classic at Castledonovan in which he and his classy opponent Mick Russell, Drinagh each set up a new record for the course with bowling of exceptional quality. Daly had first established the new record in going over the finishing line with his fourteenth shot but it was superseded moments later when Russell topped the mark in the same number of throws by eighteen metres. The Drinagh bowler lost a subsequent championship score at Dunmanway to Eugene Daly, Colomane. The quarter finals of the Junior championship saw Brendan O'Driscoll, Drinagh, beat Christy Coleman, Saleen, the same player who narrowly lost the All-Ireland Junior final of 1967; Jimmy Canty, Lyre, got the better of City player Andrew Twomey; Ted Roche, north Cork, went into the semi-finals at the expense of London champion Jim O'Donoghue; and two of the best known players in the Junior grade, Mick Coughlan and Donie Madden contested the remaining semi-final place with North East bowler Coughlan proving best on the day. He proved best on subsequent days also for the Fermoy man had a huge win over Coachford bowler Ted Roche and then got clear by a bowl of odds over the other semi-final winner Brendan O'Driscoll, to win the Munster Junior title at Crossbarry.

In the Ulster Junior championship of 1976, Aidan McVeigh, Armagh, son of the renowned Joe of Knappagh fame, and subsequent long term Secretary to the Northern Branch, An Bol Chumann, had made his way through to the provincial final by virtue of convincing wins over Malachy Quigley, Armagh and Malachy Comiskey, Portadown. Comiskey had been strongly fancied for the title following impressive wins over Pat Toal, Grangemore, and the fast bowling Paul Gillespie. McVeighs opponent in the provincial final was Donal Toal, Tirgarve, who had been getting great length into his shots when beating Liam Donnelly, Allistragh and Jim Campbell, Lisadian. It was those long drives which proved so valuable in the end when Toal overhauled a huge early deficit to merely win on the last shot after McVeigh had extended him all the way. Toal went on to win the special overall contest for Ulster champions that year but there was disappointment when he was unable to travel for the All- Ireland final in August. The title went to Fermoy when Mick Coughlan was awarded the honour in a walkover. The Intermediate championship in Ulster produced some shock results with favourite Gerry Boylan going out to a great display by Donald Gribben, Farmacaffley, whilst Larry Lyttle, Armagh, surprised Al Mallon Kilmore, with the ease of his extended lead and finishing margin. Oliver O'Neill, Armagh easily defeated Sean Webb, Annahagh, and in a combat of rare speed, the two city bowlers of powerful deliveries, Sean Doran and the late Brendan Digby each fought out a score of exceptional dimensions. It was Brendan Digby who was the more powerful in the end and he further maintained his form through the semi-final in a last shot win over Larry Lyttle, only to go one better in a superb final performance when forging well ahead of Oliver O'Neill who had qualified with a shot lead over Donald Gribben. In the Munster Intermediate championship it was Billy Hurley of Dunmanway and London who was setting the pace. He had beaten Pat Murphy, Templemartin by a narrow margin on the final throw after both men were on level marks for the last shot in their semi-final score at Ballinadee. In the Munster final at Kilbrittain there was no such close finish. Declan O'Donovan made a marvellous start but Billy Hurley responded with equally fine bowls at crucial stages to open up a substantial lead and subsequently win easily.

It was more of the same in the All-Ireland Intermediate final at Ballyshonin on 28th August 1976. Brendan Digby never reached the standard of his accurate and powerfully strong bowling in the provincial championship some weeks earlier and it was without pressure that Billy Hurley collected the National title for Cork and indeed the bowling fraternity in London.

But whatever about the nature and quality of the 1976 National finals already played, the real gem had yet to come. A senior championship final of which there has been few equals. It goes back to May of that year when Mick O'Driscoll, Carrigtwohill, beat Dermot O'Sullivan at Ballinadee and followed it up with another stirring win over his relative and namesake from Blackpool at the Waterloo course. That victory put Mick O'Driscoll into the Munster senior final for the first time. His opponent in that final had a stunning run of successes. Donal O'Leary, the Intermediate champion of the previous year, had beaten Mick Barry in the first round of the senior championship and then overcame the formidable talent of Liam Daly at Beal na Blath. He was then faced with the complete and accomplished bowling skill of Denis Scully in the provincial semi-final at the same venue, and despite being virtually equal in strength with a consistently magnificent loft, O'Leary was given a less than even chance of mastering the Fairhill expert. But master him he did. Not only was the result significant but more particularly the convincing manner in which it was achieved. That win, on 10th July, 1976 set Donal O'Leary up for a magnificent Munster senior final clash with Mick O'Driscoll at Newcastle eight days later. It was a surprise line-up but O'Leary was undoubtedly the senior player of the year and O'Driscoll was having his best year ever with very creditable senior league performances and he too had recorded recent wins over Scully and Barry. The final was one befitting the record of each of them. It was a thrilling contest watched by a crowd that equalled the enormity of the play. O'Leary nearly did it in what would have been a fairytale year but he had to watch agonizingly as O'Driscoll's final bowl closely hugged the grass verge on its way to trundling over the mark by a mere eighteen inches in a most exciting climax.

The Ulster senior championship offered a great deal less in excitement. Harry Toal (junior), the Intermediate provincial champion of the previous year, had somehow managed to outweigh the superior play of the title holder John Gribben in the first semi-final and Danny McParland went through again to the final with a comfortable win over Aidan Toal. The final was a non- event. Harry Toal sustained an injury at work which ruled him out of bowling for some time and a walkover was granted McParland who was then contesting his first All-Ireland senior final for four years but, incredibly, his ninth in all since the series began thirteen years earlier in 1963. The speculation for the All-Ireland senior final at Ballyshonin on 29th August 1976 was intense. It was the showpiece of the bowling year. Mick O'Driscoll, the Carrigtwohill master of the bowl was considered to be the Ballyshonin specialist. He had never been beaten at the venue and all his best performances were over that particular course near Blarney. But even in 1976 those who cherished a much vaunted Cork supremacy were acutely aware that of all the northern players, Danny McParland was still the greatest challenge even if all his old wizardry had not necessarily been fully retained.

The All-Ireland final started out with less than spectacular bowling from both men but after six shots the score developed into an encounter that produced some of the finest bowling ever seen at Ballyshonin or anywhere else. Each player covered a distance of the course in five shots which was a feat almost beyond belief. Over the second half of the course McParland beat the finest series of shots O'Driscoll had ever played on a road at which the Cork bowler had never lost a score. And he tried valiantly not to lose that one. It was the best finishing performance of his bowling lifetime and yet every magnificent drive seemed to goad

McParland into greater effort as he amazed the crowd with breathtaking shots that protected the much threatened lead he had held since the eighth shot of the score. The Armagh man defended his lead to the finish against the most intense test and in a way which created speculation that his last six shots over the course might never be beaten. It was a splendid way in which to win his fourth All-Ireland senior title. And immediately afterwards Danny McParland announced to those within hearing range of his impromptu comment, "That's my last." The remark provoked intense interest as press representatives, officials, supporters and admirers sought clarification of what they had just heard. But McParland was not one for giving extended interviews and they were left to ponder upon the real meaning of his short but typically crisp declaration. It had indeed been his last. He entered the senior championship the following year but didn't qualify and it was early in 1978 that his official retirement was confirmed. That thriller of 1976 was Danny McParland's last appearance in an All-Ireland final and, fittingly, he won it to crown a most brilliant career which had enthralled road bowls followers for nearly twenty years. His mastery of the bowl was devastating in its power and uncanny in its expertise. Danny McParland had beckoned a whole new era in the sport which provided a tremendous source of inspiration to those less accomplished, and an immense sense of fulfilment to all admirers of peak quality bowling. In winning the first All-Ireland senior final in 1963 he had embarked upon a title pursuit that was to see him collect three more National titles and contest no less than five of the remaining ten championship finals. A phenomenal record that ensures the great Danny McParland is, and will remain, an enduring reality of outstanding sporting achievement.

The Potential for Greatness

The sport of road bowling, in common with most other competitive games, has engendered a catalogue of notable participants who have acquired distinction through the sheer quality of their individual performance over the years.

The formula for eminence is multifarious, and the requisite attributes diverse, but astute judges are adept at early recognition of the potential for player greatness. Such was the case when the dynamic young southern discovery, Denis Scully, from Fairhill, near Cork City, first demonstrated his bowling skills in the late sixties. The road bowls following was enthralled at the prospects bidding for this exciting young player. Those closest to his playing activity in Cork were enthusiastically predicting a great future for Denis Scully. That he was already one of the top four senior players in the south was a clear indication of his proven ability and enormous potential.

Denis Scully had been the subject of the greatest plaudits ever accorded a bowl player so young, and of such limited experience. He was reported to show greater potential than did the illustrious Mick Barry when at the same youthful age, and that in itself was a wonderful commendation. It was claimed too that he then commanded the biggest following of any player in the country.

How delighted then was the bowling fraternity in the north when news was released that the sensational young nineteen your old Denis Scully was to play in

Denis Scully.

Armagh for the first time. It was in October 1968, for the Charlemont Hotel Cup, and his opponent over the Knappagh course was to be the current Ulster Senior Champion, Danny McParland. It proved to be a score in which the Armagh man had failed to disburden himself of the inferior play that plagued his All-Ireland Senior Final at Nadd against Johnny Creedon just two months earlier.

But for Denis Scully it was so satisfying and for northern spectators it was particularly fascinating.

This is how the *Ulster Gazette* of 31st October, 1968 reported the score and, in particular, focused upon the skilful exhibition by Denis Scully:

> *There can be no doubt that for a player of his age and, as yet, very limited experience in big- time bowling, this young Cork sportsman, Denis Scully, is one of the finest players we have ever seen. Not so much based upon his actual performance at the weekend against Danny McParland, but more for the sheer potential which is clearly evident in his every effort and the rock-like determination with which he approaches each aspect of his game. With an almost professional attitude, and portraying perhaps greater qualities than any other current player, it is well nigh impossible to find a fault with him in any facet of the game. This is a combination of attributes which must surely bear him to the top very soon. It would appear that he is destined to bowl his way into a position of dominance in senior ranks whilst still one of the youngest players ever to do so. As yet his relatively diminutive physique tends to hinder him fully taking the game by storm but with maturity, and additional inter-provincial experience, he is surely going to create a tremendous impression in every bowling competition for which he enters.*
>
> *Denis Scully is already a delight to watch with his superb delivery, pinpoint accuracy, and surprising strength. And never before have we seen a player with such determination and patient concentration on every single shot. His preparation for each and every delivery was on a par with something we have seen on our television screens from the Mexico Olympics during the past two weeks. For this young bowler, with so much of his sporting glory still ahead of him, it was a most rewarding stance. Scully's performance at the weekend was a great one. It is very easy to point out that he failed to make the finishing line in twenty-four shots but this was his first inter-provincial score and consequently his first time ever to play at the Knappagh venue. Taking that alone into consideration we must acknowledge the sheer quality of his performance; but there is more to it beyond that. For those who watched his play closely they will be convinced of his enormous speed, precise accuracy, and, in this particular event, hapless breaks with some of his well placed shots. They will also admit that only twice in twenty-four shots did he slightly misplace a bowl and in most cases when he failed to get great length into his shots it was where the camber of the road was against his delivery and the options were very limited. On a few occasions he played perfectly but just failed to get away. One of the really outstanding features of Scully's game is his tremendous strength and undoubted ability to cope with the hills. When, before,*

Michael McSweeney, Cork, President of Bol Chumann Na hEireann and great admirer of Denis Scully's Bowling ability is pictured at the 1995 All-Ireland Finals at Dunderrow, near Kinsale in County Cork. In the background is bowling enthusiast, Tim O'Leary, Bandon, a son of Denis 'Sonny' O'Leary, the great bowl player at the beginning of the twentieth century.

have we seen any player to equal those two uphill shots on the sixth and the thirteenth throws?

In this one event Denis Scully has demonstrated a combination of qualities which make this young Cork lad the greatest prospect in the game today. After the score Danny McParland could offer no excuses other than to say he just couldn't get behind his bowl - and then he quipped, "the only shots I could get behind were Scully's!"

The powerful young Denis Scully went on to deliver his promise with some superb performances in subsequent years. In the qualifying scores for the Macardles National Tournament in 1969 he conquered Donie Madden at Togher and then enthralled a massive crowd at Cobh, on 2nd March, with a brilliant win over another top senior bowler, Derry Kenny, who was the first winner of the prestigious trophy in 1968. But the biggest test of all still faced the young Fairhill idol when Mick Barry won through against the strong bowling of John O'Donoghue at Fermoy. It was what everybody in the game had been longing for. Barry, the durable incumbent of bowling supremacy being challenged for the first time by the youthful Scully, widely hailed as heir apparent to his place upon the pedestal. Perhaps, Barry, now faced his greatest test of all! But there the speculation ended. The anticipated showpiece at Youghal became a non-event when Barry sustained an injury and Scully was through to the National final at Armagh on Sunday 16th March, 1969.

In the final he was challenged by Danny McParland who had emerged as the northern qualifier from the top eight senior players nominated to contest the Tournament. McParland had beaten John Gribben in the northern final after they had come through qualifying scores over Mickey Hughes, Aidan Toal, Oliver O'Neill, Brendan Digby, Harry Toal and Billy Quigley.

In that National final Scully went on to emulate Kenny's achievement in 1968 when he soared into a big lead after eight shots and, despite difficulties with the Knappagh course, was never pressed as he crossed the line with more than a bowl of odds of spare.

In the 1969 International event in Holland, Denis Scully performed splendidly for Ireland in all the events and he further enhanced his European reputation in 1970, at Cork, when he came second in the German loft and also made a vital contribution to Bol Chumann winning first and second place in the Road Bowling event. In the German loft Scully temporarily broke all existing records with a massive lift of 88.5 metres.

There was disappointment though for Denis Scully in the 1969 Munster senior championship final when he succumbed to the bowling power of Mick Barry at Waterloo, and it was all of four more years before he won his first provincial senior title. That 1973 championship is one he will fervently cherish, not least for his brilliant semi-final win over Seamus Sexton who had earlier ended the title hopes of Mick Barry in a second round tie at Berrings. Scully had already beaten Barry three times in succession in major scores that season, the third of which was at Ballincollig in July. It was a series of wins which appeared to justify the widespread belief that Scully was establishing a performance rating superior to Barry with every indica-

Denis Scully, Cork, in the European Bowling Championships at Cork City in 1992.
Photo: Denis McGarry.

tion that he would remain there for a long time to come. There was even speculation that Barry's long and undisputed ascendancy over all the other players of his generation had ended. Indeed such was the sheer quality of the Fairhill bowlers consistent performance it was the emergent contention that the bowling monopoly enjoyed by Barry was shifting exclusively to Scully. He did lose the fourth score in the series to Barry, albeit a poor one, on Sunday 22nd July, 1973 at Ring and it is that fact which made his championship win over Sexton so important. It had the effect of re-establishing his supremacy and that was confirmed through another marvellous display in the Munster final against John Kenny at Fermoy. That was the year of the delayed All-Ireland finals and the senior decider was further deferred when Scully sustained an injury and required hospitalisation. That postponed event was played at Ballyshonin, Co Cork on Saturday, 12th October, 1974, with Scully emerging victorious over Armagh's Harry Toal. It had been Scully at his brilliant best. He wiped out all previous records for the road in what was possibly his finest score.

Into the mid-seventies young Denis Scully was still being heralded as the new bowling idol but alas his period of ascendancy was short lived. He again won the Munster senior title in 1977 but lost that All-Ireland final by more than two shots to Harry Toal, (junior), a son of his 1974 vanquished, at Castleblaney, Co Monaghan on 2nd October, 1977.

Denis Scully's fleeting rise to fame had earned him but one All-Ireland senior title. He did gain some consolation when he re-emerged in 1988 to win the All-Ireland Intermediate championship final against James McCann, Moy, County Tyrone, on Sunday 10th July at the Skibbereen venue of Bauravilla.
Happily though, Denis Scully was back on the Irish International team for the European Bowling Championships at Cork in 1992. He was there on merit, having been selected by virtue of his diligent preparation and intense practice performance. Perhaps his total collection of trophies is not yet complete.

The bowling career of Fairhill's Denis Scully was to warrant widespread acclaim and, on considered reflection, merits due acknowledgement.

The Emergence of Contemporary Talent

The virtual dominance of the senior championship, for more than a dozen years, by a prime few of the leading bowlers in the country was eventually interrupted in the late seventies when the subordinate grades began to yield a range of competent players fully capable of taking National honours in senior competition. The players to emerge over that period and subsequently share the All-Ireland senior titles had, almost without exception, figured prominently in the lower ranks of the championships in the preceding years.

There was a paucity of bowlers in Ulster of true senior standard at the time but that fact didn't detract from the competitive quality of the outstanding player to eventually emerge as the able challenger for National senior honours. It had been fairly evident for some time, and particularly following his win in the Under 18 championship of 1974, that Harry Toal, (junior) was a player with outstanding potential who had the necessary power to succeed at senior level. But for injury he was quite capable of achieving National success in his first year as a senior bowler. He proved the point the following year, in the 1977 Ulster championship when he beat Danny McParland and Aidan Toal in true fashion and on 10th July that year, in a rousing provincial final, he dislodged the formidable challenge of Gerry Boylan who had been so impressive in a great semi-final win over Brendan Digby.

The Munster senior championship that year was also generating new talent at senior level and one of those was Billy Hurley, with Junior and Intermediate titles already to his credit as well as a special award for being selected West Cork Sports Star in 1976. He created the premier surprise of the senior championship with a convincing win over the experienced Donie Coveney at Macroom but lost out in the quarter final to the reigning Munster champion Mick O'Driscoll at Ballineen. That win brought O'Driscoll through to a semi-final tussle with Dermot O'Sullivan who had not previously won honours in any grade but showed promise of an end to his personal dearth with a fine win at Ahiohill against John Kenny. The other side of the draw saw Seamus Sexton oust Johnny Creedon at Beeing before gaining a semi-final place on beating Pat O'Sullivan at Ballyshonin. He was joined in that semi-final by Denis Scully following a win at Newcastle against Derry Kenny. They were two particularly intriguing semi-final pairings with no shortage of bowling talent and a newcomer in the form of Dermot O'Sullivan, hungry for his first major success at any level. But even his utmost determination and considerable bowling skill was not sufficient to curb the power and accuracy of the reigning champion at the demanding Ballinadee course on 31st July 1977 as Mick O'Driscoll, once again, qualified for the Munster senior final. He then pensively awaited the clash a week later, at New Tipperary, between the masterly Denis Scully and Seamus Sexton who, apart form a hint of unpredictability, had every attritube of a great bowler. It was that degree of inconsistency on Sexton's part, and the lack of it in Scully's bowling, that helped determine the outcome. In the end it went Scully's way and his performance was such that he was considered to have a great chance of toppling the holder O'Driscoll in the Munster senior final at Ballyshonin. And that he did. It was a big disappointment for Mick O'Driscoll who had hoped to go one better than the previous year when he bowled his best ever in the All- Ireland final and still lost. His marvellous record at Ballyshonin was by then well and truly shattered. But for Denis Scully it was a renewed opportunity to complement his sparse title list and he confidently faced that prospect.

The All-Ireland senior final of 1977 was played on the Oram road, just outside Castleblaney, Co Monaghan on Sunday 2nd October and it is one that Denis Scully will have no great desire to recall. Not only did he drop a few of his shots too low for distance he also, untypically, scattered a number of others. Those errors alone may have cost him the score in any case but Harry Toal (junior) was taking no chances. After requiring a little time to settle he soon reached his peak form and with powerful lengthy bowls, coupled on occasions with skilful negotiation of challenging corners, he stretched ahead to win by more than two shots. A new champion had emerged and the nature of his hitherto performances suggested he would reign for quite some time.

Surprisingly though, Harry Toal (junior) did not make it through to the National senior final in the following three years. The challenge for senior honours was really wide open. In the 1978 Ulster senior championship Harry Toal was virtually gifted a place in the final when, following a tremendous score, Gerry Boylan faltered on the last shot with a particularly short effort which cost him the score. And Pat Mallon was in marvellous form throughout his score against Aidan Toal to eventually win with ease and face the daunting undertaking of a provincial final challenge against the reigning All-Ireland champion. But Pat Mallon was never one to dread such an assignment and over the Blackwatertown road on Sunday 13th August 1978 he caused a sensation in not only winning the Ulster senior title but bowling Harry Toal completely out of contention by a margin of over two shots.

The All-Ireland senior final was scheduled for Ballyshonin, Co Cork that year and the Munster finalists had little reason to be concerned by a result that determined their challenger to be the man who was so unimpressive in the Intermediate final the previous season. And perhaps their complacency was justified. It had not been one of the more competitive Munster championship campaigns. Several players reported injuries and Denis Scully was definitely out for that reason. John Kenny was also nursing an injury but he made it to the provincial final only to be beaten at Waterfall, on 19th August 1978, by Pat Butler who was in his first year as a senior bowler. It was unusual, but both contestants had reached the All-Ireland final on their first entry to senior ranks. However it proved to be a final that both men will wish to forget. Played on Sunday 27th August 1978 it was considered by many to be the poorest bowling final of that or any other year. A lack of experience may have been one factor but each player evidently struck an off-day and it was Butler who was least badly affected. That alone earned him his first All-Ireland

The determination of champion bowler, Pat Mallon.
Photo: Ann McManus/Irish News

senior title. Both men, and their supporters, knew they were capable of a great deal better.

Incredibly it was not until twelve years later, in 1990, that the revitalised Pat Butler emerged when he then embarked upon a series of wins that was to lay claim to him being acknowledged as the supreme bowler of the period. Pat Mallon didn't wait as long. He was back in the All- Ireland senior final of 1979, a year after that undistinguished performance at Ballyshonin, and keen to redeem his credentials as a legitimate senior bowler. He had already done that in the eyes of northern followers with a championship win over Harry Toal (senior) and after again scorching through the Ulster senior final with another great win over Harry Toal (junior) who was strongly fancied following his doubly impressive defeat of Gerry Boylan and Aidan Toal. That provincial final was played on the 29th July, 1979, over the Blackwatertown road, the same course designed for the All-Ireland decider, and an occasion that was to mark the first National bowling finals to be played in Armagh since 1971.

The news of Pat Mallon's win had not posed any significant threat to the confidence of the Munster camp most of whom were mindful of the insipid encounter at Ballyshonin a year earlier. Standing by was the new Munster senior champion John Creedon who had won the provincial final against Donie Coveney on Sunday 22nd July 1979 at Beal na Blath. It had been eleven years since John Creedon previously contested the National senior final but he had been quite impressive in his new found eminence and the odds on him winning his second All- Ireland senior title were very favourable. But the resilient Pat Mallon was making the second attempt at winning his first and the fierce determination was obvious.

A huge crowd converged on the Blackwatertown road for the All-Ireland final on Sunday 5th August, 1979. They had been deprived of major fixtures on home ground for so long and it was a welcome scene for those seeking to restore normality in the organisation of National bowling finals.

The score got off to a rather ordinary start with Mallon shaky at the outset and Creedon going into a timid lead. Soon afterwards the Armagh man began to settle and he was rapidly into the stride more familiar to his followers. Urged on by his supporters Mallon opened up a threatening lead over Creedon who was superb in flashes but susceptible to an occasional error that prevented him getting back into a truly challenging position. It was Mallon who continued to dominate and over the final quarter he consolidated a two shot lead to win by that margin amidst great jubilation at a local victory and a rejuvenating northern success in the first senior final played in Armagh since 1969.

Throughout that period of years the Intermediate championship had been generating some fine scores with close finishes and superb individual performances. In the 1977 Munster championship Corney Bohane beat Donie Madden at Dunmanway; Liam Daly outplayed Pat Butler at Ballinadee; Denis Collins ousted Pat Murphy at Enniskeane; and John Murphy got the better of Declan O'Donovan at Ballineen. But the biggest crowd puller of the series was the clash of two particularly classy players, Bill Daly and Donie O'Mahony, one considered to be consistently good and the other intermittently great. It was the occasional greatness that saw Bill Daly through that one but he subsequently lost a quarter final score to Joe Twohig at Dunmanway. He in turn lost to Corney Bohane at Enniskeane and the remaining place in the provincial final was filled by ex-senior player Christy Keating who had recorded wins over Liam Daly at Ballinadee and John Murphy at Togher Cross. The Munster Intermediate final at Macroom on 21st August, 1977, saw the tenacity of the more youthful Bohane prevail over the subdued experience of Keating and the challenge for National honours was a daunting engagement at Castleblaney in October.

The Ulster Intermediate championship of the same year produced many close finishes. Donald Gribben, Farmacaffley, narrowly beat Colm Grimley, Lisadian before toppling another fast bowler in Patsy McKenna of Knappagh. Harry Toal (senior) sprung a surprise with a mere three metres win over the powerful bowling of Al Mallon, Kilmore, and further confounded the critics by pressing the former Junior and Intermediate champion Gerald McKee to a last shot fright before losing by the minimum margin. McKee had earlier ended the championship ambitions of fellow city player Oliver O'Neill. Meanwhile Pat Mallon, Tyra, was commanding attention with splendid wins over Billy Quigley, Armagh and Stephen Donnelly, Allistragh, but the real confirmation of his ability came in his Ulster final victory against the vastly experienced Gerald McKee.

The 1977 All-Ireland Intermediate final at Castleblaney on Sunday 2nd October, produced a sharp contrast in fortunes. Pat Mallon never at any time hit the form that was so prevalent throughout the Ulster championship and Corney Bohane was overwhelming in his power with a consistent standard of bowling that far exceeded his personal best. No less than four shots divided the pair at one stage and even when Pat Mallon did get into a reasonable rhythm of play it may have succeeded in halving the deficit but Bohane's performance was such it was never going to make any impression on the result.

In a well contested and highly competitive Ulster Intermediate championship of 1978 it was Al Mallon, Kilmore, who came through to the final for the first time in five years following wins over Sean Devlin, who played for Armagh in the All-Ireland Gaelic Football final in 1977, and Gerald McKee who was surprisingly beaten for speed on the day. But the real surprise of the championship had to be the spiritness of the irrepressible Harry Toal (senior) who despite being virtually written off at the outset of the competition had come right through a field of proven quality and then went on to deal the clincher in the provincial final, on Friday 21st July, 1978, when he took the challenge of the winding Blackwatertown road in his stride and beat the local favourite Al Mallon for the title.

The Munster Intermediate final of that year was played at Ballinadee on 13th August and resulted in John Murphy, a defeated semi-finalist the previous year, going out at the ultimate stage to Declan O'Donovan who had himself lost the provincial final two years earlier.

The All-Ireland final at Ballyshonin, Co Cork on Saturday 26th August, 1978, was expected to be a tough test for Harry Toal (senior) who, despite the regularity with which he could reach the conclusive stages of National finals, that elusive win over a Munster opponent had yet to be realised. And so it remained. Once again his form deserted him and in Declan O'Donovan he found a competitor far too good on the day who was able to coast unperturbed to his first National title.

But if the veteran bowler Harry Toal had still been awaiting an All-Ireland award so too had Al Mallon who, despite figuring at the top for many years with consistently sound performances, was also devoid of any remarkable success at championship level. But a renewed opportunity was the reality of the 1979 Intermediate championship when he beat Colm Grimley and Gerald McKee before gaining the provincial title on 29th July with a last shot win over John Gribben in a most exciting score played before a large crowd of enthusiastic spectators. The Munster Intermediate title that year had gone to the late Christy O'Driscoll who had a credible win over P J McCarthy at Ahiohill. The report of that final hadn't prepared the Ulster champion for anything more than the normal challenge of Intermediate standard and with a home venue in Mallon's favour he was widely fancied. But this one was different. In that All-Ireland final on Saturday 4th August 1979, over the Blackwatertown road, Christy O'Driscoll not only launched into it with a spectacular opening shot but proceeded to combine pinpoint accuracy with optimum power on every single throw from that to the finish. It was a devastating performance which inevitably pulverised Al Mallon who had done well to stay level to halfway but lost contact beyond that point to lose by more than two shots. The magnitude of the late Christy O'Driscoll's achievement is placed in perspective when it is considered that he covered the same course in two shots less than the new All-Ireland senior champion did the following day. And even more significantly he had gone over the line in the same number of shots as did Danny McParland in that record shattering performance of 21st February, 1965. A wonderful all round bowling accomplishment.

There was more than ample inspiration for Junior players throughout the late seventies as they viewed performances in the higher grades. But such was the competitive nature of that particular category the undistracted concentration of participants was a necessary requisite for sustained involvement. And there was a huge field of contestants in each of the Ulster and Munster Junior championships of 1977. In the quarter finals of the northern championship Johnny Mills virtually threw away his score with a disastrous finish which handed a semi-final place to Stephen Toal and he made full use of his redeemed opportunity by going on to beat Larry Corr who had impressed in his win over Pat Toal. But coming through on the other side of the draw was relative newcomer Paddy McKeown who had defeated Aidan McVeigh and Patrick Comiskey before winning the provincial title in a close encounter with Stephen Toal. But if that result was close it had nothing on the All-Ireland final at Castleblaney. The Armagh mans opponent in that particular struggle was Simon Buckley, Cork city, who had won the Munster junior title at New Tipperary through good wins over west Cork bowler Derry Connolly at Macroom, and east Cork representative Barney McCarthy at Fermoy.

The National final on Saturday 1st October was a closely contested affair.

Shandon Steeple, Cork City.

Photo: Bord Fáilte.

Going into the last bend Paddy McKeown was offered a wonderful chance of victory but he failed to seize it and the inspired Simon Buckley rallied with a tremendous final throw which won the score and the All-Ireland Junior title by a magical margin of three metres.

The competition in subsequent years was no less intense. In Ulster it was Oliver Gribben who came through in 1978 for his first provincial win since taking the Under 18 title in 1973. He had beaten Patrick Comiskey in a close score, throughout which both players were equal for speed, but on the day Gribben was the steadier of the two and he won by almost a shot. The Munster Junior championship generated its own particular drama that year in which the closing stages were contested by regional winners Paddy O'Donovan, City; Noel O'Brien, South West; Bunny O'Driscoll, Mid.; Wally Shannon, West; Paddy O'Riordan, North; and John Butler, East. The provincial final went to Noel O'Brien who was awarded the score at Togher Cross less than three shots from the finish when an official ruling had deemed him the winner. The Clonakilty player, undoubtedly one of Cork's best junior bowlers over a long period, went on to justify his merit by beating Oliver Gribben, younger brother of experienced players John and Donald, through much superior speed over the Ballyshonin course. That All-Ireland Junior title of August 1978 had rewarded Noel O'Brien for a consistent series of good quality performances and it was evident even then that he would gain further acclaim.

If anything, the 1979 Junior championship was even more rival than those that had gone before. In a fiercely contested Ulster campaign the eventual finalist, Oliver Grimley, had taken care of the challenges offered by Noel Carr, John Lennon, John Grimley, Paul Gillespie and Larry Feighan in a hard earned path to the provincial final. His opponent, Paul McVeigh, had an equally difficult trail including demanding scores against Noel Mallon, Ciaran Rocks and Malachy McIlvenna. In the final over the Blackwatertown road on 29th July 1979 Paul McVeigh came out best and the manner of his win was sufficient to prompt speculation that he could take the National title the following week over the same course.

The Munster junior final at Macroom on Saturday 28th July, had seen Joe O'Connor, Cork City, stimulate ideas that he too was capable of winning the All-Ireland title, even away from home, when he beat Timoleague bowler John O'Sullivan who was regional winner in the constantly vying South West section.

The All-Ireland Junior final at Blackwatertown on Sunday 5th August 1979 fulfilled in total the week long speculation about the legitimate claims of each player to National honours in their particular grade. Both McVeigh and O'Connor rose superbly to the occasion despite the wet and dreary conditions which prevailed throughout the contest. It was close and exciting with some fine shots produced by each and, as in all good matches, it was down to the last shot. The Armagh man, son of the celebrated Joe McVeigh, must have utilised a combination of his father's wisdom and his own personal skill to produce an effort that surprisingly scored the finishing line and to all intents and purposes appeared to seal a stunning victory. But Joe O'Connor wasn't finished. He gave his last shot everything and awaited the reaction of his supporters as they watched the bowl mount the grass verge close to the finish and then roll over the mark by a mere three metres in a most exciting finale to a thoroughly contested score. A narrow and tremendously jubilant win for Cork.

If ever there was a measure of success and a manifest commitment to a policy of youth involvement in bowling it must rest with Tadhg O'Duinin, Cnoc an Lur, and all the other members of the Gaeltacht region who affiliated to Bol Chumann Na hEireann in 1976 and within a year had a young man contesting the Under 18 All-Ireland final. The dedication of the bowling members of the region was further recognised in 1991 when they were entrusted with the onus and responsibility of conducting the All-Ireland finals for three consecutive years and did so with aplomb and effectiveness. Their representative in the 1977 All-Ireland Under 18 final was Brendan O'Callaghan, Gaeltacht, a strong and steady player who had won the Munster title on merit over the cool, reliable and accurate Sean Bohane, from the West Cork region.

The Ulster Under 18 championship of 1977 saw Liam Boylan come through and it was no surprise. He had won it the previous year also and in the season before that had taken the provincial juvenile title. The experience of those two National finals undoubtedly exerted in his favour in the All-Ireland final at Castleblaney on Saturday, 1st October, 1977. The opposite applied to Brendan O'Callaghan. He was lacking in such experience and it showed on the day. Liam Boylan was in great form as he cruised into a big lead which he gradually extended all the way to the finish to gain a National title that had eluded him so narrowly the previous year.

If the Under 18 title belonged to Liam Boylan in 1977 it was almost totally dominated by other members of the same Lislea, Co Armagh family the following year when the two brothers Dessie and Martin beat all comers including Mickey McGleenan, Anthony O'Neill and Seamus Fox, to contest the Ulster final between them. That unusual but not unique event was played on Friday 21st July, 1978, and it was the older of the two brothers Dessie Boylan who took the title.

The last four in the Munster Under 18 championship were Tony O'Brien, North East; Tom O'Callaghan, North; Jerry Dullea, West; and Michael Buckley, City. The eventual winner was Michael Buckley, a player who went on to win the All-Ireland senior championship in 1983, and that potential was evident at Ballyshonin in 1978 when he took the Under 18 National title in a full shot win over Ulster champion Dessie Boylan.

The Cork city player was back in the provincial Under 18 final the following year at Macroom but lost to Baltimore bowler Pat Bohane. And in Ulster it was Jarlath Devlin, Armagh and Brian Grimley, Madden who contested the final having beaten Philip Rafferty, Madden and Mickey McGleenan, Armagh, respectively. The surprise winner in that final was Brian Grimley and despite a lively delivery it was feared he would lack the necessary speed to go all the way for the National title.

In the All-Ireland Under 18 final of 1979, over the Blackwatertown road on Saturday 4th August, it was Grimley who started best but the greater speed of Bohane was obvious and once the Baltimore man got his accuracy sorted out he went into the lead on the fifth shot and remained there to the finish for a relatively easy win.

By the year 1977 there had already been completed a successful decade of thoroughly competitive Juvenile championships in which the admirable commitment and evident ability of youngsters in the sport had established, in its own right, a popular competition at National level. The earnestness and enthusiasm of the Under 16 competitors also offered valuable opportunity for considered assessment of individual bowling potential and this evaluative exercise added cogency to a competition of great interest.

In that 1977 Juvenile championship, the Boylan family, who had been enjoying a tremendous run of success throughout that particular period in northern bowling, virtually dominated the Under 16 competition when brothers Martin and Dessie each reached the Ulster final. And the will to win was in no way diminished when they both served up tremendous play in a close contest which went to the final throw. Even then only a mere four metres divided the pair and it was Martin who held the lead when it mattered most. An unfortunate injury ruled him out of the All-Ireland final that year but in 1978 he was back again having won the Ulster Juvenile title for the second year in succession with a narrow win over Martin McVeigh in a closely fought score. The young man so sorely disappointed by the postponement of the 1977 National final was west Cork player John Hegarty, a strong and highly talented bowler of exceptional ability who had beaten young Tom O'Callaghan, Dromahane, to gain the Munster title at New Tipperary on Saturday, 20th August, 1977. He got his chance a year later for the National title but it was Armagh's Martin Boylan who gained the award when he proved superior on the day over the Ballyshonin course in Co Cork. Remarkably, Martin Boylan put two All-Ireland Juvenile titles back to back on that weekend of 27th August, 1978 when he gained a shot win over the Munster champion John Young, Drinagh, to also take that years National Under 16 title against a strongly fancied young Cork player who had emerged from a semi-final quartet which included Eddie Buckley, City, Larry O'Brien, North East, and Jerry O'Sullivan, North Cork, all of them highly regarded under-age bowlers.

The 1979 All-Ireland Juvenile final was the first in that particular grade to be played at an Armagh venue in over eight years. The previous occasion, in 1971, had seen Patrick Comiskey beat Jim Twomey to keep the title in Ulster and it was with renewed confidence that northern followers viewed the prospect of another home win. The Ulster championship of 1979 had ended in a three way final after Patrick Digby had beaten Malachy Quigley (junior) and Philip Rafferty edged out Neil Hunter with Kevin Cully coming through on the last shot to oust Colm Toal. In a very competitive provincial decider it was Philip Rafferty, Madden, who came out best in a performance which augured well for his chances of taking the National title. But the credence of his opponent in that All-Ireland contest at Blackwatertown on Saturday 4th August, 1979, was clearly evident in advance of the encounter. Even before Pat Creedon, North Cork, had beaten Doire O'Duinin, Gaeltacht, at Togher Cross there was widespread belief in his title prospects and this reliance was further strengthened when he took the Munster Juvenile title at Ballyshonin against the East Cork champion Ciaran Hennessy. Guided by the intuition and practical experience of his father John Creedon, Clondrohid, All- Ireland senior champion in 1968, it was obvious the Blackwatertown road or Portmor course would pose few difficulties in his quest for National Juvenile honours. Pat Creedon adapted perfectly to the course. It was probably his best ever performance to then and with it he gave little hope to Philip Rafferty who was very soon into a shot deficit and struggling to prevent further loss. Pat Creedon went on to win rather easily and gain the All-Ireland Juvenile title for 1979. It was with very special interest that he watched his father John Creedon attempt, twenty four hours later to win the All-Ireland senior title over the same course but alas that momentous achievement was denied the Creedon family by the superior bowling of Armagh's Pat Mallon.

The decade of the seventies had been one of mixed emotions and variable experiences for followers of the sport. For many people the ten year period bore sadness, dismay, pessimism and frustration. Conversely it was also a period which generated hope, resolution and a sense of accomplishment in the challenging circumstances of the time. It was a period too in which the sport lost some of its finest supporters. Barney Grimley, whose son Colm contested the 1970 All-Ireland Junior final, and who was a life long supporter of the sport, died suddenly while attending a score at Knappagh on Sunday 27th January, 1974. The first competition for a Cup presented by the family in his memory was won by Gerry Mallon, Kilmore in a three- way final in 1976. The late seventies also recorded the death of Hedley McCay, B.L., who was a valuable member of the Executive, An Bol Chumann, since the early sixties. He was a District Justice and a linguist who was particularly fluent in French and German. The practical assistance of Hedley McCay in helping to establish the International Bowlplaying Association is widely acknowledged. The Executive of Bol Chumann Na hEireann suffered another great loss with the death in July, 1979, of Pat Kerrigan, T.D., a most respected and dependable individual who offered only considered opinions in any debate. A founder member of Cork city region and the first Secretary to that body he was largely instrumental in resolving contentious issues which had arisen in 1972 between northern and southern administrators. A gentleman and true sportsman, Pat Kerrigan was always conciliatory in nature without ever diminishing his advocacy for fairness. Another significant loss to Bol Chumann in that period was the passing of Dan O'Mahony from Ballygibbon, Blarney, who, for many years in the nineteen sixties, served as liaison officer for the north in matters of personal communication and clarification.

The more satisfying aspects of the seventies period centred upon the successful conduct of the All-Ireland championships in each of those turbulent years and the return, at the end of the decade, to the fixtures arrangement of playing the National finals on alternate years in Armagh and Cork. The stable leadership and mollifying management adopted by the late Joe Horan and John Gribben, each of whom presided over the Northern Branch of Bol Chumann for consecutive periods during that time, had been fundamental to the preservation of championship bowling in a most crucial term for the sport in the north.

A Shot for the Record Books

The longest shot in any score of road bowls will invariably play a vital role in determining the eventual winner on the day. Such has frequently been the case.

Claims abound as to the longest shot on record in any bowling event. They are all entitled to an assertion of authenticity and there is little point in comparing or contrasting any of the avowed claims. No two shots; no two stretches of roadway; no two sets of circumstances can ever be sufficiently similar in a score of road bowls to justify a serious attempt at concluding the definitive overall best.

There will be those historians who will point to the incredible finishing shot by Mick McCarthy-Quirke of Kilgariffe, Clonakilty in a Clancool score against Mick Deasy, Bandon, on St Patrick's Day 1925, or perhaps his long bowl, four from the finish, at the same venue that year, against Blackpool bowler, Jimmy Mahony. Followers of the great Tim Delaney, Fairhill, will recall his fourth shot at Knappagh in 1928 against Armagh's Peter Donnelly. Another great northern bowler of that era, Jimmy Smith, is on record as saying he "never saw anything like Delaney's shot that day."

Southern followers may cite either of two fantastic shots, on the seventh and eighth, by Denis O'Donovan, Fisher's Cross, on his way to winning against Mick Barry at Dublin Hill, Cork in June 1954. Others will choose to reflect on the highlights of the long shot competition at the Festival of West Cork in Clonakilty, the first of which, in 1964, was won by Bobby Crowley, Enniskeane. And the many admirers of the great Mick Barry, Waterfall, near Cork city, will adduce several of the massive drives he unleashed towards the finish of the 1965 All- Ireland senior final on the Keady road, Armagh. Indeed some of those devotees may rate more highly Mick Barry's opening throw in the Munster senior final that year at Dunmanway against Denis O'Donovan, Bandon. Not without recognition is Denis Scully's win in the 1976 Bandon Festival Long Shot Competition with a bowl of 287 yards (262 metres) and either of his two uphill shots in the final for the Charlemont Hotel Cup at Knappagh in October 1968. Also due consideration is the dramatic penultimate shot by Seamus Sexton at Beeing on 7th October which ended the Munster senior title hopes of Mick Barry in the 1973 championship. Another remarkable distance shot was that by Joe Donnelly, Kilmore, who completely transformed a doubles score over the Blackwatertown road on Sunday 23rd March, 1980. Donnelly, who later won the All-Ireland Junior 'B' title in 1988, put his partner, Noel Collins into an unassailable lead against the McIlvenna brothers, Brendan and Malachy, with an approximate shot of 355 yards (325 metres) from the "long lane" to almost "the bridge" on the road to Port Mor.

No less an authority than Eamon O'Carroll, the former long term Secretary to An Bol Chumann Na hEireann confirms a throw of just over 500 yards (457 metres) by Cork's Johnny Creedon, along a flat road in Holland. Another long shot of International interest was the massive opening effort of 252 metres by Johan Bruns

Danny McParland.

NKB, Netherlands, in the first quarter final of the Paddy Whiskey World Road Bowling championship at Whitechurch, Cork, on Friday 28th June, 1985.

Many enthusiasts are likely to include on their short list of longest shots the superb drive by Armagh's Harry Toal on his fourth bowl in the All-Ireland final of 1985 against Bill Daly at Whitechurch. Others will point to the fact that Gerry Boylan, Armagh, took the award for the longest shot in the Paddy Whiskey World Road Bowling Championship in 1987 with a throw of 346 metres. Included too will be the brilliant effort by Armagh's Michael Toal midway through the 1988 All-Ireland senior final on Sunday 31st July at Tassagh against Cork's Mick O'Driscoll, or indeed the Armagh man's magnificent uphill finishing shot in the All-Ireland Final at Ballingeary against World road bowling champion Bill Daly, when, faced with a rising, curving roadway of more than 200 metres, he topped the mark by 17 metres on a misty late evening of 14th July, 1991.

Yet another shot of exceptional distance over twisting terrain was played by Michael Toal on the Cathedral Road, Armagh in the final of the Joe MVeigh Cup against James Buckley. It was on Easter Sunday, 19th April 1992 and the score was watched by journalist Thomas Quirke who reflected on the event in *The Times Saturday Review* of 23rd May, 1992:

By 4pm the crowd was being entertained by St Jarlath's Independent Pipe

Band. Then, suddenly, there he was, all 6ft. 5in and 16´ st. of him; the pride of Armagh - Toal the Bowl.

...... As the bowl flashed past their ankles, his supporters roared, breaking into cheers when they saw how far it had gone ...... But with the end almost in sight, Toal had fallen behind eighty yards. It was then he sent an inch-perfect bowl along the ashphalt. It bounced off the wall, shot over Stuarts Bridge, and ran beneath three cars coming down the road. It had travelled 400 yards, almost to Barney Grimley's Corner. It was one of the greatest throws in road bowling history.

But for all the claims, the most outstanding memory and satisfactorily authenticated record has got to be that of Danny McParland's massive shot over the Moy road, Armagh, on Sunday 16th August, 1964, in the City Tournament against Aidan Toal. The spectacular shot was all of 510 yards (466 metres) and represented an accomplishment which satisfied the criteria for consequent inclusion in the Guinness Book of Records.

The nature of that tremendous feat merits a comprehensive review of the circumstances. This is partly how Road Bowls correspondent "B.T." reported the event in the *Armagh Observer* of 22nd August, 1964:

Easily the greatest attraction in present day bowling in Armagh is a clash

The solid iron bowl of twenty-eight ounces (793.8 grms) which was thrown a record distance of 510 yards (466 metres) by Armagh's Danny McParland in 1964.

The exact location on the Moy Road, Armagh, from which point Danny McParland played his record shot that travelled considerable length beyond the distant bend in this picture.

between All-Ireland Senior champion Danny McParland, Armagh City, and Aidan Toal, Tirgarve.

When their City Tournament meeting on Sunday was announced it was thought the score would have lost a great deal of public appeal in view of Toal's recent three defeats in a row. However, bowls followers thought differently and the tremendous crowd which packed the spacious Moy Road for the fixture was treated to the finest exhibition of bowling since the same two met in the Keady Tournament almost six months ago.

But this one had even more to offer. In one of the most sensational finishes ever seen, McParland turned what appeared to be certain defeat into dramatic victory with the longest shot on record, a bowl which travelled every inch of 510 yards. There is no doubt that this unbelievable drive which took him from a shot and forty yards in arrears to a fifty yard lead for the final throw will remain a monument to the greatest bowl player the North has ever produced.

This was really a great exhibition of bowling from both men and one point it made abundantly clear is that they are the perfect partners for the big charity score in Cork on 6th September. The bowling from each man was truly exceptional. As against Mick Barry's record for the road this time last year both men were ahead of it at Allen's Corner in four shots. At Bond's Hill Toal was a shot ahead of the record while McParland had equalled it to that stage. At the three-quarter stage Toal had gone almost two bowls ahead of Barry's record for the course and over the final stretch, where each man unexpectedly erred, both came close to the finishing line in twenty-two shots.

With only four shots to go to the finish the champion was trailing by well over a bowl. Toal held the same substantial lead within two bowls of the finishing line and now, more than ever, the score appeared to be well and truly over. McParland who was on the verge of conceding defeat, decided on an all-out effort. Over the smooth, wide open section of the Moy Road his bowl travelled a quarter of a mile through the crowd before going on to stop within thirty yards of the finishing line at the Milestone. An incredible drive and one which Toal failed to reach in two shots to set up one of the most sensational finishes for years.

The crowd, seething with excitement, watched tensely as Toal found himself in the amazing position of being at a fifty yard disadvantage for the final throw. His last shot was a good one but McParland's final effort did enough to snatch him victory in the most spectacular win of his remarkable career. For some time after the score spectators continued to discuss the dramatic finish and, hours afterwards, a number of separate groups were studying that astonishing shot from all angles.

The Impact of an Inspirational Leader

A fervent desire and impassioned ambition for comprehensive organisation and authoritative management in the sport of road bowling was a personal crusade incessantly pursued by the late Flor Crowley until that worthy objective was achieved and firmly established.

Few sporting or other organisations will ever be graced with an inspirational leader of such immense stature and untiring diligence. Flor Crowley, a native of Behigullane, Dunmanway, Co Cork, and a national teacher at the local school for many years, is credited with being instrumental in founding, in 1954, An Bol Chumann Na hEireann, the Association responsible for bringing to the sport a formal and dignified level of organisation which has grown in stature ever since. When Flor Crowley died on 25th July, 1980, he was still leader of the great sporting association so much of his life had been devoted to upholding. For more than a quarter of a century he had been Chairman to An Bol Chumann Na hEireann and during that lengthy period he was unceasing in his efforts, uncompromising in his obligations, and consistent in his achievements.

Not content with merely steering the association in the south, he set about, in conjunction with his group of dedicated officials on the Executive Committee, to promoting the prospect of championships being extended to a National context. The informal soundings, persistent contacts, persuasive expressions, and convincing assurances of Flor Crowley were particularly significant in the historic developments which resulted in the inauguration of All-Ireland championships which have now obtained for well over thirty years.

Consistently evident was his appreciation of the importance to bowling of ample press coverage. Equally, the sports editors of various newspapers readily recognised the literary attributes of a man so competent in conveying to readers the reality of events. Flor Crowley possessed an acuity of observation and perceptive interpretation that was exceptionally skilled in its practice. His previews and reports on road bowling in the *Cork Examiner, Evening Echo, Southern Star, Kerryman, Sunday Review*, and other publications, imparted to readers a sense of emotion and an assurance of authenticity that was so real as to be equivalent to the total experiences of being present at the unfolding event. And those events extended to an International dimension such was the progress under his administration. Flor Crowley had initiated bowling contacts with Germany and Holland in the sixties and his perseverance with that new ambition resulted in the first International bowling events being played in Losser, Nederland in 1969 with further European championships conducted throughout the intervening years and now established on a four year frequency.

Even with such an overall commitment to bowling administration and com-

Flor Crowley.

The grave of Flor Crowley in St. Patrick's Cemetery, Bandon, County Cork; founder of Bol Chumann Na hEireann in 1954, and Chairman of the Bowling Association until his death in 1980.

munication, Flor Crowley had many additional interests which made him one of the best known personalities in Cork and far beyond those boundaries. He was a formidable athlete, being Irish champion in the Goulding hammer and proved his ability on the rifle range by winning the All-Army Individual Rifle Championship at Gormanstown in 1969, a feat he repeated three years later. A noted historian Flor Crowley had written articles on such events as the Crossbarry and Kilmichael ambushes and was author of the publication, *"West Cork Long Ago."*

The sport of road bowling however was his enduring and passionate interest. A good competitive player of championship standard he once joined his teaching colleague, and fellow bowling administrator, Eamon O'Carroll for a doubles score in which they were each partnered by a pupil from the school in a novel attraction that generated great enthusiasm. For more than fifty years Flor Crowley was associated with the sport and as this man of intense determination strode the bowling roads of Ireland he portrayed an authority and commanded a respect commensurate with his office.

In a tribute to Flor Crowley in the *Southern Star* of 2nd August, 1980, pen-name "Ciaran" revealed how the late Chairman, less than three weeks before his death, had asked him to pass on the following message to his bowling friends. "Tell all those who have offended me that I forgive them and I trust that any man I have ever offended will forgive me."

As Flor Crowley was laid to rest in St. Patrick's Cemetery , Bandon, on a hilltop overlooking his home in Green Gardens where his widow Mary still resides, foremost among the many mourners were the followers of road bowling who owe so much in return for his life-long dedication to the sport.

One of the more prestigious competitions now played over the bowling roads of Cork is a tournament for the Flor Crowley Cup. In truth, Road Bowls, played anywhere in Ireland, will forever remain a testament to his memory.

Vying for Bowling Acclaim

The level of competition throughout the early eighties had grown in fervency with the introduction of additional championship grades and the presence of many new players in pursuit of bowling acclaim.

The Ulster Senior championship in 1980 had been springing surprises and the corresponding news from Munster confirmed that many of the big names had also gone out of the competition there. In Ulster it was reigning All-Ireland Senior champion, Pat Mallon who put paid to the hopes of Harry Toal in a most impressive display at Knappagh but he was subsequently trounced by Gerry Boylan, Lislea, who had won virtually nothing since his provincial Junior championship win seven years earlier. The manner of that particular victory suggested he was back in a big way. The other semi-final in Ulster had seen Aidan Toal produce one of his best ever displays over the Knappagh course to gain a fairly comfortable win over Al Mallon, Kilmore, a player of outstanding ability but remarkably without a National title in any category. The Ulster Senior final on Sunday 17th August, 1980, was close and exciting without ever being spectacular. Played over the Knappagh road it had been considered to be the most open final for years with both Toal and Boylan enjoying great form in most outings that season. The lead interchanged several times during the score with Toal more prominent entering the final quarter. But the consistent Gerry Boylan was the more impressive performer on the finishing stretch and he came through for a relatively safe win to take the Ulster Senior title for the first time.

In the Munster Senior championship of 1980 Mick O'Driscoll, east Cork was already through to the provincial final and he was joined by west Cork bowler Dermot O'Sullivan who mastered the challenge of Pat Butler at Beal na Blath. Mick O'Driscoll had to beat Donie Coveney, the man most fancied to win the championship, and that semi-final victory had engendered renewed hope of a title win. Neither finalist had been in the limelight for some time and few followers considered either of them to be likely final contestants. In the end it was the speed of Dermot O'Sullivan, over the testing parts of the Ballyshonin course, that proved decisive against the acknowledged accuracy of Mick O'Driscoll and the west Cork player had gained his first provincial title at any grade.

The All-Ireland Senior final at Ballyshonin on Sunday 24th August, 1980, was a daunting prospect for both men who had never before played at this level of competition and the huge attendance tended to exacerbate the tension surrounding the event. Dermot O'Sullivan was striving to gain unprecedented personal acclaim and Gerry Boylan was particularly keen to gain the senior crown to add to three National titles gained in other grades by his brother Liam. The contest was a good one which thrilled the large crowd with an interchanging lead and some mighty shots. Boylan had a great opener for the lead but O Sullivan produced one of the longest shots of the entire score to reverse the placings on the second throw. The Cork player was first to blunder though and Boylan went a shot up only to see his opponent rally for a part in the finish. Playing his last shot from more than seventy metres in arrears, O'Sullivan put in a terrific bowl which just missed the line. Boylan still had it all to do but he made no mistake with a great drive which deservedly gained him his first and only All- Ireland Senior title.

Gerry Boylan was back in the provincial final the following year and bowling better than ever. In his semi-final clash with Aidan Toal who had already eclipsed Pat Mallon, the reigning champion had his best ever score at Knappagh when he crossed the finishing line in twenty-two shots. Both men were brilliant throughout the first half of the score but Boylan was unbeatable over the final quarter and hopes were high for another National senior title. But the enigmatic Harry Toal was back after a long absence and his semi-final win over Sean Webb was an indication of his claim to another title. He finished with six tremendous shots which propelled him into a two shot lead for a most encouraging win. It was an Ulster Senior final that hosted the two undisputed leading bowlers of that era. The open nature of the contest was reflected in the magnitude of the attendance at Knappagh on Sunday 12th July, 1981, for a provincial final featuring the 1977 and 1980 All-Ireland champions. Boylan was first to break off with an enormous bowl which Toal failed to cover in two. And then Boylan faltered with two shots which Toal had no difficulty covering in one. A bowl of odds opened up as Toal, spurred on by the embarrassing start, was settling into his old form and even though the lead wavered it never diminished significantly. A desperation shot by Boylan near the finish in an attempt to rescue the outcome failed to materialise and the chance of two consecutive titles was gone. But Toal's performance had augured well for another National Senior title.

So too had the conduct of the Munster Senior final laid claim to the merits of a National title for Cork. "A memorable occasion" was how one veteran of the game had described the Munster Senior final at Ballyshonin on Sunday 12th July, 1981. It was an apt description for one of the finest spectacles of sporting endeavour ever witnessed on a bowling road. It was record bowl playing before a huge crowd of spectators which relished every shot of a pulsating contest. Not once did the pressure of the occasion impinge on the manner of play exhibited by either bowler in a tremendous score which saw Seamus Sexton take the laurels over an equally impressive Mick O'Driscoll. A Munster final the nature of which both contestants can reflect upon with justifiable pride.

The All-Ireland bowling finals scheduled for Armagh on the first weekend of August, 1981, were postponed at short notice in deference to the volatile situation deriving from the death of prisoners on hunger strike in Long Kesh. By that particular weekend eight prisoners had died on hunger strike and the mounting community tension had rendered any sporting occasion to be of little relevance. However the finals were subsequently re-scheduled a month later and went ahead at the original venues in Armagh.

The All-Ireland Senior final of 1981 was one of contrasting fortunes for the contestants. Harry Toal got off to a very ordinary start but soon settled into a pattern of consistently accurate and particularly fast bowling that was to be recorded as his best performance of the year. It was a very different matter for the north Cork bowler from Nadd, Seamus Sexton. Despite an early lead of more than a shot he had surrendered all of that after three bowls and went one down before halfway. Sexton's play, well below his full potential, was never going to regain the lead without some serious error by Toal but the Armagh man's confident display was so complete that such an opportunity never arose. It was Harry Toal's second All-Ireland Senior title and he had won it in style over a packed Knappagh course on the first Sunday in September.

It was six years before Seamus Sexton again appeared in an All-Ireland Senior final but Harry Toal was back to contest the next two. He had just managed to pip Gerry Boylan on the final throw of their Ulster semi-final encounter in 1982 and was through to a provincial decider against Aidan Toal who had a convincing win over Martin Boylan, the Ulster Intermediate champion of the previous year. The Ulster Senior final at Knappagh on 8th August 1982 was often thrilling and for a long time unpredictable. The reigning champion Harry Toal gained an early lead but Aidan Toal regained the initiative to go a bowl up on two separate occasions only to misjudge a soft bowl and create an opportunity which his opponent seized upon to set him on the way to victory. Harry Toal was ready to defend his National title at a Cork venue having won his two previous All-Ireland senior honours at Castleblaney and Armagh.

The Munster Senior final at Ballyshonin on the same date was down to two men with impressive records, Donie Coveney and Jim O'Driscoll (junior), each of whom had been enjoying tremendous form. Having gone out at the semi-final stage to Mick O'Driscoll two years previously Donie Coveney made no mistake that particular season with a devastating performance against Eamon Bowen in which his last five shots were particularly outstanding. That was the kind of form he carried into the provincial senior final over the same course and, coupled with his greater experience, he took the title over a very determined Jim O'Driscoll.

The very large attendance expected something special from the All-Ireland Senior final at Ballyshonin on Sunday 22nd August, 1982. Harry Toal, Armagh, was reigning senior champion and packed a lot of power into his bowling. Donie Coveney had covered the course a month earlier in a remarkable sixteen shots and two weeks later never once looked like losing the provincial final. But the huge crowd was to be disappointed. Toal was only a shadow of his true form and trailed behind his opponent from the first shot. Coveney was not error free either but he could afford the occasional lapse as he eased ahead to win by two bowls of odds. It was Donie Coveney's tenth season in senior ranks and he had at last been rewarded with his first, albeit his only, All-Ireland Senior title. The same two players met again in inter- provincial scores at Easter of 1983 and 1984 and each recorded a home win at Knappagh and Ballyshonin.

Remarkably, both Coveney and Toal figured in the closing stages of the 1983 Senior championship but there was to be a new champion emerge that year. In the Munster semi- finals Pat Butler, the 1978 Senior title holder, beat Seamus Sexton at Newcestown whilst Michael Buckley ousted the reigning champion Donie Coveney, at Ballyvolane, each of them winning by the clear margin of two bowls of odds. There was sufficient evidence in those two semi-finals to suggest the Munster Senior final could well be a memorable one. And the capacity crowd which turned up at Beal na Blath on Saturday 23rd July, 1983, thought likewise. But the event was disappointing in many ways. Torrential rain had delayed the start for well over an hour and the score became a rather protracted encounter. The early lead went to Buckley, then Butler produced four great shots to draw almost level, but during the latter half the gap opened up again. Butler's normal composure was less evident in the second period and Buckley won by less than a shot. It was Michael Buckley's first Munster Senior title and he had sufficient power and ability to go further.

In Ulster, Harry Toal was endeavouring to retain his provincial senior title and he was confronted in the final by Pat Mallon, the 1982 All-Ireland Intermediate champion, who had often been the surprise victor in their numerous encounters. But this time was different. The score produced nothing spectacular over the Knappagh course until Toal eventually got into his rhythm and after that he lined his bowls to stride away from Mallon for a three shot win.

The All-Ireland Senior final at Knappagh, Armagh, on Sunday 31st July 1983 was intriguing to say the least. It was a new scene for the strong bowling Michael Buckley, and the enigmatic Harry Toal was apparently back to his best and eager to win his third National senior title. But, as in so many anticipated performances, the reality was less spectacular. Neither played to their full potential as each of them missed opportunities at varying stages but the crucial factor in the outcome was a very powerful drive by Buckley within four shots of the finish. This great bowl consolidated his lead and inspired him to faultless bowling from that to the finish giving Toal little opportunity to do other than save the bowl of odds. Michael Buckley, Cork city, was a new name on the National championship roll of honour.

The 1984 Senior championship saw the return of Bill Daly to the fray, a bowler with enormous potential as was affirmed in his 1975 Under 18 National title win. A Garda, assigned for a time to border duties, he was subsequently transferred to Glanmire and not only rekindled his interest in bowling but also re-established his presence as a formidable contestant at the highest level. In the 1984 Senior championship he recorded a semi-final win over Donie Coveney at Ballyshonin to take him into the Munster final against Eamon Bowen, Carrignavar. Bowen had narrowly come through his semi-final clash with Mick O'Driscoll at Ballyvolane when a strong finish earned him a last shot victory. The last shot was also the deciding factor in the Munster final but much more dramatically so. Played at the Rising Sun on Saturday 25th August 1984 the lead had rested with either player through the score and for the final throw it was Bowen who held the advantage. Daly played his last shot and scored the finishing line by twelve metres. It looked relatively easy for Bowen but he spun his bowl fiercely to the grass verge and fell well short of the line to forfeit the score and a Munster Senior title.

The surprise of the Ulster Senior championship centred upon Aidan Toal being back in the All- Ireland final for the first time since 1969, all of fifteen years after he had lost to Mick Barry at Armagh. Even more surprising was the nature of his Ulster final win over Harry Toal, the reigning provincial champion. Given little chance he outclassed Harry with a power packed performance at Knappagh on 26th

August 1984 in which his consistently forceful play built up a two shot lead over an opponent who could find no way back over the latter half.

The line-up for the All-Ireland Senior final at Ballyshonin on Sunday 9th September, 1984 was one of contrasting perspectives. Each player had been striving to win their first National senior title. But Bill Daly, at 26 years old, was in his first ever final at senior level. Aidan Toal, at 42 years old, and bowling for more than a quarter of a century was in his third final, and in the twilight of his career. The respective provincial final performances gave either player a chance of victory but Daly was strongly favoured to win the title at his first attempt. And he did. It was an astonishing display of class bowling which had the massive crowd admiring the quality of the performance. Toal took the lead on the first but rapidly conceded the advantage with a poor second and further attempts to get back in contention were to no avail against Daly's precision play which assured him a comfortable win by two bowls of odds.

The quality of Bill Daly's performance was further underlined in the 1985 championship when he came through Munster yet again following wins over Christy Mullins, Bantry, at Kilbrittain, and against Pat Butler at Beal na Blath. Showing tremendous speed he retained his provincial title in the final against Eamon Bowen at Whitechurch, six miles from Blarney, on 11th August 1985.

The Ulster Senior championship resulted in Harry Toal taking the provincial title for the fifth time in nine years when he beat Pat Mallon, Aidan Toal and Jim

Billy McAuliffe, Glanworth, Co. Cork.

McCann, Moy. The Ulster final at Knappagh on Friday 2nd August 1985 had seen McCann threaten for a period only to drift away in a poor finish as Toal swept over the distance with some massive shots.

The little village of Whitechurch hosted the 1985 All-Ireland Senior final on Sunday 18th August and it was a determined Bill Daly, anxious to defend his title and gain two consecutive wins, who was faced with an equally resolute Harry Toal, replenished with all the power that had imbued his best bowling performances. The event was sponsored by Murphy's Brewery which added further value and prestige to an already lauded championship. Both men opened brilliantly with Daly gaining a four metre lead which he soon extended to a bowl of odds. But a massive drive by Toal on his fifth shot reversed the placings, and the trend of the score, as Daly wilted and began to lose ground rapidly. Toal continued to play superbly on a road he had experienced for the first time and though Daly finished with an ankle injury, there was no doubting the power of the Armagh man's bowling on the day. It was Harry Toal's third All- Ireland Senior title and his first at a Cork venue. It was also his last for in his only subsequent final appearance he was well beaten at Armagh in 1990 by Pat Butler.

The Intermediate championship in the early eighties lacked nothing in competitive bowling. Christy Mullins, Bantry, a fine bowler who was equally adept at gaelic football, hurling and handball had gone through to the Munster final in 1980 but was thwarted for the title by the south west Cork champion Pat McCarthy. In Ulster that year it was Sean Webb, Annahagh, who strode to victory over a disappointing Larry Corr, Rock, after he won a thrilling semi- final with an incredible last shot to pip Donald Gribben. The All-Ireland Intermediate final at Ballyshonin on Saturday 23rd August 1980 proved to be a glorious experience for Cork's Pat McCarthy who settled into a pattern of excellent bowling to win with ease over Sean Webb who never rose to the quality of his provincial performances. The following year it was Tim O'Halloran, Upton, who won the Munster title in a disappointing provincial final at Whitechurch against Eddie Ryan of Youghal. In Ulster it was Martin Boylan, one of the few members of that Lislea family without a bowling title, who rectified that particular matter when he gained the provincial Intermediate title with sufficient spurts of brilliance to account for the experienced Gerald McKee and the inconsistent Jim McCann. The All-Ireland Intermediate final at Knappagh on Saturday 6th September 1981 went to Tim O'Halloran but only after the lead had swung in both directions and two poor shots near the finish had sunk the hopes of Martin Boylan.

Pat Mallon, the All-Ireland Senior champion of 1979, won his way to the 1982 National Intermediate final by virtue of steady wins over Donald Gribben, Larry Corr, and a provincial victory over Malachy McIlvenna who had won the Ulster Junior title the previous year. His opponent in the All-Ireland Intermediate final at Ballyshonin on Saturday 21st August 1982 was John Murphy who had beaten his namesake Pat Murphy in the Munster final at Crossbarry. The final was a tremendous encounter. Both men bowled exceptionally well. Many suggest it was Pat Mallon's best ever performance and even with that it was only on the final throw that John Murphy gave way. It was a great win for Mallon but equally so for Ulster which had failed to gain an All-Ireland Intermediate title for over a decade.

In 1983 Pat Murphy, Cork city, won the Munster title after beating Eddie Ryan at Midleton and Pat Sutton at Ballyshonin. The Clonakilty player, Sutton, had a clear semi-final win over Billy McAuliffe at Beal na Blath but went down by a bowl of odds to Pat Murphy in the final. The experienced Ulster senior player Aidan Toal had contested the Intermediate championship for the first time in 1983 and swept through the opposition with relative ease when he had more than two shots to spare over semi-finalist Martin Boylan and finalist Sean Webb. In the All-Ireland Intermediate final at Ballyshonin on Sunday 14th August 1983 he had no such easy assignment. Toal led on the first shot and was only five metres in arrears nearing halfway but several exceptionally long bowls by Pat Murphy reinstated a shot lead for the Cork city player and that margin remained intact to the finish.

The record of northern bowlers in the Intermediate grade was not an impressive one and the standard of play in the 1984 Ulster final did nothing to inspire renewed hope. Pat Mallon had won a semi-final in great fashion over Sean Webb whilst Martin Boylan was equally impressive in the other final eliminator against Jim McCann. Despite the bowling credentials of each player the final is one both of them will wish to forget. Played over the Knappagh road on Sunday 29th July 1984 it was a score frequently punctuated with errors and in the end it was Boylan who got through. With the All-Ireland Intermediate final scheduled for the same venue on Sunday 5th August 1984, northern followers had no illusions about the predicted outcome. And that was good news for Nelius Hurley from the little village of Ring near Clonakilty who was pursuing his first National bowling title in any grade. Hurley had beaten Donie O'Mahoney before going into the Munster final with a win over James Sullivan at Beal na Blath. In the other semi-final it was Paddy O'Leary who defeated Eddie Ryan at Youghal. That provincial final at Ballyvolane had all the excitement reserved to the last. With Paddy O'Leary more than sixty metres ahead for the final throw the outcome appeared inevitable but Hurley unleashed an astonishing effort in a bid to pull it off and succeeded in doing so to gain his first major title. But the challenge of an All-Ireland final at an away venue had yet to come. The drama in this one unfolded at the outset. Martin Boylan, who lacked support following his rather indifferent performance in the Ulster final, made a disastrous opening to amazingly go almost two shots down in the first quarter. Hurley was bowling with great determination and his supremacy was only threatened when Boylan eventually got going with some good play over the second half. But the margin remained relatively safe and Hurley won by a bowl of odds to be hoisted shoulder high by his west Cork supporters on this his first All- Ireland title win.

The Ulster Intermediate championship of 1985 produced some great scores over varying courses involving Sean Webb, Donald Gribben, Patrick Comiskey, Oliver Gribben, Henry Lyttle, and Paul Grimley. The surprise of the championship was Henry Lyttle, son of the great Pat Lyttle of bowling fame in the forties and fifties. But the final, on Thursday 27th June 1985, was down to Patrick Comiskey, Portadown and Paul Grimley, Madden. It was a great score. Comiskey had been the most improved player of the period and it was known he would need it all against the consistent Grimley. He was faultless on the day to eventually win by a shot and this victory provided Patrick Comiskey with an opportunity of adding a National title at Intermediate level to his All-Ireland Under 16 championship success in 1971. The only threat to that ambition was one Mick O'Driscoll of Mayfield. He had beaten the renowned Derry Kenny at Waterloo in the Munster semi-final before sensationally ousting John Murphy, Brinny, in the provincial final at Ballyshonin on 28th July 1985. There was an amazing conclusion to that final. John Murphy had led the entire score and was more than two bowls up on his opponent. But somehow Mick O'Driscoll got back into it and won the final throw over the line for an astounding title success.

The All-Ireland final at Armagh on Sunday 4th August 1985 was played in a constant downpour. The Cathedral road was thronged but enthusiasm was dampened despite some quality bowling. The lead interchanged several times in the early stages but Mick O'Driscoll went to the front on entering the last quarter as his exceptionally lengthy drives superseded some great bowls by Patrick Comiskey. The last three throws by O'Driscoll were unbeatable and these sealed his victory by a bowl of odds.

Throughout the period of the early eighties there emerged some spectacularly new bowling talent in under age championships. The standard of play had been superb and the potential for greatness was evident in the performance of some championship winners.

In the Under 16 Ulster championship final of 1980 Francis Kiernan, Madden, came from behind on the last shot to narrowly beat Colm Toal, Grangemore, and in Munster it was Pat Lawlor who emerged from a talented group including Michael Davis, Jerry Desmond and Paul Malone. The All-Ireland final Ballyshonin on Saturday 23rd August was dominated by Francis Kiernan who led from start to finish against Pat Lawlor to record one of his best ever displays. The Madden youth got off to a great start with four marvellous shots in succession which built up a comfortable lead that was rarely threatened over the final stages. The All-Ireland Under 18 final was played the same day but the margin of victory in that was a great deal closer. Brian Grimley, Madden, was the surprise winner in Ulster when he gained a fully deserved win over Martin Boylan, Lislea, whilst Dan O'Halloran, mid Cork, came through in Munster following a win over the north east Cork champion Vincent Connolly. It was all to play for on the last shot at Ballyshonin. Grimley held a slight advantage going to the line but the longest throw came from O'Halloran and the National title was his.

The following year saw a player of outstanding promise emerge in the Under 16 Ulster championship. A very young Michael Toal, who had created a tremendous air of expectation in winning his first ever bowling score against Sean Mackle over the Blackwatertown road on Sunday 13th January 1980, was already a championship contender in 1981. Still some months short of his twelfth birthday he was through to the provincial final in the Under 16 championship. But his limit had been reached in that particular season. In the final he was faced with Dermot Grimley,

Michael Toal, Armagh, has won numerous national titles in road bowls but his first All-Ireland sporting success was in 1976 when he won a gold medal at the National Community Games in Mosney, Co. Meath. The silver medal winner on the left is Kevin Walsh who played at midfield for Galway in the 1994 All-Ireland Gaelic Football Semi-Final at Croke Park.

Madden, who had been very impressive in a semi-final win over Brendan McOscar, An Port Mor. The difference in experience was evident as Grimley justified his favouritism with a win by a well deserved bowl of odds. The Under 16 championship in Munster was equally exciting that year. In one semi-final D.J. Flynn had got the better of Cormac O'Donovan at Dunmanway. But the really exciting prospects had contested the other semi-final at Ahiohill. In that particular encounter it was Pat Thompson, west Cork, who snatched a last shot win over city player James Buckley and he held his form into the provincial final at Newcestown on Friday 17th July 1981 when he gave further indication of his potential with a win over the south west Cork bowler D.J. Flynn.

There was the prospect of a thrilling All-Ireland final and it lived up to all its promise. The Cathedral road in Armagh was the venue and they battled it out closely all the way. Fittingly, it went to the last shot. Thompson was slightly in arrears and bowled first with a magnificent effort that seemed to put paid to any hope of victory for the Ulster champion. But Grimley responded with an unbelievable drive to surprisingly top the mark by more than twenty metres. And that was only part of a Grimley celebration on that weekend in September 1981. The Under 18 Ulster championship title that season had gone to his brother Paul following great wins over Sebastian McKeown, Declan McCoy and Colm Toal. In Munster it was Ciaran

O'Driscoll, south west Cork, who had beaten Frank Kelly at Dunmanway before going on to win the provincial title at Newcestown against James Sullivan who had been highly impressive in his semi-final defeat of Paddy Daly.

The All-Ireland final at Armagh was one that Paul Grimley had diligently prepared for. And he was justly rewarded with magnificent bowling throughout the score which he dominated for the most part despite a strong O'Driscoll rally near the finish. It was a great year for Paul Grimley in which he also won the Macardles trophy and the Gaffney Cup. But the season was a particularly gratifying one for the late Pete Grimley, a lifelong follower of the sport who had the proud experience of seeing two of his sons collect All-Ireland road bowling titles in the same year.

The sensation of the 1982 Ulster Under 16 championship was the title win by Armagh city young bowler Dominic Donnelly who followed the best that Brian Kiernan, Madden, had to offer and beat him on the last shot for a win that few would have predicted with any real confidence. In Munster, D.J. Flynn had gone one better than the previous season by gaining a place in the provincial final with a narrow win over Noel O'Rourke at Aherla. But his run ended there when James Buckley, who had easily beaten John Paul Healy at Beal na Blath, maintained his winning form at Ballyshonin to take the Munster title. The All-Ireland Under 16 championship final was played at the same Cork venue and consequently there was little to favour the chances of the young surprise champion from Armagh. And yet in the opening shot of that event, on Sunday 22nd August 1982, he played one of the longest first throws ever seen on the road only to have the salutary warning of what was ahead of him when the enormously strong James Buckley amazingly beat the mark by thirty five metres. It was clear then that James Buckley was a player of outstanding ability. "A great prospect if properly handled" said Brendan Roche in the *Cork Examiner.* "The best Under 16 bowler we have seen for a long time" said Aidan McVeigh in the *Armagh Observer*. The outcome of that particular score - the National title for Buckley by a wide margin - speaks for itself. And so too does his bowling record ever since.

The same season had seen Cork's Pat Thompson gain compensation for his All-Ireland final defeat the previous year. He made amends in the 1982 Under 18 National final at Ballyshonin on 21st August when, showing enormous improvement, he bowled with great precision and evident maturity to win by more than two shots over the Ulster champion Philip Rafferty of Madden.

The 1983 season, not surprisingly, belonged to James Buckley. He dominated two championships that year. In the Under 16 grade Buckley beat the west Cork champion Kevin O'Riordan and in the county final he accounted for north Cork representative Padraig Buckley who had beaten Pat Moynihan from the Gaeltacht region. He then went on to win the Munster final at Rathcormac by a wide margin over John McDonagh, Limerick, and the nature of that victory made Buckley a clear favourite to retain his National title. In the north Brian Kiernan was not without a measure of success either. He too had dominated two provincial championships having beaten Michael Toal in the Ulster Under 16 final and two weeks later took the Under 18 title over Fergal McCreesh, Navan. A remarkable coincidence that the same two players, James Buckley and Brian Kiernan, should contest two All-Ireland finals, at Under 16 and Under 18 grade, in the same year. The Under 16 final was first to be decided. That was over the Cathedral road, Armagh on Sunday 31st July 1983 and despite consistently good bowling by Kiernan it was the exceptional power of Buckley that produced shots almost on a par with senior standard to win by more than a bowl of odds. Two weeks later James Buckley made it a spectacular double. In the All-Ireland Under 18 final at Ballyshonin on Sunday 14th August 1983, Brian Kiernan had no answer to the power and precision of a sixteen year old who had evident ability to cope with virtually any category of competition. All throughout the Munster championship James Buckley was consistently outplaying his opponents in the Under 18 grade beating Donie O'Driscoll at Ballyshonin in the county final and then Frank O'Sullivan, Limerick, in the Munster final at Rathcormac. It was by then a remarkable record for a bowler so young. Three All-Ireland titles and still only sixteen. Little wonder then he was being acclaimed "the most promising player ever to grace the bowling roads of Cork". And he was back again in 1984. He beat that tough cool player from mid Cork, Donie O'Driscoll in the Under 18 Munster final at Ballyshonin by a narrow margin on the final throw. His opponent in the All-Ireland final? None other than Brian Kiernan. He too was back again having taken the Ulster Under 18 title against Michael Toal in a contest of the highest order where both young men competed shot for shot to the last. It was an awesome task that faced Brian Kiernan in the National final at Ballyshonin.

Michael Toal, Armagh, pictured on the day he won his first All-Ireland Road Bowls title — the 1984 Under 16 National Championship Final.

James Buckley's ability was better known to the Madden man than to most others but he was undaunted at the prospect. At halfway only a few metres divided the pair but a mistake by Kiernan fluffed his chances and with diminishing confidence he lost further ground as Buckley went on to win by a flattering two bowls of odds. James Buckley had by then, at seventeen years old, won no less than four All-Ireland bowling titles. Not surprisingly he later added All-Ireland Intermediate and Senior titles to his remarkably outstanding record.

The Under 16 championship of 1984 was also unveiling young bowlers of great promise. In Munster a fine young player in Patrick Moynihan from the Gaeltacht region came through a formidable quartet comprising Denis O'Sullivan, Dermot Long and Finbar O'Donovan, to take the provincial title. In Ulster Michael Toal was in trouble until three massive drives rescued him against Aidan McCreesh and he then went on to beat Malachy Gribben in the provincial final. The All-Ireland final at Armagh on Sunday 5th August 1984 was another rescue effort by Michael Toal when he found himself over two bowls behind the superb opening play of Pat Moynihan. Then amazingly he completely wiped out the deficit with a series of colossal drives towards the finish to produce a result that seemed well nigh impossible. It was Michael Toal's first All-Ireland title and the nature of his championship performances had prompted bowls correspondent Aidan McVeigh to declare it was "surely the first of many". Toal responded to that encouragement in no uncertain terms. Despite being only fifteen years old he blazed a trail through the Ulster Under 18 championship of 1985 with a win over Malachy Gribben before surprisingly ousting the reigning champion Brian Kiernan and then continuing his power bowling with an impressive win over Paddy O'Neill for the provincial title. In the Munster Under 18 championship it was Brendan O'Regan who was doing likewise. The west Cork bowler had beaten David Molden and then won a closely contested county final against Eddie Murphy before going on to beat Dermot Daly of Limerick in the Munster final at Buttervant. In the All-Ireland final at Armagh on 4th August 1985 Michael Toal again produced a blistering display in which his early narrow lead over Brendan O'Regan was gradually extended to more than two bowls of odds at the finish.

The Under 16 All-Ireland championship final the same year was played at Whitechurch, near Blarney. The surprise winner in Ulster was Navan player Pat McCreesh who had beaten Terence Rafferty in the semi final and then won the provincial title with two superb finishing shots against Martin Mullan. The Munster champion in 1985 was Dermot Daly of Limerick who was coached throughout the championship by Fachtna O'Donovan the 1966 All-Ireland Junior champion. The National final, on Sunday 18th August, was a great match. The lead was small at any point of the score and on the final throw Daly put down what looked like the winner. But McCreesh responded with a courageous effort that topped the mark by nearly thirty metres to give his huge Navan support great reason for joyous celebration.

The early eighties had undoubtedly produced some spectacular bowling across all categories in the sport. And, additionally, one of the highly appreciated admin-

John Gribben (right), Northern Branch Chairman of Bol Chumann Na hEireann, had the unusual experience in 1984 of presenting awards to five members of the same Toal family. Michael (left), All-Ireland Under 16 Champion; Eileen, Ulster Women's Senior Finalist; Declan, Special Award Recipient; Aidan, Ulster Men's Senior Champion; and Rosheen, Ulster Women's Senior Champion.

Photo: Michael Campbell.

istrative gestures by An Bol Chumann Na hEireann was their hosting a special dinner for all the northern followers at the All-Ireland finals in 1982. The function, at Christy's Hotel Blarney, was presided over by Bol Chumann Chairman Brendan Roche and was the Associations way of acknowledging the stirling efforts that had been made to nurture the sport in the north during difficult times. A magnificent gesture and one which underlined the social and cultural features of a great sporting organisation.

The period also saw confirmation of long term sponsorship of the All-Ireland championships in Munster by Murphy's Brewery. Since 1985 the event has been known and publicised as the Murphy's Irish Stout Bowling Championships. In the north the championships have been sponsored by Bank of Ireland; Armagh Oil Company; K'Mac Glass; Cross Refrigeration Limited; Northern Building Supplies; and latterly very significant sponsorship has been offered by Philip White Tyres Limited in conjunction with Falken.

Another sponsorship deal entered into by Murphy's Brewery was that of the Cork Viaduct loft on Sunday 8th September 1985. More than 10,000 spectators watched the 23 year old German athlete Hans Bohlken clear the viaduct with a 28 ounce bowl to collect a trophy and £5,000 in prize money. A £1,000 prize for lofting a 16 once bowl over the viaduct was shared by joint winners Bill Daly, Eamon Bowen and Dan O'Halloran.

In all, it had been a very successful period for the sport with its competitive bowling and the associated sporting, social and cultural perspectives both at home and abroad.

A Bowling Champion of the World

The Paddy Whiskey Trophy for the World Championship.

The announcement of a World Road Bowling Championship in 1985 signalled a mammoth remove from a very early perspective of the sport being a parochial activity peculiar to relatively small and diverse pockets of interest in rural Ireland.

The first such World Road Bowling Championship was held at Whitechurch on the outskirts of Cork city on the weekend of Friday 28th to Sunday 30th June 1985 and was one of the principal events in the "Cork 800" celebrations to mark the 800th Anniversary of the City's First Charter. It was an enormous undertaking and stupendous promotion by Bol Chumann Na hEireann under the direction of the then Chairman Brendan Roche and one which was aided and supported by the International Bowl Playing Association; the then Minister for Sport, Donal Creed, T.D., and the Lord Mayor of Cork, Alderman Liam Burke, T.D., whose term of office encompassed the "Cork 800" celebrations. Not least in importance to the whole occasion was the magnificent sponsorship by Irish Distillers Limited whose Group Managing Director, Richard Burrows assured the venture of his organisations financial support and general goodwill.

The Paddy Whiskey World Road Bowling Championship was undoubtedly the biggest event in the history of the traditional road game and attracted many thousands to the normally quiet County Cork village of Whitechurch which nestles almost as close to Blarney Castle as it does to Cork city. The spectacular promotion drew participants from the Netherlands, Germany and Ireland with bowlers from Scotland entering the 1987 championship.

The pageantry of the official opening had been impressive and it set the scene for a weekend of bowling that was to provide an insight to the variation in techniques, styles, methods and skills of the top players in the world, each of them vying for an honour unprecedented in the history of the sport.

In this prestigious championship the major surprise emanating from the quarter finals was the defeat of all four German entrants particularly that of Wilfred Muller of the FKV team who had been rated as the most likely player to win the Paddy Whiskey Trophy and first prize of £2,000. The defeated quarter finalists had shared a prize of £1,000 but into the semi-final play-off went Johan Bruns NKB, Netherlands, who won against Ulrich Nagel, Germany; Aidan Toal, Ireland, who had beaten Manfred Thieb, Germany; Henk Lammerink, NKB Netherlands, who beat the favourite, Wilfried Muller; and Bill Daly, Ireland, who had ended the championship hopes of Adrian Peters, SKB Germany.

Road Bowling Champions of Europe at the start of the World Championship at Whitechurch, Co. Cork in 1985. Included (from left) are Willfried Muller, Germany; Manfried Thieb, Germany; Henk Lammerink, Netherlands and Adrian Peters, Germany.

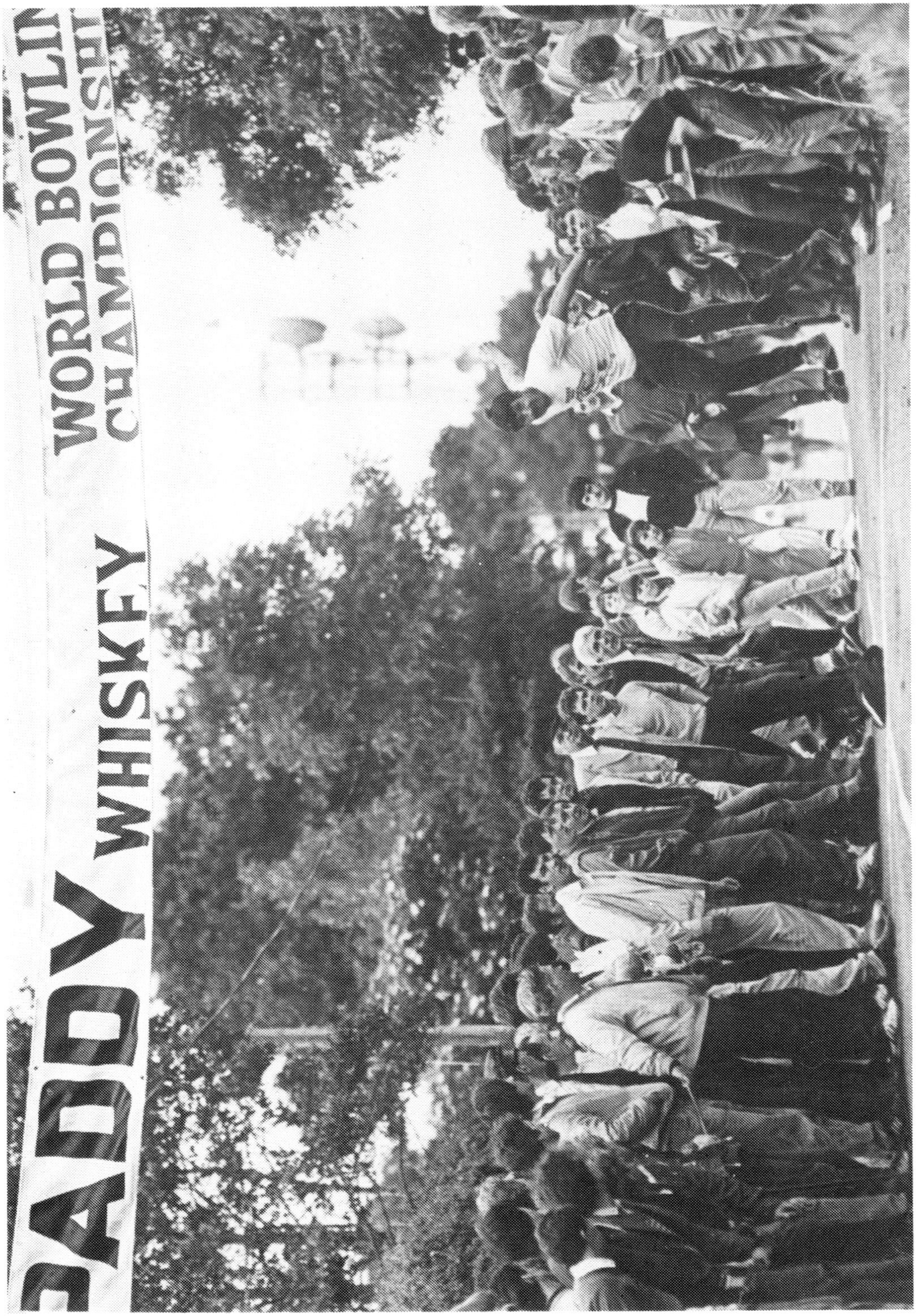

Aidan Toal, Armagh, with his opening throw in the Paddy Whiskey World Road Bowling Championship at Whitechurch, Cork in 1985. Photo: John Sheehan.

The semi-final draws pitched fellow country men against each other and the first of these saw Henk Lammerink go through against Johan Bruns whilst Bill Daly was particularly impressive in his defeat of Aidan Toal. The final of the Paddy Whiskey World Road Bowling Championship, on the afternoon of Sunday 30th June 1985, had attracted media attention from various parts of the world as Bill Daly, Ireland, took his place at the starting line alongside Henk Lammerink, Netherlands, for a title that no other bowler ever had the opportunity to win in the past. The crowd of spectators was massive as each player made the break-off in this unique event. First it was Daly who led but Lammerink was on his way back into it with a close encounter rapidly unfolding when suddenly the absorbing contest was over. Henk Lammerink had been forced to withdraw through injury. As many thousands of gaelic football fans were filing out of venues all over the country they heard the announcement on RTE radio sport that Bill Daly of Glanmire, Cork, Ireland, was bowling champion of the world. It was no fault of Bill Daly that the conclusion was so unsatisfactory and it was disappointing in the extreme for Henk Lammerink that his claim to a world bowling title had ended so abruptly.

The morning after the big event the Cork Examiner of Monday 1st July 1985 had this to say:

> *Bill Daly a 27 year old Glanmire Garda was crowned the first World Road Bowling champion at Whitechurch, Co Cork yesterday when his Dutch opponent Henk Lammerink withdrew with a thigh injury just before the turn. It was a very disappointing finish because the 26 year old Dutchman had threatened to ruin Daly's ambition and a close score appeared to be unfolding. The drama started halfway out when the powerfully built Lammerink unleashed a mighty effort*

Bill Daly (left) and Aidan Toal at the finish of their Semi-Final clash in 1985.

which shoved him 150 metres ahead of the Irish champion but he winced with pain and from there on it was only a matter of time before Daly was declared champion. Lammerink at first had his thigh strapped but this failed to ease the strain. A doctor was called and he advised him not to continue though Lammerink wanted to play on. At the time Daly took full advantage and surged into a lead but not before he was given a very tough match.

In addition to various television crews from around the world the event also captured the attention of Hugh McIlvanney whose more global report in the Sunday Times of 7th July 1985 included specific reference to the course and the champion:

Last weekend's world championship course took the contenders 2,750 metres out from the start and its three miles or so was a marathon compared with most of the many scores advertised weekly in The Cork Examiner. Daly, whose 13st 6lbs is well distributed over a sturdily athletic physique, was never going to be inconvenienced by the extra distance, especially as he was the only competitor who employed the full wheel-like swing of the arm traditional in Cork, and so regularly generated superior power with "the bullet." The Continentals and Aidan Toal, the 42 year old Armagh veteran, all favoured the short under-arm release. It is reckoned to give greater scope for imparting the spin that helps to take the bowl round bends, vitally prolonging the running life of a shot. But Daly is strong in that department too, and outstanding when the need is for lofting, the technique that hoists the bowl into the air to carry over rugged or treacherous stretches of road or even, when the conditions are right, over the verges and hedgerows to cut out the angle of a sharp bend.

The new bowling champion of the world was feted at an elaborate presentation function in Christy's Hotel, Blarney at which the hosts, Irish Distillers Limited, were represented by the firm's Group Managing Director, Richard Burrows and other dignitaries included Donal Creed, T.D., the then Minister for Sport; Brendan Roche, Chairman, Bol Chumann Na hEireann; Liam Burke, T.D., Lord Mayor of Cork; John Gribben and Paddy Comiskey, the then Chairman and Treasurer respectively of the Northern Branch, An Bol Chumann Na hEireann; and players, mentors and officials from the competing countries. It is little wonder that Bill Daly was named as Jury's Sportstar of the Month in July 1985. Such was the level of success associated with the entire event a prompt announcement was made by Bol Chumann Na hEireann and Irish Distillers Limited that the Paddy Whiskey World Bowling Championship would again be held in 1987.

The venue once again was Whitechurch, County Cork, on the weekend of Friday 19th to Sunday 21st June 1987 and the top bowlers representing several nations included title holder Bill Daly, keen to retain his crown and eager to vindicate a victory that was somewhat anti- climatic two years earlier. Graham Jarvie beat fellow Scottish player Keith Lindsay in the early rounds and also eliminated at that stage was Ulrich Nagel, Germany, who lost to Bandon bowler Declan

O'Donovan, whilst Adrian Peters, Germany, made an early exit at the hands of Henry Lohius, Holland. Gerry Boylan, of Armagh, the Ulster senior road bowling champion of 1987 presented with a towering physique that prevailed over even the most powerfully built players of any nation. He absorbed the course at Whitechurch in a fine quarter final win over Graham Jarvie, Scotland, and it was no great surprise that he recorded the longest throw of the championship with a bowl of 346 metres for which he collected a special £200 prize. The surprise of the quarter finals was the defeat of Declan O'Donovan by Harm Henkel, Germany. Another German bowler, Gerd Oltmanns, also qualified for the semi-finals when he beat

A commemorative plaque on the exterior wall of Buckley's hostelry in Whitechurch, Cork.

Frans Fox of the Netherlands. But dominating the remaining quarter final was the title holder Bill Daly who ended the hopes of Dutch bowler Henry Lohuis.

The first semi-final resulted in a surprisingly easy win for Armagh's Gerry Boylan over the German player Gerd Oltmanns and the nature of his victory left him supremely confident going into the final. The second semi-final was a real thriller and easily the most entertaining contest of the entire championship. Bill Daly, Ireland, was faced with the challenge of Harm Henkel, Germany, who had been so impressive in the quarter final. On the way out to the first line it was Daly who led, and on the turn he was again extending his lead until the superbly fit German began to unleash a series of tremendous shots. Each one more impressive than the other Henkel deservedly took the lead and powered forward for a distinct advantage that might ultimately assure him of victory. But Daly's title wasn't yet relinquished and in a storming finish he just regained the lead at the vitally important moment to go through to the final.

It was an all Irish final for the individual title of World Road Bowling Champion. A fact that in no way detracted from the appeal of the event. An enormous crowd had gathered for the fixture and prominent amongst them was a plethora of media personnel. Bill Daly of Cork against Gerry Boylan of Armagh. The semi-finals had indicated that this bowling encounter on Sunday 21st June 1987, had all the ingredients for a classic. But Boylan got away to the worst possible start - a very poor opening throw. Daly had twice gone into a useful lead and at halfway it was substantial. Despite courageous efforts by Boylan to get back on terms it was Daly who was gaining in distance and stature to go well clear at the finishing line. Bill Daly was again the Paddy Whiskey World Road Bowling Champion and this time there was no disputing the merits of his achievement. It had been a gruelling experience of marathon bowling over a four day championship but the reigning champion was up to it all in skill and stamina.

That sustained period of supreme fitness and fine tuned bowling skills earned for Bill Daly of Cork the unique individual title of World Road Bowling Champion in 1985 and 1987.

It had been a glorious era of International competition that brought a new and exciting dimension to the sport in Ireland.

Expanding the Championship Range

The positive influence exerted by championship bowling as it unfolded over the years is emphasised in the realisation that within twenty years of the first ever All-Ireland championship being played there had been established no less than eight National championships offering competition to players in virtually every category of the sport.

The most congested bowling division had always been that of Junior grade and it was a necessary development in 1980 when a new 'B' grouping was added to the championship range. That decision had served to promote more open competition in both Junior sections with enhanced opportunity for players to gain provincial and National honours.

The Junior 'A' championship that year had been particularly competitive. In the Munster semi-finals Pat Corkery had edged out Sonny Butler at Ballyvolane whilst Chris O'Donovan was doing likewise against Bunny O'Driscoll at Argideen. In the provincial final at Ballyshonin on Friday 8th August it was west Cork bowler O'Donovan who came through against north Cork representative Corkery and that win took him to the National final at the same venue on Sunday 24th August 1980. A place in that same final was at stake in a hectic Junior 'A' championship in Ulster. Going through to the provincial final were Martin Kinchin, Tassagh, who surprisingly beat Sean Oliver, Grangemore, and Shane O'Neill, Tullysaran, who had gained a shock win over the tournament favourite Johnny Mills. It was Kinchin who controlled the Ulster final with steady play throughout the score to gain him a lead that was seldom threatened by O'Neill. No such command though in the All-Ireland final. It was almost totally dominated by the strong bowling of Chris O'Donovan and whilst Martin Kinchin rallied he had too much to do to recover sufficiently.

The Junior 'B' final that year was equally disappointing. Kevin Mackle from Kilmore had won the northern final over Michael Rocks, Keady, but in the National decider he found the opposition much too powerful. Tom Walsh had beaten Paddy Kelleher and then John O'Callaghan to win the Munster title and the west Cork bowler maintained his form at Ballyshonin to easily win the first National 'B' final against Kevin Mackle who could find no answer on the day. The following year it was less one-sided. There was a huge entry in Ulster and steadily emerging out of the ranks was one Tom McKeever, who came through the final stages with victories over Ciaran Rocks, Tassagh, Laurence Carragher, Newtownhamilton, and Shane O'Neill, Tullysaran. That provincial final win over O'Neill was gained on the last shot following two tremendous finishing drives by McKeever over the Cathedral road in Armagh. That was the venue too for the All-Ireland Junior 'B' final on Saturday 6th September 1981. And coming through from Munster to contest that final was Cork city player Anthony O'Neill, who had returned after a long lay-off to beat Dan Connolly at Ahiohill and then Jerome O'Mahony at Carrignavar. The

National final at Armagh was a close and unpredictable contest in which both players occasionally erred. With a narrow margin separating the pair for most of the way it was O'Neill who got there on the final throw. The Junior 'A' National final was also played at Armagh that year. The most impressive bowler throughout the Ulster championship had been Madden's Malachy McIlvenna and he maintained that form to take the provincial title following wins over semi-finalist Al Mallon and finalist Liam Boylan who lost out on the final throw. It was Cork city player Mick O'Driscoll who won the Munster title over Donie O'Mahony and his performance throughout the provincial championship rendered him strong favourite for the All-Ireland final on Sunday 7th September 1981. But neither player produced their best play over the Cathedral road and it was McIlvenna who eventually forfeited his chances with a serious error near the last which enabled O'Driscoll to pull away for a great finish to win the title.

In 1982 the surprise of the Junior 'B' championship in Ulster was the success of Fergal McGuigan, Newtownhamilton, who won a place in the provincial final with a win over Ciaran Rocks at Monaghan. But his great run ended when faced with the experienced Paul Mills, Benburb, who came from behind for a fine win. The Munster title that year had gone to Finbar Doyle who had rather easily beaten Denis Cronin at Macroom before winning by a lesser margin over Finbar Collins at Coachford. The All-Ireland final at Ballyshonin on Saturday 21st August 1982 was close and exciting. In exceptional play from both men the lead wavered before the final throw by Mills just missed the finishing line. It was an assured and confident Doyle who put his final effort over the line to take the National Junior 'B' title to north east Cork. The likelihood of the Junior 'A' title also going to north east Cork in 1982 was a genuine consideration when Patsy Coleman won his way to the National final after beating Justin Cremin, at Innishannon, Simon Buckley at Carrignavar, and Pat Sutton at Ballyshonin. The concluding stages of the Ulster championship had produced mediocre performances from players with the potential for greater bowling competence. Brendan McIlvenna had won a semi-final against Neil McVeigh but so too had Colm Grimley, Lisadian, gained a similar win over Paul Grimley, Madden, and it was he who went on to take the provincial title in a disappointing contest. The All-Ireland Junior 'A' final at Ballyshonin on Sunday 22nd August 1982 held an emotionally motivating reality for Patsy Coleman. At that time the most recent success in the Junior 'A' championship by a bowler from east Cork had been in 1967 by his late brother Christy who died unexpectedly in 1982. Some fifteen years later, and just months after his brother Christy had died, it was Patsy, formerly of Saleen and then living in Midleton, who held the same Munster title. He went on to win the National title by a convincing margin to complete a great season of top class bowling. Tragically he was to win no more. This exceptionally dignified gentleman of the sport had himself died unexpectedly within less than twelve months of that memorable win. The bowling ability and genteel nature of Patsy Coleman is a lasting exemplification of how the sport can be played and portrayed.

It was fitting that the All-Ireland Junior 'A' title won by the late Patsy Coleman in 1982 should be retained by a bowler from east Cork the following year. Paddy O'Leary from Youghal was the man to do it when he won his way through Munster with wins in the later stages of the provincial championship over James O'Sullivan, Tim O'Brien and then Billy O'Driscoll at Rathcormac. The closing stages in Ulster were down to two intriguing semi-finals. One of these was a thrilling contest which was decided on the last shot. Henry Lyttle, Armagh, had put down a marvellous drive but unbelievably James McCann, Moy, surpassed it. The other semi-final was poor in contrast; missed opportunities, successive blunders, and for all that, it too was decided on the final throw when Neil McVeigh, Armagh, edged out Oliver Gribben, Farmacaffley. The provincial final was unimpressive in quality and it was the relatively unknown Moy player James McCann who made the least errors to gain the title. The National final between McCann and O'Leary on Saturday 13th August 1983 at Ballyshonin was closely contested until the end of the third quarter. From that point McCann rapidly lost ground as O'Leary gained in confidence to go on for a clear win. The Junior 'B' All-Ireland Final of 1983 was played in Armagh. And back pursuing Junior honours that year was Martin Kinchin, Tassagh, who lost the 1980 National 'A' final at Cork. He had beaten Brian Grimley, Madden, in a semi-final before winning the provincial title against Jim Cullen, Ballyheridan, on the last throw of a close and exciting score. The Munster champion was Michael O'Connor from Dromahane, near Mallow. He had been particularly impressive in beating Pat Calnan at Templemartin and again showed excellent form in the County final defeat of Stephen Barrett. In the Munster final at Rathcormac he had a bowl lead at the finish over Limerick's Michael O'Leary. The All-Ireland Junior 'B' final was over the Cathedral road on Sunday 30th July and it was Martin Kinchin who held a fluctuating lead which extended to a bowl of odds at the finish as Michael O'Connor faded towards the end.

In 1984 the Junior 'B' championship saw Monaghan bowler Robert Cochrane win his way into the Ulster semi-finals after a surprising run of victories at Threemilehouse which included narrow, but nonetheless impressive, wins over Pat Donnelly, Ballynahonebeg, and Joe Shortt, Keady. But that proved to be his limit for the season when he went out to Frankie Kiernan, Madden, who in turn lost the inter provincial final to Maurice McKenna, Knappagh, a brother of the 1967 Junior champion, Patsy McKenna. In the Munster 'B' championship Peter Ruby had a semi-final win over Kevin Leahy at Rylane whilst Ted Hegarty just got up on the last shot to beat Freddie Shannon at Templemartin. But that close call inspired him for the Munster final at Tower and it was the Clonakilty player, Hegarty, who took the title against the north east representative Peter Ruby. Ted Hegarty led for a long way in the All-Ireland Junior 'B' final at Armagh on Saturday 4th August 1984 and was fore bowl for the last shot over the Cathedral road but Maurice McKenna laid down a perfect effort which gained him victory.

The Junior 'A' final of 1984 was contested by two provincial champions who had been showing great power and accuracy throughout their respective qualifying scores. Donald Gribben, Farmacaffley, and Gerald McKee, Armagh, had fought out a memorable score in a semi-final clash which was acknowledged as the best for a long time previous. Not only did Gribben come through that one but he was equally exciting in the way he contended with the challenge of Neil McVeigh, Armagh, in the provincial final. The other provincial champion, and one equally impressive, was Mick Murphy from Donoughmore in Co Cork who won the Munster title over east Cork bowler Willie Dennis at Fermoy. Much was expected from the All-Ireland Junior 'A' final at Ballyshonin on Saturday 8th September, 1984. But northern champion Donald Gribben got away to a disastrous opening in contrast to a superb start by Mick Murphy who unleashed a massive drive. That introduction dictated the trend of the score and though Gribben came back into it the result was rarely in doubt as Murphy protected a one shot lead to the finish.

It was an alarming statistic but the northern champions in the Junior 'A' category had by then, at the end of 1984, failed to win a National title in the grade for ten years. Stephen Donnelly, Allistragh, had been the most recent northern success and that went back to 1974. But hopes were raised when Gerald McKee came through Ulster in 1985 from a formidable field which included in the closing stages John Gribben, Martin Kinchin, Colm Grimley, Sean Doran, Larry Corr, Paul Mills and Patsy McKenna. McKee's provincial final win against Kinchin was a narrow one but the score featured some very lengthy shots. However it was the Munster championship which had all the unusual features that year. The county final had the unlikely pairing of Donal Crowley and Stephen Barrett, neither of whom were forecast as potential champions. And for a moment it seemed that both of them had won! In an exciting finish at Newcestown firstly it was Barrett who was hoisted shoulder high and seconds later Crowley was in the air through his supporters. The final bowl by Crowley had gone into the hedgerow some ten metres behind his opponents mark giving rise to premature celebrations by Barretts supporters. Their joy was short lived when it was realised that Crowley's bowl had rocketed through the summer growth to beat Barretts mark by just over a metre. After that particular scare Donal Crowley, from the south west region, went on to win the Munster final against Mick O'Leary from Limerick. He went one stage further in the All-Ireland final at Armagh on Saturday 3rd August 1985 when he had an easy task to win the final shot over Gerald McKee who never at any time was able to reproduce the quality play associated with his earlier championship performances.

The protracted Junior 'B' championship of 1985 eventually whittled the large entry in Ulster down to the semi-final stage when Larry Carragher, Newtownhamilton, beat Paul Gribben and the remaining finalist was confirmed through Jim Gartland's win over Dermot Grimley. It was Gartland who had toppled all the more favoured prospects and he did it again in the provincial final by a small margin against Carragher. But the All-Ireland final at Whitechurch on Saturday 17th August was an assignment of a very different nature. Tim O'Halloran, the Munster champion, was a very strong bowler who got tremendous distance into his shots and he used it to telling effect to record a victory by a wide margin.

The championship season had no sooner concluded in 1985 when the bowling fraternity was saddened to learn about the unexpected death of Brendan Digby, Armagh, who had graced the bowling roads with his quality play and unobtrusive demeanour for so many years. Brendan, who died on 27th October, 1985 aged 42 years, had contested every championship for which he was eligible and competed in two All-Ireland finals at Cork venues. He was runner-up to Seamus Sexton in the Junior final at Ballyshonin in 1971 and played for the Intermediate title against Billy Hurley at the same venue in 1976. Brendan was also a member of the Armagh team of bowlers at the fourth International championships at Jever, Ostfriesland, Germany in 1974.

The 1986 All-Ireland Junior 'A' final had seen Malachy McIlvenna, Madden, back at the ultimate stage of the championship for the first time since 1981. He had beaten Patsy McKenna by over a bowl in the Ulster final and at Whitechurch on Saturday 12th July 1986 he took on Tom Hayes, Ross, who had a comfortable win over Robert Shorten in the Munster final at Dunmanway. The margin in the National final was again a definite one as Hayes opened up a two shot lead over McIlvenna and held it to the finish. The Junior 'B' final that year was contested by Jarlath Devlin, Ballycrummy and John Desmond, Midleton, Co Cork. Devlin had beaten Stephen Toal, in the Ulster final but the impressive reign of successes by Desmond in Munster had been notable. He beat Mick McCarthy, Youghal, by a bowl at Waterfall, and in the county final at Coachford had a clear win over Dan O'Driscoll, Gaeltacht, before going on to win the provincial title by a similar margin over Rory Barrett. The leeway in the All-Ireland final at Armagh on 2nd August 1986 was less decisive but nonetheless sufficient when Desmond again came through to win by almost a bowl to take the National title.

In the year following, Stephen Toal was again defeated in the Ulster Junior B' final this time by Paul McVeigh who was then bound for a Cork venue no doubt mindful of the historic bowling performances in the same county by his father, the great Joe McVeigh, in the late fifties. But John Deasy of Cork had his own agenda and he recorded a two shot win in the All-Ireland Junior 'B' final at Whitechurch on Saturday 11th July 1987. The Junior 'A' National final that year had bowling talent in abundance. In Ulster James McCann, Moy, Co Tyrone, was in great form and confirmed his standard with a classy win over Sean Webb in the provincial final. But few players were displaying the supremacy of Kieran O'Gorman, south west Cork, as he swept his way through the Munster championship. A former gold medallist with the Irish youths team at the International games in the Netherlands in 1980 he enthralled a capacity crowd at Ballinacurra, Upton, when beating Donal O'Leary, Waterloo, and then gave a superlative display against Billy McAuliffe, Glanworth, in the Munster final at Crossbarry to win by nearly a bowl of odds. The All-Ireland final at Tassagh on Saturday 1st August 1987 was played in a continuous torrential downpour but James McCann contended with all the challenges until Kieran O'Gorman laid down a tremendously long throw near the finish to gain a bowl of odds and take the title in impressive fashion.

The unrelenting dominance of southern bowlers in the Junior championship was extended in 1988 at Bauravilla, near Skibereen. Martin Boylan, Lislea, had renewed hopes of a rare northern victory by virtue of his comprehensive defeat of Sean Webb in the Ulster final but Dan Burke, Cork Gaeltacht, had been equally

At the start of the 1987 Junior 'B' Final at Whitechurch are (left) Paul McVeigh, Armagh, and John Deasy, Cork, with the referee in centre.

Photo: Denis McGarry.

Larry Corr, Rock, All-Ireland Junior 'B' Finalist in 1989, with his mentor John Kane, Armagh.

impressive, though by a much smaller margin, in his Munster final win against Willie O'Donovan at Ballyshonin. It was a National final dÇbut for Burke but he belied that fact over the Bauravilla course on Saturday 9th July 1988 when he produced eighteen stunning shots of impeccable bowling to leave Boylan trailing by two bowls in arrears at the line. There was consolation though for northern bowlers when the Junior 'B' title was won later that year by Joe Donnelly, Kilmore, who had beaten Noel Carr in the Ulster final and then maintained his good form in the All-Ireland final at Tassagh on Saturday 30th July 1988 to gain a shot lead over Dan Vaughan, Cork Gaeltacht, and hold it to the finish.

The exacting standard of Junior bowling in Munster was never more positively underlined than during the 1989 season when the calibre of players and the nature of contests in the closing stages of the championship were each of the highest order. In two exciting semi-finals Jerry Hegarty, Carbery, had beaten west Cork bowler John Carroll at Cottage road, Clonakilty, whilst Noel O'Brien defeated Cork city player Simon Buckley at Ballinacurra, near Upton. The Munster final had all the ingredients for a thriller and that prospect became a reality. Noel O'Brien, a member of a great bowling family in Clonakilty, and European road bowling champion at Garding, Germany in 1984, was finely tuned in his pursuit of a historic double win at Junior ranks. He had won the 1978 Junior title and was very much in line for repeat National honours. But between him and that historic opportunity rested one Jerry Hegarty whose bowling credentials were second to none. It was indeed a thrilling Munster final at Dunmanway. O'Brien went a shot down at one stage to the brilliant play of Hegarty but in a superb overall performance of fifteen magnificent shots the Clonakilty player fought out a tense and rousing finish to win the score of the year by a mere twenty-seven metres. It was that kind of form he brought to the north for the All-Ireland Junior 'A' final at Tassagh on Saturday 5th August 1989. It was a three way contest. Ted Hegarty was the London champion and Fergal McCreesh, Navan, had beaten Martin Boylan by a shot for the Ulster title. But even the double opposition was not enough to thwart Noel O'Brien in his pursuit of a historic second National win at Junior ranks when he established a shot lead over each opponent and won his coveted title by that comfortable margin. It was not all lost for London bowlers that year though. Michael O'Brien, the London Junior 'B' champion, had beaten the Munster champion, Pat O'Brien, Youghal, on the last shot at Ballincurrig. In Ulster it was Larry Corr, Rock, who came through the provincial final against Dermot Grimley, Madden, but the London followers gained their consolation in the All-Ireland Junior 'B' final at Skibbereen on Saturday 8th July 1989 when Michael O'Brien won the title by two bowls of odds.

The classy bowling of Dan Keneally was maintained into the Munster Junior 'A' final of 1990 when he overcame the challenge of Michael Coughlan at Ballyvolane. The Ulster title that year had gone to Brian Kiernan, Madden, following a win over Paddy O'Neill, Armagh, but a polished performance by Keneally in the All-Ireland final at Bauravilla on Saturday 7th July 1990 saw him take a lead on the second throw that he never relinquished as he went on to win his title by a bowl of odds at the finish. There was an exciting contest for the Junior 'B' title of 1990 between

Michael O'Leary, Waterford, bowling to win the 1991 All-Ireland Junior 'B' Title at Armagh.
Photo: Ann McManus/Irish News.

Jim O'Driscoll, Cork, in action during the 1995 All-Ireland Junior 'A' Final at Armagh.
Photo: Philip Wilson/Ulster Gazette.

Brendan McIlvenna, Madden, and John O'Brien, Carberry. The Munster final was won on the last shot by O'Brien over south west Cork bowler John Hurley whilst McIlvenna beat Gerard McVeigh, Armagh, and Peter Mallon, Grangemore, on his way to the Ulster title. The All-Ireland Junior 'B final over the Cathedral road, Armagh, on Saturday 4th August 1990 saw Brendan McIlvenna go into a full shot lead only to surrender it to a series of fine shots by John O'Brien over the final quarter which left him the winner of the title by almost a bowl of odds.

The 1991 All-Ireland Junior 'A' championship final saw the return of two former National champions to the fore when Corney Bohane, the 1977 Intermediate title holder, was confronted by Paul Grimley the 1981 Under 18 National champion. Bohane had got there through a great act of survival in winning an enthralling last shot struggle with Humphrey O'Leary in the Munster final at the Miles. And it was a storming finish that earned Grimley the Ulster title over Pat Mallon when he beat him at Armagh by two shots. It was over the same Cathedral road course in Armagh that the National final was played on Sunday 4th August 1991 and a great contest ensued. Both men bowled superbly with little between them and it went to the last shot. It was only then that Bohane was edged out when Grimley's final effort made it over the line to record a victory that was greeted with a tremendous roar by the home crowd. Paul Grimley, Madden, had done it in brilliant fashion and Corney Bohane, Carbery, had pressed him all the way. It was a particularly significant win for Ulster. No northern bowler had won the Junior 'A' National title for seventeen years and the exuberance of the home following was fully understandable. That eventual breakthrough proved to be an inspiration for the following year when Brian Kinchin, Tassagh, after beating Eddie Carr in the Ulster final, went all the way to take the National title against Denis O'Sullivan. O'Sullivan had put in a solid display to beat Brendan O'Callaghan, Gaeltacht, by a shot in the Munster final at Ballyclough and was strongly fancied to take the National title. But the All-Ireland final at Ballingeary on Saturday 11th July 1992 was surprisingly dominated by Kinchin who gained an early shot lead and led all the way to eventually win by two bowls of odds. It was a remarkable change of fortune for northern bowlers to win two elusive Junior titles in successive years following such a protracted period of failure. But the trophy was not on permanent loan. Paddy O'Neill, Armagh, had won the Ulster title in 1993 over Stephen Toal and in the All-Ireland final at Armagh on Saturday 31st July, he lost out to John O'Brien, Ballydehob, who had beaten Eamon Connolly at Macroom in the Munster final, and was much too steady for the inconsistent Armagh man in the National final.

Corney Bohane on the first shot of the 1991 All-Ireland Junior 'A' Final at Cathedral Road, Armagh.

Shane O'Neill, Armagh, the defeated finalist in the 1991 Junior 'B' National Final.
Photo: Ann McManus/Irish News.

Joe Shortt, Keady, hurling in Poc Fada over the Cooley Mountains in August 1988.

Photo: Irish News.

Over the same three year period all the Junior 'B' National titles had been won by Munster bowlers. In 1991 Shane O'Neill, Tullysaran, was the Ulster standard bearer in the grade when he beat Michael McKinney, Armagh, in the provincial final. The Munster champion was Michael O'Leary who had beaten Tim Cahalane, at Aherla by nearly two shots, and he retained that speed and composure into the All-Ireland final at Armagh on Saturday 3rd August to win the National title by a bowl of odds. The final of the Junior 'B' championship provided a most interesting clash the following year. In Ulster it was Joe Shortt, Keady, who had won the provincial title over Armagh's Gerard McVeigh, and being a supremely fit and competent sportsman, equally adept at hurling, football, snooker, handball, poc fada, and bowling, the Keady man commanded a huge following in his quest for All-Ireland honours at Armagh on Saturday 1st August 1992. But the opposition that day was equally compelling. The player to win through in Munster was none other than Derry Kenny, the exceptionally stylish and competent bowler who had contested the 1963 All-Ireland Senior final at Armagh. It was Joe Shortt who started best in the National final and entering the closing stages he was very much in control with a commanding lead. Just then it all changed. Kenny put down a brilliant shot near the finish. A great bowl but hardly sufficient to alter the outcome. Incredibly, and certainly untypically, Shortt misplaced two shots in succession to astonishingly forfeit his lead and reverse the bowl of odds in Kenny's favour. It was an amazing reversal of fortunes and as a bewildered Joe Shortt pondered the dramatic outcome a much relieved Derry Kenny celebrated his unexpected victory.

It was the turn of Nial Smith, Navan, to challenge for National honours in 1993 when he won the Ulster Junior 'B' title over Port Mor bowler Brendan McOscar. The task was a daunting one following the performance of Munster champion Philip O'Donovan at Crossbarry against Carbery player Michael Crowley. It had been a thrilling provincial final and it took a great last shot by O'Donovan to give him the title. No such requirement in the All-Ireland final though. Played at Ballingeary on Saturday 10th July 1993, O'Donovan was a clear favourite and he justified that confidence with a convincing win over Smith who never really got to terms with the unfamiliar course and was always in difficulty.

There was every confidence in the ability of the Ulster Junior 'B' champion of 1994 following a most impressive win by Malachy Lappin, Keady, over Brendan McIlvenna, Madden. The Keady man carried that same determination into the All-Ireland final at Armagh on Saturday 30th July when he again produced excellent bowling to beat the Munster champion Liam Barry, east Cork, by almost a bowl of odds. The same year saw Philip O'Donovan, Cork, win the Junior 'A' National title at Bandon on Saturday 9th July 1994 when he laid down a series of very lengthy drives to leave the Ulster champion Paul Grimley trailing for most of the score. The following year it was the turn of his brother Tim Pat O'Donovan to challenge for National honours when he won the Munster Junior B' final. His opponent in the All-Ireland final at Dunderrow on the Bandon to Kinsale road was a young northern bowler who was back to his best after an indifferent period in the sport during which he had rarely figured since winning the Under 18 National title in 1989. For this contest on Saturday 8th July 1994, Johnny Kelly, Armagh, had himself well prepared and it showed. He had been masterly in his defeat of a very competent Joe Shortt in the Ulster final and in this one he was equally adept. But it wasn't enough. In Tim Pat O'Donovan he had met a man who was superb on the day and despite a faultless display by Johnny Kelly he lost out on the final throw. That was a close and exciting finish at Dunderrow but it didn't rate with the drama and tension created by Pat Mallon, Grangemore, and Jim O'Driscoll, Cork, in the closing stages of their All-Ireland Junior 'A' final at Armagh. Played in the sweltering temperatures of Saturday 5th August 1995 it had been a great score for most of the way with Ulster champion Pat Mallon having to make a comeback after an early deficit. Both men missed the finishing line when it seemed certain that each of them, in turn, would score it to win the title. When neither of them did the crowd was then treated to another shot for the contest and, in further drama, Pat Mallon failed to get his bowl near the required play to rapidly forfeit his chances from a position that was more favourable to him than he had enjoyed throughout the entire score. The rest was easy for Jim O'Driscoll as he virtually lofted the bowl over the mark to claim his All-Ireland title.

More than twenty years of Junior championship bowling at All-Ireland level has invariably generated the characteristics of competitive sporting endeavour that are almost exclusive to this intriguing sport.

A Cultural and Sporting Breakthrough

A perplexing peculiarity associated with the bowling venues of early years is that they were almost totally devoid of women spectators at any of the scores however appealing the events may have been to committed followers. It was a social and cultural norm which had unwittingly evolved and inadvertently become established within the sport.

That undesirable pattern no longer prevails nor has it done so for almost the last quarter century. But the ensconced cultural and social barriers to the logical development of female participation in the hitherto male orientated sport were not features that readily and rapidly evaporated. When first mooted by forward thinking people of both sexes the reactions varied from covert rejection, through indifference, to outright enthusiasm for such rational proposals and sensible attitudes. And any reflection on evolvement of the sport in recent times must surely acknowledge that one of the more refreshing developments in the game has been the inauguration of women's championships and the outstanding success this competition has been from every angle that the sport can be evaluated.

The All-Ireland Senior Women's championship final of 1995 was perhaps the finest bowling contest in any category of the sport for a very long time with its marvellous bowling, exciting exchanges, constant elation, athletic performers, and a close tense finish to enthral the enthusiastic spectators.

It was fourteen years earlier that the first National Womens final was played and for some time before that the women of Cork had been encouraging entrants and organising tournaments on a regular basis. Many areas within the various bowling regions initiated practice sessions and low profile events in an effort to generate interest and evaluate the potential for development. Amongst these was the launching of a Womens tournament at Ardcahan, Dunmanway in 1976 and the formation of a Women's bowling club at Ballinacurra in 1978. It was in 1980 that the north responded to the welcome developments in the south and within months they were making preparations for the first Ulster Womens championship. Joan Shannon from west Cork region was the player to win the Munster title in the first year of the All-Ireland championship series in 1981 and she was due to travel to Armagh for the inaugural National final. The play- off in Ulster took longer than expected. There had been a sizeable entry for the first championship which had generated its own festive enthusiasm and particular enjoyment. At the semi-final stage Ann Boylan, Lislea, had beaten Patricia Grimley and Bernie Dynes surprisingly ousted Cathy McSorley, Drumcairne, who had been giving great displays throughout the earlier rounds. The first Ulster Women's final at Cathedral road, Armagh on 19th July 1981 was evenly contested for most of the way but near the finish it was Bernie Dynes, Drumbreda, who edged into the lead and held it to the line to narrowly beat Ann Boylan.

Joan Shannon, the first All-Ireland Senior Champion in Women's road Bowling is pictured with Bol Chumann officials John Gribben, Armagh (left) and Jerry Desmond, Cork.

The first ever All-Ireland Women's final on Saturday 6th September 1981 over the Cathedral road in Armagh was a memorable one in which two excellent sportswomen set the standard for future years. Bernie Dynes had bowled well at the outset and took a shot lead but a very fit and determined Joan Shannon regained the advantage to eventually win by a bowl of odds. The first National Womens bowling title had gone to Joan Shannon, Ballineen, and that notable achievement is now a significant factor in the history of the sport in Ireland.

Yet another momentous occasion in Women's bowling was reached less than a year later when a promising young county Cork girl, Linda Ahern, won the Under 18 west Cork regional championship. Linda, aged twelve, and perhaps the youngest to then compete in Womens championship bowling won the regional title on 3rd July 1982 in a wonderful personal accomplishment that made her the pride of the region she represented. That Munster championship of 1982 had seen the reigning champion Joan Shannon again reach the final by gaining a last shot win over Noreen Buckley at Beal na Blath. But coming through in the other semi-final was Gretta Hegarty who beat Noreen Murphy at Aherla and she went on to win the 'A' final at Ballyshonin after Joan Shannon had put in a strong but vain attempt to retain her title. The Munster 'B' championship semi-finals resulted in Sheila Kiely defeating Ann Murphy at Newcestown and Sandra Dempsey accounting for Breda

Malone at Macroom. Sandra Dempsey went on to win the 'B' final but then lost out in the overall contest to 'A' winner Gretta Hegarty.

The Ulster Womens championship in 1982 was again well supported and very competitive. Bernie Dynes again reached the final when she beat Eileen Toal, Grange, by less than two metres in the contest of the year in Womens bowling. In the second semi-final, Cathy McSorley, Drumcairne, had led to almost the finish but was edged out by Rosheen Toal, Grange, before the line. It was a new title holder who emerged that year when Dynes relinquished her provincial crown to consistently accurate bowling from Toal in the Ulster final.

The All-Ireland final at Ballyshonin on 21st August 1982 brought together two competitors who were to get to know each other very well in future seasons. It was a remarkable final in many ways. Spectators crammed the players at the point of delivery to gain a view of the contrasting styles but even more bewildering was how Rosheen Toal let slip a substantial lead to be beaten on the last shot. It was a great contest and the impressive Gretta Hegarty, Lyre, had a fine bowl near the finish to set her up for that narrow win.

The Munster 'B' championship in 1983 was down to Colette Twohig and Joan Savage but in the end it was Gretta Hegarty again who took the overall provincial title. She had beaten Sheila Kiely by a bowl of odds in a semi-final at Templemartin whilst Catherine Coffey, who had a two shot lead near the finish, just held on by a mere two metres to beat Breda Malone at Ballyvolane. It was two experienced players for the 'A final but Gretta Hegarty had the advantage and she went on to win that one, and the overall event, as well as the Munster final at Rathcormac against Veronica McDonagh of Limerick.

Gretta Hegarty, Cork, Bowling at Armagh in 1983

The Ulster championship had attracted new entrants in 1983 and those making a debut to competitive bowling included Deirdre McKenna, Caroline McKee, Shirley Powell and Margaret Rafferty. But it was experienced bowlers who made it to the provincial final when Rose Duffy came through to be followed by the holder Rosheen Toal. The Grange player went on to retain her title and renew the challenge for National honours with renowned rival Gretta Hegarty. That All-Ireland final was played at Armagh on Saturday, 30th July 1983. Toal gained an early lead but then wasted the advantage and soon Hegarty edged in front to finish strongly for a clear win by just under a shot. The outcome marked two consecutive National titles for Gretta Hegarty and for Rosheen Toal a perplexing experience of two successive defeats at the ultimate stage of the championship.

There were many familiar names and some predictable results from the Munster Women's championship of 1984. Joan Shannon had beaten Catherine Coffey by a bowl at Crossbarry; Eileen Linehan had won by a shot over Ann Twomey at Ballyshonin; Mary Barry had a narrow win against Joan Savage at Templemartin; and Agnes Hurley had a big win over Mary Collins at Dunmanway. But the real surprise of the championship had been the defeat of reigning All-Ireland champion Gretta Hegarty by Agnes Hurley from Ring near Clonakilty who had emerged as the most improved player of the year. She proved the point effectively by the manner of her subsequent win in the county final over the experienced city player Mary Barry, and the provincial final against the relatively inexperienced Veronica McDonagh from Limerick.

All that confirmation of marvellous form demonstrated by the Munster cham-

Caitriona Powell, Armagh, and Caitriona O'Rourke, Cork, at the start of the 1992 All-Ireland Women's Under 18 Final at Armagh.

Photo : Denis McGarry

pion was of little consolation to the remaining players in the closing stages of the Ulster championship. Siobhan Gribben, Farmacaffley, had made an excellent debut in out performing Shirley Powell, Drumbreda, and it was two inter-county camogie stars who met up when Teresa McVeigh, Armagh, lost out to Eileen Toal, Grange. But again it was Rosheen Toal who beat them all to win her third successive Ulster title. This time it was Agnes Hurley between her and a first National title but Rosheen was denied yet again at the decisive stage. In Agnes Hurley she met a true champion who bowled with great style and immense composure. It was her first National final that Saturday 8th September at Ballyshonin but the nature of Hurley's play belied such actuality as she led from start to finish.

Surprisingly, in view of a class performance in 1984, Agnes Hurley didn't retain her Munster title the following year. But a familiar figure was back again and bowling better than ever. Gretta Hegarty had just made it on the final throw against Joan Shannon at Templemartin but then in the 'A' final at Upton she covered the course in a remarkable seventeen shots to win by two bowls of odds over Noreen Buckley. The Womens 'B' final had been won by Rita O'Sullivan at Shannonvale when she defeated Betty Healy but Gretta Hegarty denied her any further championship aspirations in the overall final at Enniskeane before going on to regain the Munster title with a fine win over Veronica McDonagh, Limerick, at Buttervant.

The 1985 Ulster Womens championship had produced some great encounters involving a mixture of new and experienced bowlers. Deirdre Gribben, Farmacaffley, in her first year, had ousted former champion Bernie Dynes whilst Assumpta Cullen, whose daughters Susan and Fiona both contested the 1995 All-Ireland finals, produced a superb performance against Rose Duffy. Another newcomer, Eithne Lyttle, beat Shirley Powell on the last shot after a great score. And also making a successful debut was Feena Gribben, Farmacaffley, whose accurate bowling maintained a winning lead over Cathy McSorley. But through it all was one Rosheen Toal chasing a fourth Ulster title and eager for her first All-Ireland win. She had beaten Betty Rath and Teresa McVeigh in the closing stages of the competition and retained her provincial title by the minimum margin over the impressive Siobhan Gribben.

The All-Ireland final at Cathedral road Armagh on Saturday 3rd August 1985 had a familiar look about it. Rosheen Toal, who had won a County Armagh Junior championship camogie medal the previous year and whose sporting prowess had been the subject of an extensive profile in the *Armagh Observer* of 4th April 1984, was back again. So too was Gretta Hegarty who was herself the subject of a sports feature in the Irish Farmers Journal and this magnificent bowler from Lyre, near Clonakilty, was seeking her third National title in only five years of championship bowling. There was one clear favourite for the title. One of the performances that day was afterwards described in the press as "the finest exhibition of bowl playing that would do justice to any player in whatever category of the sport." This time it was Rosheen Toal. She had excelled in this one leading from start to finish and steadily increasing a lead that was to give her the most important win of her career. After losing three successive National finals Rosheen Toal had at last won her first

Gretta Cormican, Cork, (right), receives the 1989 All-Ireland Women's Senior Championship Cup from John Gribben, then Chairman of Northern Branch, An Bol Chumann Na hÉireann; and Assumpta Cullen, Armagh, National Finalist, is presented with her award by Frank Mulgrew, Bank of Ireland, Armagh.

All-Ireland title and little wonder that Gretta Hegarty was one of the first to warmly congratulate her.

The win had generated a great deal of additional interest in Women's bowling in the north. A special promotional Committee affiliated to Bol Chumann was then established with Rose Duffy as Chairperson, Cathy McSorley, Secretary, Eithne Donnelly, Treasurer and Kevenna McSorley as public relations officer. The Neilus Duffy Cup was presented for Womens competition and the first tournament for the new trophy was won on Sunday 6th October 1985 by Maria Powell who beat Assumpta Cullen in the final.

The same Assumpta Cullen, Rock, was back in the Ulster Senior final of 1986 but it was no great surprise that the reigning All-Ireland champion retained the provincial title by a comfortable margin. Rosheen Toal, Grange, was seeking her second National title but so too was Joan Shannon, Ballineen, who was back in the final having won the first ever All-Ireland championship five years earlier. Her win in the Munster final represented an incredible reversal of the trend in the score. Gretta Hegarty, the undisputed favourite to win, had established a two shot lead but in three magnificent finishing bowls Joan Shannon just pipped her for the title on the line. It required no such superior finish to clinch the All-Ireland title at Whitechurch on Saturday 12th July 1986 when Joan Shannon dominated the course of events over Rosheen Toal to win by two shots. But retaining the National Senior Womens title in successive years has been the sole preserve of Gretta Hegarty and she removed any threat to that supremacy by regaining the Munster title in a two shot win over Joan Shannon at Newcestown on 24th July 1987. It was an impeccable display of authoritative bowling by a player of great proficiency who was gaining in stature as the years progressed. That was the nature of the challenge confronting Assumpta Cullen in the All-Ireland final at Tassagh on Saturday 1st August 1987 and it proved too great on this her first appearance in a National final. But Assumpta was back the following year with renewed vigour and enhanced experience after winning the provincial title in a great score against Bernie Dynes at Tassagh. And this time the opposition was different even if no less daunting. There had been a big upset to normal calculations in the Munster championship. Gretta Hegarty had beaten Susan Barry for the Senior title but in the overall final at Newcestown she lost to Joan Savage, Donoughmore, who had won the Junior title, and consequently she was the title holder in both categories.

In a delayed start to the All-Ireland Senior final at Bauravilla, Skibbereen on Saturday 9th July 1988, when atrocious weather conditions hampered the break-off it was Joan Savage who set out in front and led all the way to win by a margin of just under two shots. This champion of Junior ranks had really proved herself at senior level. But there was to be no retention of the National title for a second successive year. In 1989 most of the principals were back dominating the closing stages of the Munster championship but Joan Savage was not amongst them. Susan Barry, a member of the Irish team in the 1988 European championships, recorded a sixty metre win over Sandra Dempsey at Aherla and at Ballineen, Philomena O'Driscoll went down to Gretta Cormican (nee Hegarty) who was bowling better than ever. The Munster final at Macroom had an air of quality about it. Susan Barry, a bowler of outstanding ability but still seeking an elusive provincial and National title, challenging the acknowledged supremo in Womens bowling, Gretta Cormican who within nine years had won a Gold Medal in the European championships at Garding in West Germany in 1984, three All- Ireland Senior titles in 1982, 1983 and 1987 and an additional Munster Senior title in 1985. She collected another in 1989 with that provincial win over Barry. In Ulster it was Assumpta Cullen's third successive appearance in the All-Ireland Senior final and despite the awesome record of her Munster opponent she faced that challenge at Tassagh on Sunday 6th August 1989 with a fair degree of confidence. And that assurance was justified in the reality of the event. Cullen won the first shot and going into the last throw only two metres separated them with Cormican in the lead. Cullen scored the line and it seemed the All-Ireland title might be hers but Cormican, with all the conviction that such experience engenders, was able to top the mark by eight metres for that fourth National title.

Another quality player came through the senior ranks in 1990 when Sandra Dempsey beat Mary Brady and Susan Barry to win the Munster title. And in a three-way Ulster final Rosheen Mackle (nee Toal) was again to the fore in beating Bernie Dynes and Eileen Toal over the Moy road. But the advantage of a home venue was probably relished by Sandra Dempsey who lived close to the Bauravilla course and bowled there with the host club. The task of winning that All-Ireland final on Saturday 7th July 1990 was made easier for the home player through a poor opening shot by Mackle as Dempsey maintained the advantage to win by a shot. It was

Sandra Dempsey, Cork, the 1990 All-Ireland Women's Senior Champion being presented with the Cup by Brendan Roche, then Chairman of Bol Chumann Na hÉireann.

Sandra Dempsey's first All-Ireland title and a very popular one in front of her strong support.

The first All-Ireland Womens Under 18 championship was launched in 1986 and in that inaugural final at Armagh on Saturday 2nd August, Orla Galvin, Gaeltacht, won the title over Michelle McSorley, Drumcairne, who had gone through in her first year of competitive bowling. The following year it was Cork's Mary Brady who won the title at Whitechurch on Saturday 11th July 1987 when she beat Bronagh Cullen, Armagh who had been well supported following two exciting wins over Bronwyn McGirr and Paula Gillespie. Bronagh Cullen went out the following year to the powerful bowling of Feena Gribben, Farmacaffley, who also beat Shauna Houlahan at Tassagh. In the All-Ireland final at the same venue on Saturday 30th July, 1988 it was Delia Buckley from Cork city who was to challenge for the title. She had beaten Irish Senior International Mary Brady at Ballyshonin and then in a marvellous Munster final at Ovens just got through on the last shot against Brid Walsh, Gaeltacht, who had played an excellent score throughout. Feena Gribben led the final for the first four shots and in a close and exciting contest the lead changed four times before two very fine last shots by Delia Buckley assured her of victory. The new All-Ireland Womens Under 18 champion was back again the following year, having successfully defended her Munster title, but a great new prospect had emerged in Ulster. Geraldine McCluskey, from Armagh city, at sixteen years old, had created tremendous speculation with her proven ability to deliver a fast bowl with the expertise of a well trained and experienced player. A niece of renowned senior players of the fifties, Mick, and Danny Reilly, she had demonstrated in her

The 1987 Ulster Women's Under 18 Champion Bronagh Cullen, (left), with Provincial Finalist Paula Gillespie and the then Honorary Treasurer of Northern Branch, An Bol Chumann Na hÉireann, Paddy Comiskey.

Geraldine McCluskey, Armagh, (left) and Delia Buckley, Cork, with the referee at the start of the 1989 All-Ireland Women's Under 18 Final at Bauravilla, near Skibbereen, Co. Cork.

run through the provincial championship that the potential for National honours in the sport was realistically attainable. And she wasted no time in gaining that distinction. In the All-Ireland final at Bauravilla, Skibbereen, on Saturday 8th July 1989 her performance was virtually unbeatable when she gained a last shot victory over reigning champion Delia Buckley who bowled superbly in an effort to retain her title. It was the first win by a northern player in the Under 18 championship since its inception four years earlier and Geraldine McCluskey, delighted at her success, was young enough to defend the title the following year. And that she did. In resisting a very strong challenge by Paula Gillespie in the provincial final she then faced another very young bowler who was exceptionally skilled and surprisingly strong in her bowling ability. At only fourteen years old, Shirley McAuliffe, Glanworth, Co Cork had been highly impressive in her win over Mary Browne, Gaeltacht, in the Munster final at Monkstown when she led from start to finish to win by a bowl of odds. The All-Ireland final at Armagh on Saturday 4th August 1990 had everything that is good in the sport; two particularly sporting contestants; excellent bowling by both players; an exciting contest; courageous perseverance; and history being made in the process. Geraldine McCluskey had retained her All-Ireland Womens Under 18 title, the first to do so, and covered the course in an unprecedented fifteen shots with young Shirley McAuliffe, who won many admirers for her sporting demeanour and consistent bowling, less than a bowl in arrears.

The same Shirley McAuliffe was an unfortunate loser in the 1991 Munster Under 18 final at Ovensbridge when she was beaten on the final throw by just fifteen metres. But the winner that day, Sharon O'Driscoll, at only fourteen years old, was a most promising bowler whose coolness in action was surpassed only by the speed and class of her bowling. That was the nature of the challenge facing Geraldine McCluskey, Armagh, as she pursued a record three in a row National titles following her last shot win over Paula Gillespie in the Ulster final. It was a great final at Ballingeary on Saturday 13th July 1991 as first McCluskey set the pace only to be challenged for the lead in the closing stages as O'Driscoll fought back. A tremendous penultimate shot by Sharon O'Driscoll made all the difference and it set her up for the lead and eventual victory in her first All-Ireland final appearance.

The Womens Senior final in 1991 was decided by the narrowest of margins. Rosheen Mackle had again beaten all opposition in Ulster, including the experienced Assumpta Cullen in the provincial final, and in the All-Ireland final at Armagh on Saturday 3rd August 1991, the Munster challenger was Mary Brady who had been given a close run by Orla Galvin in the provincial final at Gloun. In a great finish to the National final it was less than a metre that divided the pair at the end of the score in which Mary Brady had just failed by that minimal margin to get to the mark reached by Rosheen Mackle on her final throw. The victory marked a ten year period of Womens Senior championship bowling during which Rosheen Mackle had won seven Ulster titles and gained All-Ireland Senior honours in two of those successful years.

The closing stages of the Ulster Under 18 championship in 1992 was down to five exciting players in Shauna Gribben, Toni O'Reilly, Shauna Powell, Fiona Cullen and Caitriona Powell. The Munster champion that year was Caitriona O'Rourke,

Rylane, who has one of the most delightful styles with a composed method and manner of bowl delivery that matches the poise of her overall playing performance. But in Caitriona Powell, Drumbreda, who won through in Ulster, she was faced with a fit and eager opponent who had also reached the final for the first time. Played in Armagh on Sunday 2nd August 1992, it was Powell who first went a bowl up but then a good recovery by O'Rourke brought the margin down to twenty metres before the Armagh girl reasserted her position to stay in front for a win on the final throw. There was consolation for Caitriona O'Rourke later in the year when at the Bol Chumann Na hEireann Awards dinner in the Blarney Park Hotel in October she was deemed to be most accomplished female exponent of the game in 1992 and presented with an award for that distinction.

The Senior final that same year had produced something special. The two senior contestants had clashed in a close and exciting National Under 18 final the previous year. Geraldine McCluskey who had produced a classy performance in the Ulster final to oust Rosheen Mackle, was poised for her first senior title. But causing a tremendous stir in Munster was Sharon O'Driscoll, west Cork, who, at fifteen years old was out performing many experienced players, including Susan Barry in a semi-final at Ahiohill, and the next big assignment was Sandra Dempsey, Carbery, who had beaten Shirley McAuliffe at Macroom. That Munster final at Lyre, near Clonakilty was an exceptional encounter. The score drew a record crowd and the bowling by each player was superb. In the end it was O'Driscoll's superior power that consistently pushed her ahead for a clear win to maintain an unbeaten championship record. The All-Ireland Senior final at Ballingeary on Saturday 11th July 1992 had all the promise of a thriller. Geraldine McCluskey, a particularly fine player with St Brigids Camogie team in Armagh, and one of the best prospects in Womens bowling anywhere, was up against the youngest ever Munster senior champion but one who was unbeaten and had a considerable advantage in speed and match practice. And the tense final went to a last shot showdown. It was a late rally that brought McCluskey back to overhaul O'Driscolls early lead and in a dramatic finish the Armagh woman just got there by the narrow margin of two metres. There were ecstatic scenes as Geraldine McCluskey's supporters celebrated her first National Senior title win but alas it was short lived revelry. James Reilly, an uncle of Geraldine, who had been her mentor throughout a successful bowling career, died at the Cork venue a short time after conclusion of the score his niece had just won. It was a traumatic experience in reversed emotions for young Geraldine and a tremendous shock to all followers of the sport. The remaining National finals scheduled for the venue were automatically cancelled. James Reilly had been a character in his own inimitable style and his loss was sadly felt. At his funeral in Armagh the Chairman of the Northern Branch, An Bol Chumann Na hEireann, John Gribben, in a becoming departure from normal routine, paid fitting tribute to James Reilly in a graveside oration.

The following year held little bowling interest for Geraldine McCluskey. It was the opposite for Cork's Sharon O'Driscoll. The Drimoleague girl regained the Munster Under 18 title in 1993 when she won the provincial title after resisting a very strong challenge by Karen Daly at Reenascreena. In Ulster the surprise Under

Rosheen Mackle delivers the bowl in the 1991 All-Ireland Women's Senior Final at Armagh.
Photo : Ann McManus/Irish News

Geraldine McCluskey, Armagh is carried shoulder high by enthusiastic supporters following her victory in the 1992 All-Ireland Women's Senior Championship Final at Ballingeary, Co. Cork.
Photo : Denis McGarry

Caitriona Powell, Armagh, breaks off with her first shot in the 1992 All-Ireland Women's Under 18 Final.
Photo : Denis McGarry

Dr. Mike Bull, Fitness Professional

18 winner was Majella Mallon, Keady, who had beaten Fiona Cullen, Rock, in the provincial final but the National test was too much for her. Played at Ballingeary, Co Cork on Sunday 11th July 1993 the vast difference in playing experience and bowling strength between the two contestants was a telling factor as Sharon O'Driscoll won the All-Ireland Under 18 title for the second time with relative ease. A clear manifestation of Sharon O'Driscoll's bowling superiority was her success in the Munster Senior championship the same year. In taking that title she was in a line for a unique double in the 1993 Womens championships. Paula Gillespie, Armagh, had won the Ulster title over Rosie McClelland, Tassagh, and the All Ireland final at Armagh on Saturday 31st July had attracted special interest. Among the spectators was fitness professional Dr Mike Bull who directed the filming of bowling excerpts including action shots of Sharon O'Driscoll. The filmed television report was presented on 'UTV Live' four days later when Mike Bull focused on the physical preparation necessary for effective participation in the sport of road bowls. There could have been few better subjects than Sharon O'Driscoll. Despite being forty metres in arrears in the All-Ireland final as Paula Gillespie set the pace right up to the three-quarter stage it was the evident fitness and superior bowling strength of Sharon O'Driscoll that began to take precedence as she finished by far the stronger to win the National Senior title for the first time. To do so in the year that she had also won the National Womens Under 18 title was a marvellous personal achievement and marked the accomplishment of a unique double that will survive many attempts at emulating the feat. And as if to underline the supremacy of her bowling skill Sharon O'Driscoll was again back in the All-Ireland Under 18 final of 1994. Her opponent in the National final at Cathedral road Armagh on Saturday 30th July was the All-Ireland champion of two years earlier, Caitriona Powell, Drumbreda, who had beaten Mary O'Hagan, Ballynahonebeg, in the Ulster final. It was Caitriona Powell who set the early pace in the All-Ireland final with a good lead on the first two shots but a mistake surrendered the advantage and from that to the finish it was the accomplished bowling of Sharon O'Driscoll that dominated as she went on to win yet another National title in impressive fashion.

A number of very young players again contested the 1995 Womens Under 18 championship and one of these, Fiona Cullen, Rock, was the ultimate provincial champion when she won a great final against Bernice Gribben, Farmacaffley. Both players had been particularly impressive in their attitude, presentation and bowling ability but it was the steadier play of Fiona Cullen that gained her the title. In the All-Ireland final at Dunderrow near Kinsale on Saturday 8th July 1995 that consistently good standard was less than sufficient to cope with the bowling strength of the Munster champion, Kathleen Cooney who adapted better to the course but even then was required to produce an excellent final throw to ensure victory.

The Womens Senior championship final in 1994 had brought two familiar contestants to the fore when four times National champion Gretta Cormican was back along with Armagh's Geraldine McCluskey who had two Under 18 titles and one Senior crown to her credit. The weather conditions at Bandon on Saturday 9th July 1994 were the worst imaginable for road bowling and as a spectacle the National Women's final was seriously diminished. But that fact didn't detract from the fur-

Caitriona O'Rourke, Rylane, Co. Cork, one of the supreme stylists in the game of Road Bowling.
Photo : Denis McGarry

Susan Cullen, Rock, Armagh, at the start of the 1995 All-Ireland Women's Senior Championship Final.

Agnes O'Gorman, Cork, is greeted by her supporters at the finish of a thrilling contest in the 1995 All-Ireland Women's Senior Final at Armagh.

Gretta Cormican, pictured here in the 1994 Senior League at Crossbarry, has established a superb personal record in Road Bowling ever since the All -Ireland Women's Championships were first introduced in 1981.
Photo : Denis McGarry

ther success achieved by Gretta Cormican who registered another title on her impressive list after she mastered a score in which Geraldine McCluskey was rarely seen to her full potential.

The Womens Senior championship in Ulster was seen at its best in 1995. There had been a series of excellent scores in which the potential for championship success was clearly evident in the performance of many contestants. The final was down to Susan Cullen, Rock, and Bernice Gribben, Farmacaffley, and in these two contestants the score had everything; two youthful players, each fully committed; both of them thoroughly prepared and appropriately attired; and a single minded approach to the one focus of attention, that of winning an Ulster title and the opportunity of gaining National recognition in Womens bowling. The provincial title went to Susan Cullen. She had played the more consistently of the two and though Bernice Gribben was bowling stronger near the finish Susan Cullen had enough in hand to hold out to the line. It had been a disappointing experience for Bernice Gribben to lose two provincial finals in one season but this committed sportswoman gained early compensation when, within weeks, she had won a County championship medal with St Brenda's Camogie team, Ballymacnab, County Armagh.

The All-Ireland Womens Senior final at Armagh on Sunday 6th August 1995 will long be remembered for its quality bowling and exciting exchanges. Agnes O'Gorman the Munster champion had looked supremely strong in pre match practice but Susan Cullen, who had diligently prepared for the event, was limbering up like someone who was really looking forward to the challenge. It was a great contest. With every shot cheered to the echo the large and enthusiastic crowd was treated to a thrilling score in which the best bowling efforts of one player was instantly matched by the other. Susan Cullen had almost constantly held the lead but it was always going to be close. None more so than at the finish. Only metres separated them for the final throw and on that vital shot it was Agnes O'Gorman who did best to gain a narrow but very exciting win. The title went to Cork but the plaudits belonged to both contestants each of whom had elevated Womens championship bowling onto a new plane which sets the standard to which aspiring bowlers may hope to attain.

The rightful scheduling of Womens championship fixtures within the same programme as that for Mens competitions and the consequent sharing of promotion and support is the way forward for equality in the sport. Arguably women coaches and mentors have more to offer their own sex in bowling guidance and motivation than male counterparts could ever hope to achieve. And hopefully that trend will continue. But equally important is the opportunity to compete regularly and frequently within the midst of high profile fixtures thus providing the essential experience for coping with large crowds and pressure contests.

A number of experienced and competent women bowlers are featured on the recently released coaching video, "Splitting the Sop", which has been commissioned by Bol Chumann Na hEireann. The video contains advice from top coaches and world class players which is aimed at encouraging more young people to participate in a sport which is both physically and mentally challenging as well as thoroughly exhilarating and enjoyable.

The Champions' Classic

The rather ambiguous title to the end of season bowling classic at Ballincurrig in County Cork, which has been attracting generous sponsorship and well merited press coverage since the initial competition in 1985, tends to create in the mind of the uninitiated a perception unconnected with the reality of the sport.

Any mention of the King of the Roads competition may contrive to set minds thinking about anything from long distance lorry drivers to a wandering minstrel. Even Linda McAuley, the experienced broadcaster, when introducing the Morning Extra programme on BBC Radio Ulster on Friday 9th October 1992, considered it pertinent to clarify for listeners that *"down in Cork this weekend there's a search on to find the King of the Roads and its not a karaoke competition nor even a cycle race but the ancient sport of road bowls which has traditionally provided a sporting link between Cork and County Armagh".*

That little ambiguity aside this bowling classic at Ballincurrig near Midleton in the east of Cork county is second only in importance and prestige to the All-Ireland championship finals. The renowned tournament has already completed more than a decade of marvellous competition and efficient organisation with the event growing in stature through each passing year. It is indeed a champions classic. Each participant in the senior bowling event has earned the privilege of contesting the King of the Roads competition either through possession of provincial or National championship titles or alternatively by qualifying from a specific prerequisite tournament which is so testing in its quality as to produce a classic champion in itself.

The inaugural event in 1985 was a modest one by the standard set in subsequent years but even then it was a magnificent promotion. The contestants in that opening classic were the All- Ireland Senior champion Harry Toal, Armagh and World Road Bowling champion Bill Daly, Cork. The overall performance by Daly was in keeping with his bowling status. He had a massive opening drive and went a shot up but Toal came back to draw level after eleven throws. However Daly re-established his dominance and finished in superb fashion to win by two bowls of odds. The first ever King of the Roads title belonged to Bill Daly and the impressive Bank of Ireland Cup was his for a year - at least. In 1986 Daly was automatically accorded a place in the final as reigning champion. But the All-Ireland Senior champion that year was Declan O'Donovan, Bandon, and he was engaged in a semi-final contest with Harry Toal, Armagh, in which the Irish title holder just got through to the final on the last shot of the score. In the King of the Roads final on Sunday 19th October, 1986, Bill Daly was determined to retain his crown but the powerful bowling of Declan O'Donovan denoted a stern challenge if not a possible shock win. The destination of the title wavered precariously within four shots of the finish when O'Donovan took a shot lead but Daly managed to narrow the gap to a mere thirty metres for the final throw. The reigning champions final effort was a massive drive of 300 metres and, despite a particularly fine shot, O'Donovan was denied a significant double by just 15 metres.

Spectators await the shot with the distant guidance "sop" in place and the "road shower" in position a few metres further back.

Photo : Denis McGarry

There was a new dominant figure in the 1987 championships when Seamus Sexton, Banteer, became All-Ireland Senior title holder and a fresh challenger for the King of the Roads title. In the semi-final he recorded a clear win over the 1985 Ulster Intermediate champion Patrick Comiskey whilst Bill Daly was on course for a third consecutive classic title following his defeat of Jim O'Driscoll who had come through from the qualifying tournament. It had been a fabulous year for Seamus Sexton and he underlined his absolute dominance of the sport in that particular season by wresting the crown from Bill Daly with a very impressive two shot win.

The challenge then facing Seamus Sexton was his bid to retain the classic title the following year. He succeeded in the first leg of that endeavour when he beat Bill Daly on the last shot of a semi-final encounter. The other semi-final of 1988 was intriguing. Michael Toal, Armagh, who had just been pipped on the last shot of a brilliant Under 18 supporting contest at the same venue the previous year by Michael Wall, was into the Ballincurrig bowling classic as reigning All-Ireland Senior champion. The man he beat to gain the National title was Mick O'Driscoll and the duel was renewed in a tense and closely contested semi-final score. This time the outcome was reversed. O'Driscoll gained victory on the last shot to go through to the final. That final, on Sunday 16th October 1988, was a gripping event. And it took a classic last shot to determine the destination of the title. The record crowd was spellbound to the final moment. Seamus Sexton's bid to retain the title appeared complete when he laid down a brilliant last shot that few considered surmountable. But Mick O'Driscoll defied all predictions with a truly brilliant effort that surpassed his opponents shot by all of nineteen metres for a dramatic victory. And he was back in the final the following year when faced with the challenge of the 1989 All-Ireland Intermediate champion, James Buckley. Again it was a superb final. Played at Ballincurrig on Sunday 15th October 1989, it was Mick O'Driscoll who had edged to the front but James Buckley demonstrated a steady perseverance to come from behind and take the title by almost a bowl of odds at the finish. And James Buckley retained the title the following year having beaten Eamon Bowen in the semi-final and then gaining the verdict in the final over Pat Butler, the reigning All-Ireland Senior champion, who had defeated Armagh's Harry Toal to reach the conclusive score in the 1990 event.

The undisputed bowling ability of the same two players, James Buckley and Pat Butler, was again evident in the 1991 season when the Ballincurrig classic was down to these renowned exponents of the game. Played at a different venue due to road resurfacing James Buckley was pursuing his third consecutive King of the Road title and had surmounted a testing semi-final score against the reigning All-Ireland Senior champion Michael Toal who went out by a bowl of odds. Pat Butler had come through on a last shot win over Bill Daly to set up a final that promised a thriller. It was all of that. Both players were at their best and it was a mammoth fifth shot that sent Butler into a significant lead. The bowling by both men was faultless as Buckley continued to pressure for an opening but in the end it was he who conceded the odds that determined the result when Butler went a shot up and held it to the finish.

The quality of bowling in the champions classic at Ballincurrig was such that each year the standard of play appeared to supersede anything that had gone before. And 1992 was no different in that respect. There was a strong northern rep-

This particular road shower, Eddie Mallon, Armagh, is in no doubt about the precise direction in which the bowl should be laid down.

Photo : Ann McManus/Irish News

resentation that year. Paul Grimley, Madden, was in as Ulster Senior champion whilst Michael Toal had won through from the qualifying tournament. The prospects for a first Ulster victory were brighter than ever but the semi-final results decreed otherwise. Michael Toal went out by a bowl of odds to Pat Butler and Paul Grimley lost by a wider margin to Tim O'Halloran. The final on Sunday 11th October 1992 was something special. Played from the village out Tim O'Halloran was off to a fine start with some great shots. But there was nothing that Pat Butler didn't equal and even surpass. On the day he was the complete bowler. So assured in his decisions; so unobtrusive in his actions; so perfect in his judgement. The spectators were enthralled. They had seen skilful bowling at its supreme best. It was a measure of Tim O'Halloran's bowling ability that he could stay in touch as well as he did. Towards the end of the last quarter the margin had inevitably increased. The entourage of advisers around Pat Butler had also grown in size and as he paced the play for his next shot they were vociferous in their guidance. If Pat Butler was listening at all he showed no signs of it. Just then an elderly gentleman met him in his path and this time he stopped to listen. Pat Butler engaged the man in quiet and unhurried conversation as the numerous advisers were left standing idly by and almost irrelevant. The elderly man was Tim O'Halloran's father who had unassumingly offered Pat Butler quiet congratulations on the inevitable outcome of the score. It was a considerate moment in the midst of a competitive event. Pat Butler won the score in a record sixteen shots; but he also won the admiration of those who

Pat Butler, Cork, seen here bowling in the 1993 Final at Ballincurrig, has attained a unique record of achievement in the champions classic, "King of the Roads" Tournament.

Photo : Denis McGarry

observed a man whose judgement in sensitivity was as impeccable as that of his bowling.

It was not the only impression he made on the game during that period. Pat Butler went on to set up his own unique record by winning the King of the Roads title for a third consecutive time. He had gained a last shot victory in the semi-final against James Buckley whilst Michael Toal also went through with a bowl of odds win over Kieran Gould. The final, on Sunday 10th October 1993, was the first that Armagh had managed to contest in over eight years and the event created unprecedented interest which lived up to its promise. Toal had a bowl blocked within four shots of the finish but an incredible drive soon afterwards drew tremendous reaction from the crowd and appeared to put him right back into contention. The response from Butler was unbelievable; a perfectly judged bowl, with speed that was almost unreal, amazingly beat the mark. It was enough to conclude the verdict in a brilliant final that was to see Pat Butler gain three classic titles in succession to record a truly magnificent personal accomplishment.

The following year saw Bill Daly back in the final when he accomplished a semi-final win over the holder Pat Butler whose performance on the day was impressive but nonetheless some way short of the flawless play he so often produced at the same venue. Daly had crossed the line in a very credible eighteen shots and was again on course to regain the title that was his in 1985 and 1986. The second semi-final in 1994 saw Michael Toal set the pace in a redoubtable challenge from Michael Gould who always threatened to control but rarely dominated a score in which the Armagh man equalled Daly's semi-final performance of the same day. That equality of achievement was just the perfect advertisement for the final on Sunday 9th October 1994 and the huge attendance was proof of the appeal the fixture held for followers of the sport. The score had its moments of excitement and speculation but the eventual outcome began to take shape when Toal failed to gain full sight at the fourth bend. From then on he was under pressure to regain par with a man who was bowling too consistently to ever look like relinquishing the lead. It was a safe margin that Daly had established and he finished with confidence to win the Ballincurrig classic for the third time.

Another man with his mind set on becoming one of only three bowlers to win the champions classic for the third time was James Buckley who, in 1995, was having perhaps his best ever season in the sport. In a semi-final encounter that was far from faultless he readily compensated with some perfect lofting and his penultimate shot over a difficult ascending stretch of hazardous roadway set him up for the narrowest of wins against Bill Daly when a mere four metres put him into the final. Michael Toal had been particularly impressive over most of the course in the other semi-final until two successive blunders near the finish almost offered the score to Mick O'Driscoll who just wasn't sufficiently close to take full advantage on the final throw. There was an air of optimism amongst northern supporters that, despite being faced with a bowler the calibre of James Buckley, it might well be the year in which Ulster would win the King of the Roads title for the first time. And that expectancy was effectively strengthened right at the outset of the final on Sunday

Michael Toal, Armagh, unleashes a shot in the Final of the 1994 Champions Classic at Ballincurrig as he strives to win the elusive King of the Roads title. ***The spectator on extreme right*** *is Shirley McAuliffe, Glanworth, a superb player in Women's Championship Bowling.*

Photo : Denis McGarry

8th October 1995 when Michael Toal opened with an incredible first shot that gained him very considerable odds and immediately reversed many predictions about the outcome. But in two successive efforts the Armagh man was off target to rapidly forfeit all his lead and James Buckley was soon in front to command the score. Toal was all the time endeavouring to regain lost ground and for a long period through midway they each bowled tremendously with a marvellous succession of lengthy drives but Buckley was giving no ground. He dominated the closing stages to win by more than two bowls of odds. It was James Buckley's third time to win the title and he completes an elite group of three bowlers who can claim that distinction.

The Ballincurrig Bol Chumann and extensive organising committee of the annual King of the Roads Festival of Bowling can reflect with justifiable pride upon a record of promotion and meaningful accomplishment that testifies to the value of commitment and planning. In a gradual realisation they have progressed from a modest initial fixture to a bowling occasion that forms a significant part of the sporting calendar. It is an event which has enhanced the prestige of bowling and engendered magnificent sponsorship as well as gaining quite extensive media coverage.

Throughout the years of this popular bowling classic the organising committee have consistently included very attractive supporting contests which provide excellent competitive opportunities for players in all categories of the sport. In 1995 the committee broke commendable new ground when they included a mixed doubles score on the programme and with womens bowling gaining in momentum and overall appeal it was a timely introduction.

The Castlelyons Pipe Band has, for many years, been a musical feature of the bowling festival at Ballincurrig but that melodic celebration has yet to herald a victory in this champions classic for a bowler from Ulster.

A Random Review of Sporting Distinction

The great bowlers of the very early years had neither the same quality of renowned events or a comparable opportunity for press adulation as nowadays abounds. They are not without recognition though. Thanks to the strong oral tradition which for generations linked the present with the past, and the effort made to commit to print what was known of these great bowlers, their sporting record unpretentiously prevails. The distinction attained by some of the great bowl players of the past can be generally appreciated in this random acknowledgement of sporting achievement.

Michael McCarthy-Quirke: The tall, rangy, incredibly tough bowler from Kilgarriffe near Clonakilty may well have been the best of them all. As early as 1923 the man with the mighty sized hand was lofting the bowl beyond the 80 yard mark. His first really big score was towards the end of 1924 when he played and beat Tim McCarthy of Ring on the Timoleague road. He played Mick Deasy, Kilmacsimon, Bandon, on the famous Clancool road on 17th March 1925 and lost. It was McCarthy-Quirke's only defeat that year and he reversed the result two weeks later. At the same venue, in April and May that year, he beat Tiger Aherne, Pouladuff, and a month later recorded a clear win over Laith Rice of Blackpool. He ended the year with a fine win over Tim Delaney, Fairhill, when in September 1925 the great Michael McCarthy-Quirke had practically a bowl of odds to spare after twenty seven shots over the Clancool course.

James Mackle: A man with a great bowling rhythm and smooth co-ordination in delivering a fast running shot he was one of the skilful players around Armagh in the nineteen-twenties. Born on 10th June 1905, James Mackle lived near the mill on the outskirts of the city at Loughgall road. His first score at fifteen years old was against John Darragh and there was a series of these for years afterwards. He also beat James Daly by one yard in a great contest over the Knappagh road in 1926 and pushed Peter Donnelly to the very last throw on the Moy road in 1927. He was recipient of the Armagh Construction Hall of Fame Award in 1979. James Mackle died on 9th March, 1980.

Denis O'Donovan: The man from Fishers Cross, whose first major score was against Flor Crowley at Miltown in 1950, commanded tremendous support from all over West Cork. He was long regarded as the only serious challenger to Mick Barry, the greatest living exponent of the game. He played and beat Barry in the first Senior championship in 1954 at Dublin Hill, the renowned bowling road for the large contingent of players and spectators from Cork city. It was a memorable finish in which Denis O'Donovan's twenty seven shots equalled a record long held by Jack Murphy. There was great sporting rivalry between O'Donovan and Barry and they met frequently in tremendous bowling contests. A massive crowd gathered for

Denis O'Donovan

John Darragh

a challenge score between the pair at the Miles near Clonakilty in August 1959 when O'Donovan won by three bowls of odds. He was rarely, if ever, beaten at the Miles venue but for all that the treasured Senior Championship title remained elusive. He lost a Munster Senior championship final to Mick Barry at the High Road in 1962 and was thwarted of a Vintage title by the same player at Crossbarry in 1994. Widely acknowledged as the greatest player never to have won a Munster Senior title Denis O'Donovan was recipient of the Dairy Services Hall of Fame Award in 1992.

Johnny Darragh: One of the classy players of his time it was claimed by many that Johnny Darragh could deliver the most deceptive bowl which had the appearance of lacking power but invariably exceeded the distance achieved by numerous more forceful bowlers. Such was the style and economic delivery of the tall and lean bowling champion from Ballycrummy near Armagh for whom it was claimed few players of his era could ever hope to beat. He had many successes against top players but was a modest man who rarely explored his notable achievements and yet was ready to acknowledge the number of times he was beaten. A man with a wonderful temperament, and one particularly suited to the challenging nature of road bowls, he commanded the respect of a dedicated group of supporters who never wavered in their loyalty to him. Johnny Darragh, who died on 4th January 1985, was a recipient of the Armagh Construction Hall of Fame Award in 1980.

Tim Delaney: There have been few greater bowl players than Tim Delaney. And the game has seldom produced a finer sportsman. The pride of Fairhill, and likewise admired through every area in Ireland where the sport is played, he was one of the first great bowlers to bring a special art to the accepted skill of bowling. A man who always claimed that two moderate but accurate shots were more valuable than a spectacular scattered loft, he practised for hours in the Fair Field to improve his accuracy. And he could loft with the best. He once beat Bill Bennett with a loft of 76 yards at the park in Blarney. But bowling on the road was Tim Delaney at his most splendid. He beat the same Bill Bennett in a marvellous score at Clancool in 1928 and also in September that year was seen at his most impressive, at Knappagh near Armagh, in a historic victory over Peter Donnelly, Rock, who was one of the great northern bowlers of all time. Three years earlier, in September 1925, he lost to Michael McCarthy- Quirke in a spectacular score where each of them virtually matched shot for shot. One of Tim Delaney's earliest scores was against Jerome Collins of Blarney and he recorded a twenty yard win over Eamon O'Carroll at the opening of the Passage West bowling tournament. Even in his old age Tim Delaney continued to be a formidable figure on the bowling roads. At a special function in Midleton Co Cork on Friday 11th November 1977, Tim Delaney of Fairhill was presented with a suitably inscribed Cup to commemorate the countless bowl playing victories he achieved throughout his bowling years. Tim Delaney died in May 1985.

Tim Delaney

Andy Mallon

Andy Mallon: One of the most principled individuals in the game of road bowls or any other facet of life, was Andy Mallon of Tullygoonigan, a lifelong advocate for the sport and a renowned player over many years. A natural stylist in his compact delivery of the bowl he was a formidable opponent at the highest level of competition. An authority on the sport, without ever claiming to be one, his considered analysis of any event was totally objective and highly respected. Andy Mallon, who received the Armagh Construction Hall of Fame Award in 1989, died on 8th July, 1994. This tribute by 'B.T.. was published in the local provincial newspapers.

The bell of Saint Colm Cille's Church at Knockaconey near Armagh pealed out over the townlands of this rural parish area as 'Andy', a dear friend to the entire community, was gently laid to rest. It was an occasion which evoked nostalgic memories of the life and work of the unique individual that was Andy Mallon of Tullygoonigan, a man widely known, respected and revered for his humble nature and formidable talents.

Andy Mallon was special. By way of his dignity and calming courtesy he had endeared himself to everyone fortunate enough to have met him. So too had the skilful nature of his work ensured that he had earned the respect and admiration of all those who appreciated creativity and perfection. Andy performed many skills in his long and arduous working life- and he was expert in all of them. He was one of the few remaining truly competent thatchers in Ireland. It was an art at which he was particularly and painstakingly skilful and his work in this capacity can be seen and admired in many parts of the country.

Andy Mallon was regarded by many as a constructional genius whose innovative creations in this and other countries are a monument to the man's colossal achievements. And yet the extreme modesty of the man was never remotely affected. Andy was so gentle and serene as to be truly exceptional.

Andy Mallon's interests were many and varied. He had a particular affinity for music and gaelic sport, and was a former recipient of the Hall of Fame Award in the traditional sport of Road Bowls. It is not without significance that on the day on which Andy was laid to rest, one of his fellow parishioners was contesting the All-Ireland Senior Road Bowls Final in County Cork.

Andy Mallon now rests alongside the beauty and serenity of the Church of Saint Colm Cille which he helped so much to build. He had a very significant involvement in creating what is now the distinctive shape, character and strength of Saint Colm Cille's Church in his native and beloved area of Knockaconey. As the bell in its lofty tower continues to toll in the heart of this rural setting, the entire community, of all ages, will readily acknowledge a deep gratitude to the extraordinary nature of the noble gentleman that was Andy Mallon.

Red Crowley: A magnificent bowl player particularly throughout the nineteen thirties when he virtually dominated the sport for a considerable period. A native of Bandon, Co Cork, he lived at Clancool Terrace in the town for many years. Red Crowley shared wins in scores with Tim Delaney at Cloghroe. He is distinctly remembered in the north for his great bowling exhibition against Peter Donnelly, Rock, when he won a fine score over the renowned Knappagh road near Armagh in 1932 at a time when his unrelenting expertise was at its very best. Among his many additional sporting interests were hurling and gaelic football in which he gained medals with teams from Bandon and Carbery. Redmond Crowley died in May 1967 at a relatively young age.

Pat Lyttle: Always a committed and determined player who consistently advocated proper mental and physical preparation for any score even in the days when bowlers, whose sporting attire was virtually indistinguishable from the spectators, placed little emphasis on such fitness. Pat Lyttle grew up with the sport and his first series of competitive scores was in doubles with Jim McVeigh against Andy

Mallon and Eddie McArdle in the winter of 1934. He often played Bill George on the Loughgall road which was a virtual training ground for many great players of that era. Over the years Pat Lyttle had many contests with players like Barney Rafferty, Gerald Ward and Pat Coulter. They were the days when scores were randomly planned and the frequency of challenges usually occurred in a series until such time as one or other opponent decided it was enough. Pat Lyttle, who died in June 1987, and who was recipient of the Armagh Construction Hall of Fame Award in 1982 rarely considered he had enough of any challenges in the game he loved to play.

John McGrath: The best man in Cork city and district around 1900 it has often been claimed. Certainly one of the most famous bowlers of all time, John McGrath from Blackpool, had spectacular wins over Ger Driscoll in a score from Waterfall to Crossbarry in July 1898 and three months later beat James Barrett in a contest from Looney's Cross to Abbey Bridge. In October of 1901 he beat John Buckley, Waterfall, by a bowl of odds and one of his more significant wins was the two shot defeat of Denis 'Sonny' O'Leary at Clancool in October 1902. The great John McGrath is the subject of an oil painting by Everett Linehan in a well known hostelry, "The Bowlers Rest" in Blackpool, Cork city. It is interesting to note that paintings by the Armagh artist John B Vallely, depicting "The Armagh Bullet Thrower" adorn several private and business premises in the Primatial City and elsewhere in the country.

Michael Toal

Michael Toal: A little piece in the midst of a weekly column on road bowls in the *Armagh Observer* records that on Sunday 17th February 1980 at the Blackwatertown road "there were cheers to the echo and hats in the air when Mick Toal made a comeback after more than thirty years in response to appeals for yet another score; watched by his five sons and many old followers of the game the soft spoken Mick took up the challenge and proved that he still retains a lot of the champion class associated with his early years in the sport."

He played many other scores, most of them in the nineteen forties and some more for a long time after that. There were no trophies then and little press coverage of bowling events however appealing to the followers. Michael Toal was one of a group of enthusiasts who helped raise funds for the purchase of the first Armagh Bowls Cup which was eventually competed for in 1953. It was very different to the night in 1988 when he received the Armagh Construction Hall of Fame Award amidst a huge display of Cups for presentation to successful bowlers of that time. It was fitting that in the year Michael Toal got the award his grandson of the same name won his first All-Ireland Senior title and in doing so became the youngest ever player to achieve that honour. Michael Toal died on 15th January 1990.

Donie O'Sullivan: Affectionately known as "Buzzer" O'Sullivan he was at his best in bowling through the late nineteen thirties. He has the distinction of being the first player to throw the then 20 year old Mick Barry in a major senior score when the two met at Whitechurch in 1939. The man from Sunday's Well in Cork played and won many scores including the Whitechurch Tournament in 1940. One of his surprise defeats was as a veteran in July 1955 when he lost to Tim Mulcahy who, as a much younger player, had won the Fairhill Intermediate Tournament in 1939. The tenacious bowling of Donie "Buzzer" O'Sullivan won for him a great deal more scores than many of his peers and he ranks among the greatest of his era.

John Rafferty

John Rafferty: There has been a solid and lasting tradition of road bowls in Madden, Co Armagh and it was people like John Rafferty who consolidated that lore with consistent bowling performances that rated with the very best. Described in the national daily newspaper, The Irish News, following his death in December 1988, as "one of Ireland's most renowned road bowls players" he was considered virtually unbeatable on his home course near Madden. And as if to prove the point at the same venue during his veteran years, in November 1968, he played and beat Dick Burke but more significantly actually covered the course in the same number of shots as did two senior players on the very same day. Undoubtedly one of the most skilful players in the sport he had an independent approach to his game and often chose to play the centre of the road when most others favoured the side. The difference is he could hold the bowl there just as he did with his huge Madden following which he was always able to maintain however distant the venue. John Rafferty received the Armagh Construction Hall of Fame Award in 1985.

Jimmy Mahony: Another great Blackpool player of the nineteen twenties. He was one of those with a magnificent loft when the circumstances demanded that particular skill. To play at all against the great Michael McCarthy-Quirke was almost a criterion for stardom but Jimmy Mahony actually led the Clonakilty maestro for a long way in a magnificent score in 1925 and was poised for a remarkable victory when he had the prospect of that distinction suddenly wiped out in a brilliant finish by his opponent. He had a very strong bowl but with all that was one of the great stylists in the game and this feature of his play was evident at Clancool near Bandon when he twice played Con Keane of Drimoleague. Jimmy Mahony is regarded by many to have been one of the finest bowlers of all time.

Paul Feighan

Paul Feighan: A quiet man from the Keady Road district of Armagh, Paul Feighan played a great number of scores in the nineteen twenties and thirties but talked very little about any of them. He much preferred to discuss the qualities of other bowlers and was an astute judge of those when his opinion was sought. That evaluation he was able to do quite expertly until recent years for he attended scores involving all ages and in every championship. Many of Paul Feighan's best scores were against Bill George, Gerald Ward and Jim McVeigh but he was more at ease reminiscing about other great men of the past and of these he considered Tim Delaney of Cork to be one of the real specialists. It was the precise accuracy of Tim Delaney's "bullets" that most impressed Paul Feighan and that was a quality the Keady Road man himself possessed even though he could rarely be got to admit the fact such was the modesty of the man. Paul Feighan received the Armagh Construction Hall of Fame Award in 1987.

Joe McVeigh: A man who was everything to road bowls in the north for more than thirty years. The undisputed northern champion of the late nineteen forties and throughout the fifties he retired from the sport in 1962 but was urged to make a comeback and his return coincided with a revitalisation in the game. He played his first score when just sixteen and was still bowling in his mid-forties. The only player in northern bowling to have had an official supporters club he continued to provide them, and all spectators, with the thrill of his bowling action for the early part of the newly inaugurated All-Ireland Senior championship before he finally retired from competitive bowling in 1966. He was recipient of the Armagh Construction Hall of Fame Award in 1983. Joe McVeigh died on 26th July 1990. This is part of a tribute by 'B.T.' which was published in the local provincial newspapers.

> *For those of us who are acquainted with the bowling prowess of that great and popular sportsman Joe McVeigh his passing will have evoked memories of a man who almost made this unique sport his own. Joe McVeigh had been a marvellous champion. The scores in which he played had an awe about them that intrigued the younger spectator and thrilled the more experienced observer of the game. Enthusiasts will forever recall the detail of his great contest with Mick Barry at the renowned Knappagh road in 1954. And less than two years later the exciting and victorious return game at Cloghroe, Co Cork. Joe McVeigh had been the first Armagh player to travel to Cork and take on the might of the southern exponents in the sport. By doing so he had set records and standards that many northern players have since striven to emulate. Had fully organised championships existed throughout the bowl playing or bullet throwing career of Joe McVeigh the records would now reveal a champion who had few peers. The splendid skill, subtle strength, simple style, and exhilarating achievements of that great exponent of road bowls continues to form the basis of so much present day discussion when some of the great scores around the roads of Armagh are recalled and debated.*

Aspirations of the Young Bowler

In the early days of road bowling it would appear that most players of the time had attained a certain maturity of years and gradual inculcation to the sport before engaging in the competitive aspect of the game. All that has now changed. Local tournaments and National championships presently cater for players at a very early age and it is one of the more fascinating experiences to witness young bowlers seize the opportunity to hurl the bowl and in doing so to develop a technique and style of delivery that offers them optimum effectiveness.

For many years now youngsters have been encouraged and enabled to participate in competitions which provide them with personal enjoyment and due media acknowledgement of their achievements. The Under 16 championship has, for thirty years, been a significantly motivating factor in encouraging young people to participate in the sport. So too have many clubs which have constantly operated a youth policy and ensured regular press coverage for their endeavours. A great number of clubs in the south have been doing this for many years. In the north there are some clubs which have been exceptional in this regard. Notable amongst these has been the Rock Club on the outskirts of Armagh City. Since before 1980 they have been committed to involving very young players and have never deviated from that worthy and successful policy. So too has the Keady and Tassagh Clubs which have not only garnered a significant group of young enthusiasts over the years but also nurtured and coached many of them to a prominent level of competition and ultimate All-Ireland honours in their grade.

The Under 14 All-Ireland championship, which was launched in 1982, has provided a necessary opportunity for bowlers in this category of competition and serves as an inspiration to the young players of that age. That 1982 championship saw Martin Murphy, north east Cork, come from behind to win the Munster title over mid Cork player Fergus Twohig. The Ulster championship final provided a shock result when the strongly fancied Michael Toal went down to the young Madden player Terence Rafferty. It was two very competent bowlers who contested the Under 14 All-Ireland final at Ballyshonin on 21st August 1982 but Murphy, with the advantage in age and power, was the more impressive and he won virtually unchallenged. It was history in the making. Martin Murphy, from north east Cork, had won the first ever All-Ireland Under 14 championship title.

Emerging from a very competitive field in the 1983 Ulster championship it was again Terence Rafferty, with a semi-final win over Malachy McSorley, and he was joined in the final by Michael Toal following a victory over Paddy Donnelly. This time Toal did capture his first provincial title when superior power enabled him to draw ahead of Rafferty to win comfortably. In the Munster championship Pat Maguire, west Cork, had beaten Denis Buckley at Ahiohill to reach the final. In the

A simple sun visor for these young spectators from Keady and Tassagh at a Road Bowls Championship score in Armagh

other semi-final it was Michael Crowley who came out best against Pat O'Donovan at Templemartin and he went on to win the Munster title. The All-Ireland final at Ballyshonin on Saturday 13th August 1983 proved to be an easy assignment for Michael Crowley. The youngster from Lyre, near Clonakilty, played consistently well throughout to win by a wide margin.

There was quite a stir created in the Munster championship of 1984 when a very young Paul Shannon, an eleven year old from mid Cork, had bowled his way into the provincial final. He had beaten the acknowledged favourite Michael Coughlan at Cottage Road and was joined in the final by Gaeltacht player Brendan Moynihan who had gained a last shot win over Terence Buckley at Aherla. But the provincial final at Ballygurteen proved too much for young Shannon and it was Moynihan who went through to the All-Ireland final at Armagh. In that contest, on Saturday 4th August 1984, over the Cathedral road he was confronted by the fast bowling Mark McSorley who used his speed effectively to win the provincial final against Conor Donnelly of Ballynahonebeg, a player noted for his great delivery style and consistent accuracy. Despite his great bowling reputation Brendan Moynihan made a poor start and Mark McSorley, Drumcairne, was in command from that point to calmly go two shots up for a clear win.

The Ulster Under 14 final of 1985 brought two more young bowlers to the fore when Declan Toal, Grange, beat Stephen Druse, Rock and Liam Gribben, Farmacaffley, defeated Ben Mullan, Lisadian. That provincial final saw Toal into a two shot lead only to concede it to the cool, accurate and strong finishing Gribben, But all those attributes were less than sufficient in the All-Ireland final at Whitechurch on Saturday 17th August 1985 when Cork's Peter O'Riordan held a wavering lead until the last quarter over which he bowled magnificently to gain a clear win against a courageous Liam Gribben.

In the early days of road bowls there had been no tradition of the sport in the Newtownhamilton area of Co Armagh but when Dick Burke came to the primatial city as a teacher in 1964 he immediately took a keen interest in the game and very soon became an advocate for the sport in the south Armagh area in which he then resided. A number of high profile exhibition scores had been arranged for venues in the area and a series of tournament events ensured a consistent bowling presence with commensurate local press coverage serving as sustenance to the innovation and continued development of the sport in that particular region. Dick Burke was Chairman and press correspondent of the Newtownhamilton club for a number of years and on the death of Henry Neary in 1967 he was elected Chairman of the Northern Branch of Bol Chumann Na hEireann and retained that position for the following three years.

The perseverance of local enthusiasts had its rewards for the Newtownhamilton area in 1986 when a young player from the club, who had grown up in the midst of unfolding interest in the sport, had won the Ulster Under 14 championship. Damien Rock had faced the formidable challenge of the strongly fancied Linus O'Hagan, Ballynahonebeg, who had impressed every observer of the sport with the compact nature of his efficient delivery and the sheer performance of his quality bowling. It was a brilliant score with all the excellence of a closely contested and sporting event of the greatest essence. The nature of that provincial final victory, albeit an exceptionally narrow one, had raised hopes that Newtownhamilton was on the verge of recording its first National bowling title. The Munster Under 14 final had been won by William O'Driscoll who had a bowl of odds to spare over Derry O'Donovan at Ovens Bridge in a good contest. The All-Ireland final at Armagh on Sunday 3rd August 1986 did indeed provide a historic outcome. Damien Rock led at the finish by almost a shot to win his own special award and provide Newtownhamilton with its first National title in road bowling.

The following year it was Christy Buckley who had come through in Munster but he was faced with another exciting prospect from Ulster in Michael Rafferty, Madden, who had emerged from a final involving the two exceptional players in the category that season, himself and Tassagh's Eddie Carr. It was yet another National win for northern youngsters in the All- Ireland final at Whitechurch on Saturday 11th July 1987 when a bowl of odds separated the pair at the finish after Rafferty got clear of Buckley near the end of what had been a closely contested score.

The nature of Eddie Carrs performances indicated he had title prospects at a young age but the 1988 campaign saw him experience defeat for the second successive year at the provincial final stage. Paul Druse, Armagh had been impressive in taking the Ulster title but in Donal O'Riordan, Bantry, he was confronted by a Munster champion who had been exceptionally strong in his run of championship wins. And it was that notable strength which saved the outcome for him in the All-Ireland final at Tassagh on Sunday 31st July 1988. O'Riordan had dropped almost a shot behind the consistent bowling of Druse but the Bantry youth laid down three powerful shots in a finishing onslaught which reversed the margin at the line.

Christy Santry, Carraigtwohill, An Bol Chumann Executive, presents the Cup to 1988 All-Ireland Under 14 champion Donal O'Riordan, Bantry. In the centre is National Finalist Paul Druse, Armagh.

Two fine young prospects contested the Munster Under 14 final of 1989 when Gerard Murray succeeded in edging out Trevor O'Meara for the provincial title. The Ulster underage scene was no less impressive. Raymond Green from Madden had beaten Seamus McKee, Armagh, in a thrilling tussle for the northern title, and the All-Ireland final at Bauravilla near Skibbereen on Saturday 8th July 1989 was viewed with intriguing promise. The impressive run of consistently accurate bowling by Greene was maintained into the National final and he build up a lead of almost two bowls over Murray which he held to the line for a most convincing win.

A very fine shot to beat the finishing line was the deciding factor in the 1990 Munster final when Gaeltacht representative Alan O'Shea just managed to gain a narrow win at Gloun over mid Cork player Denis Murphy. But he was to realise the experience in reverse in the All- Ireland final at Armagh on Sunday 5th August 1990 when Paul Rafferty, Madden, who had beaten Michael Rock, Newtownhamilton, in the Ulster final, just got in to snatch victory on the final throw. O'Shea had led by a slender margin throughout an excellent contest but the score, and the title, went Rafferty's way with the important difference being determined on that vital last shot.

The following season produced some thrilling scores in the Under 14 class. The surprise in Ulster had been a strong young bowler in Barry Hughes, Keady, who had beaten the undisputed favourite for the title, Eamon Cullen, Rock. The Munster final that year was equally impressive. Played at Jagoes Mills it was a bright young find from Fairhill Peter Nagle who got through on the last shot against Michael O'Sullivan of Carbery region. That performance was sufficient to set up the Fairhill youth as acknowledged favourite to win the All-Ireland Final at Ballingeary on Sunday 14th July 1991 but such predictions tended to ignore the capacity of Barry Hughes. In ten great bowls from start to finish the performance by Hughes in that final was truly superb. The quality of Nagles play can also be appreciated when it is recognised that he was actually fore bowl for the final throw but it was then the courage of Hughes was evident when he snatched victory with a tremendous last shot. There was ample compensation for the talented Peter Nagle the following year. He again won the Munster title with impressive play throughout the championship and there was no doubting his favouritism for the National title. His opponent in the All-Ireland final at Armagh on Sunday 2nd August 1992 was a very young Eoin Carragher, Newtownhamilton, who had exceeded all expectations in beating Philip McKeever, Keady, in the semi-final and Austin McKeown, Navan, in the Ulster final. Few considered that he could adequately handle the experienced Peter Nagle and that is how the final unfolded as the margin widened and the Fairhill youth went well clear for a very authoritative win.

After going out at the provincial semi-final stage the previous year Philip McKeever made amends in 1993 by getting over that point against Enda McKenna, Madden, and then going on to take the Ulster title over Raymond Murray, Keady, with a very strong finish. It was in similar fashion that Raymond O'Dwyer, mid Cork, gained a shot win over Gaeltacht player David Tanner in the Munster final at Gloun and consequently the All-Ireland Final at Ballingeary on Saturday 10th July 1993 was wide open for predictions. The bowling strength of each player was evident but it was McKeever who eventually gained a shot lead and despite great play by O'Dwyer he could make no significant inroads on the Keady youth who held sufficient advantage to gain his first All Ireland title.

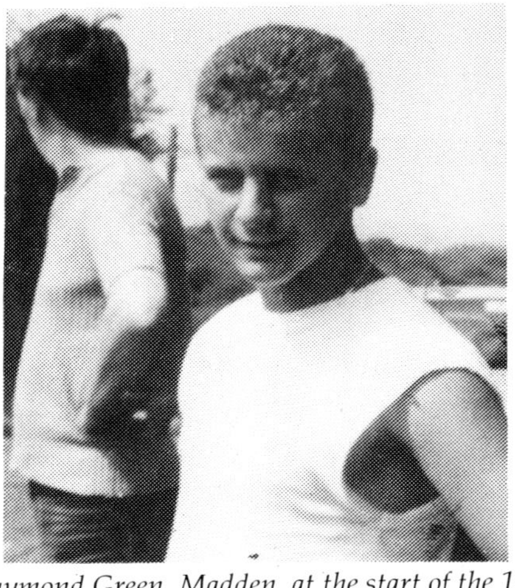

Raymond Green, Madden, at the start of the 1989 All-Ireland Under 14 Final at Skibbereen, Co. Cork.

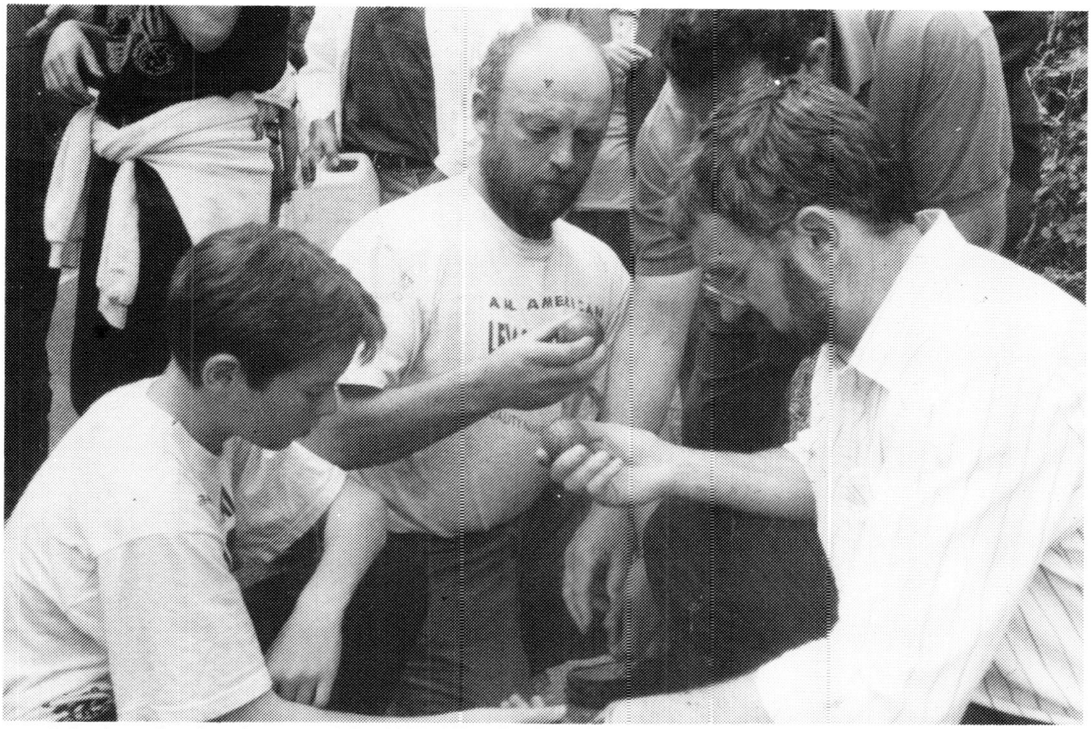

Selecting a bowl at the start of the 1995 All-Ireland Under 14 Final at Dunderrow, Co. Cork, is Ulster Champion, Adrian Lappin, Keady, assisted by Joe Shortt, (centre), and the young player's father, Denis Lappin.

Mick Young, Cork, former Senior Bowler, studies a shot with his son Tim in the Under 14 National Final as his opponent Adrian Lappin gets ready to bowl

In the 1994 championship it was Matthew Grimley, Madden, who came through Ulster in the Under 14 grade and his opponent in the All-Ireland final at Armagh on Sunday 31st July was Paul O'Rourke from Cork. It proved to be relatively easy for O'Rourke as Grimley never got into the consistent pattern of his provincial championship bowling. The following year in Ulster was something special in under age bowling. Many young players, some only ten years old, were contesting the Under 14 championship and the standard of competition was exceptionally high. There had been some thrilling contests each of which caught the imagination of followers to the extent that the focus had shifted to these earnest devotees whose spirited approach was so admirable in its practice. Adrian Lappin, Keady, who was beaten in the provincial final the previous year had made it through again. And there to join him was Fergal Donnelly, Ballynahonebeg, who had narrowly won a thrilling score against another exciting prospect Ronan McKenna. The sheer class of young Lappin was a revelation in the provincial final when he played a faultless score which enabled him to draw away from the less experienced Donnelly for a win that impressed even the most critical of spectators. The All-Ireland final at Dunderrow near Kinsale on Saturday 8th July 1995 was a challenge of a different nature. But the composed and competent Adrian Lappin always had the measure of Cork's Tim Young in a constant lead that was to extend as the score progressed. In the end the margin was two bowls of odds but the more significant feature was the classy performance of a young bowler who, in winning his first All-Ireland title, must be destined for many more National achievements in the ascending grades of championship bowling.

The sporting entertainment provided by young bowlers in the Under 14 championship spectrum has been a wonderful asset to the sport in general and points specifically to a growing interest that must generate champion players in future years. The announcement at the end of 1995 of substantial sponsorship for under age bowling by the Armagh based firm of Philip White Tyres is additional assurance that these young enthusiasts will be given the recognition and support that such honest endeavour deserves.

The Transition Towards Aptness

The Intermediate championship has always been a much respected competition in its own right and yet by its very nature it would be considered to be the means of transition to senior ranks in the sport. But in more than twenty-five years of All-Ireland championships at Intermediate level remarkably few winners of that National title have ever gone on to a repeat success in senior ranks. In fact the opposite would seem to be more the case. Players who have difficulty in sustaining the requirements of senior championship bowling often find the appropriate level of competition in the lower rank and others may experience a short sojourn in the higher grade before reverting to a level of suitability. For all that it is no less competitive and for many years has produced some great bowling contests.

The All-Ireland final of 1986 wasn't one of them though. In the Munster cham-

* *A bowling story in one rare picture. Included in this random photo taken at a Road Bowls score in Armagh are, (from left), Michael Toal, a recipient of the Armagh Construction Hall of Fame Award in 1988; Gerry Donnelly, a member of Bol Chumann Executive Committee for more than 10 years; Linus O'Hagan, Ulster Under 14 finalist in 1986 and Ulster Under 16 Finalist in 1987, Joe Feighan, life-long follower of the sport and brother of Paul Feighan, the Armagh Construction Hall of Fame selection in 1987; Conor Donnelly, Ulster Under 18 Finalist in 1989; and, (at rear), Gerry Boylan, All-Ireland Senior Champion in 1980.*

pionship final at Skibbereen it was cousins John and Mick O'Driscoll who contested the title and the latter named went a bowl up before John O'Driscoll reversed the margin with a superb finish. Donald Gribben had beaten Pat Mallon by a bowl of odds in the Ulster final but he could not repeat the form in the All-Ireland final at Whitechurch on Sunday 13th July 1986 when John O'Driscoll showed tremendous style in winning by a wide margin. Pat Mallon, Grangemore, went one better the following year when he won the Ulster title over Paul Grimley and that provided for a repeat pairing of the 1979 National senior final when it was learned that Johnny Creedon, Nadd, had won the Munster Intermediate crown. He had beaten Tim O'Halloran by a bowl of odds at Ballyshonin in the provincial final and the All-Ireland contest was scheduled for Tassagh on Sunday 2nd August 1987. Creedon had been showing renewed resilience and dedication during that season and he needed it at Tassagh. Pat Mallon had a sixty metre lead for the final throw and with Creedon bowling first he unleashed a tremendous shot against the rising ground. Despite an excellent final effort Mallon fell short of the mark by thirty metres.

In 1988 it was the former Tyrone footballer from Moy, James McCann, who represented Ulster in the All-Ireland Intermediate final. Played at Bauravilla near Skibbereen on Sunday 10th July 1988 a crowd of more than 5,000 had turned up for the event. The main reason being that Denis Scully from Fairhill was back in a National final having beaten Dan O'Halloran by two shots at Ballyvourney. But in James McCann the former senior champion found a very gritty opponent who won the lead on the sixth shot and though Scully recovered to make it over the line in eighteen throws to win the title his opponent was less than a bowl behind.

James O'Sullivan, Cork, All-Ireland Intermediate Champion in 1990. Brendan Roche (right) had, at that point, been more than twenty years an Executive Officer of Bol Chumann Na hEireann

It was only in 1989 that James Buckley re-emerged in adult ranks after a devastating show of power bowling in underage divisions more than five years earlier. But he bowled extremely well to lead all the way in the Munster Intermediate final at Ballyshonin in which he beat Donie Coveney by two shots. That performance alone indicated renewed promise of a bright senior career and he reinforced that expectation in the All-Ireland final at Tassagh on 6th August 1989 when he beat Harry Toal, Armagh by two shots after leading all the way with seventeen great throws.

Donie Coveney had the misfortune to again lose the Munster Intermediate final in 1990 at Ballyvolane when James O'Sullivan took the honours. The Ulster title had been won that year by Paddy O'Neill, Armagh, who had beaten Brian Kiernan, Madden in the provincial final. The Armagh man had a good first quarter in the All-Ireland final at Bauravilla on Sunday 8th July 1990 but a spectacular shot midway through by James O'Sullivan put him all of two shots in the lead and he extended that to the finish as O'Neill gradually faded.

The Junior champion of 1983 Paddy O'Leary made a successful run through the Intermediate ranks in 1991 when he beat Jerry Hegarty at Dunderrow before ousting Mick Young, Drinagh, in the Munster final at Beal na Blath. It was a brilliant display in seventeen shots by the Dungarvan, Co Waterford bowler and it made him strong favourite for the National title. That final was played in Armagh on Sunday 4th August, 1991 with Harry Toal, Armagh, again the Ulster champion. Toal opened well and was soon a shot up but splendid play by O'Leary brought him level. After that it was O'Leary who showed best and with two excellent drives he went well clear to hold the advantage to the finish.

The Ballingeary venue can be a testing one but if ever there was an exceptional record of incredible bowling it must surely rest with Tim O'Halloran, Bandon, who covered that course in sixteen remarkable drives. Three of them, all in succession, were phenomenal. It is little wonder he won the Munster title with that performance in 1992 but what is also surprising is the fact that the beaten finalist Jerry Murphy was only two shots behind, in a display that would have won most scores over the same road. That was the form history confronting Harry Toal who was making his third bid within four years to win the National Intermediate final. It was over that same course at Ballingeary on Sunday 16th August 1992 and the verdict went to the last shot. O'Halloran had gone a bowl up and then Toal took the lead but the Armagh man was sixty metres in arrears for the final throw. Toal put down a very fine shot which looked like gaining him his first Intermediate title but he was thwarted yet again when O'Halloran beat the mark.

The following year saw the 1992 All-Ireland Junior champion Brian Kinchin, Tassagh, challenge for the Intermediate title following his provincial final win against Paddy O'Neill. The All-Ireland final was at Armagh on Sunday 1st August 1993 and Kinchin was considered to be in with a great chance of winning the National title which hadn't been won by any northern bowler in eleven years. Michael Gould had won the Munster final over Jerry O'Leary at Waterfall and the outcome of this one was viewed as evenly balanced. It was all that until within three

Brian Kiernan, Madden, Co. Armagh drives his bowl towards the road shower in the 1995 All-Ireland Intermediate Final at Dunderrow, Co. Cork.

Photo : Denis McGarry

shots of the finish. Only fifteen metres separated the pair at that point but from then to the end it was Kinchin who faltered as Gould improved to record a clear win.

A fine new prospect came through as Ulster Intermediate champion in 1994 when Paul Rafferty, Madden, was the northern standard bearer going into the All-Ireland final at Armagh on Sunday 31st July. His opponent was Andrew O'Leary, Fermoy, who had beaten Aidan Buckley in the Munster final at Donoughmore and on that performance he was strongly favoured to take the title. But all pre-score predictions were well off the mark. Paul Rafferty, who only a year earlier had won the All-Ireland Under 16 championship, bowled with exceptional power and precision to shake off the strong challenge of Andrew O'Leary in going into a shot lead at the three quarter stage and then stretching it to twice that distance at the finish. It was a remarkable achievement for Paul Rafferty and a historic result. For one thing it

A Fairhill Double : The major bowling trophies of 1995 were won by Fairhill, Co. Cork bowlers, James Buckley (right), All-Ireland senior champion and James O'Sullivan, All-Ireland Intermediate Champion.
Photo : Denis McGarry

broke the twelve year losing sequence that Ulster bowlers had experienced in Intermediate ranks since Pat Mallon had won the National title in 1982. But more importantly for Paul Rafferty that outstanding victory had made him the youngest ever All-Ireland Intermediate champion. There are several more titles to be won by this exceptional young player.

The 1995 All-Ireland Intermediate final was the highlight of the programme at Dunderrow on Sunday 9th July when the picturesque area near Kinsale hosted five National finals over the course of the weekend. The venue was well marshalled and thoroughly prepared for the big events. A very large crowd had converged on the start of the Intermediate final between Cork's James O'Sullivan and Ulster champion Brian Kiernan from Madden. But the attendance dwindled as the excitement evaporated. Kiernan had an opening on the first throw but after that he had few opportunities as the Munster champion O'Sullivan set about producing seventeen brilliant shots that took him to the finishing line, no less than three ahead of his opponent, and in a total that would have done credit to any leading senior player in the game.

Perhaps the Intermediate category does produce Senior champions after all.

An action shot of Paul Rafferty, Madden, the youngest ever All-Ireland Intermediate Road Bowls Champion who took the title at Armagh in 1994.

Photo : Harold Ford, Portadown.

The Echelon of Ambition

A considered study of the Under 16 and Under 18 championships in road bowls over recent years provides a reliable insight into the acknowledged quality of the participants and the attractive nature of the competitions as well as the obvious potential for progression to championship honours at higher levels in the sport.

In 1986 the Munster Under 18 title was won by Finbar O'Donovan, east Cork, who had beaten Eddie Murphy at Ballyvolane. The surprise winner in Ulster was Aidan McCreesh, Navan, who pipped Michael Toal on the last shot before going on to win the provincial title against Sean Mallon by a bowl of odds. The surprise element was retained into the All-Ireland final at Whitechurch on Sunday 13th July 1986 when McCreesh won the title on the last shot over O'Donovan. The Under 16 National final that year was at Armagh on 3rd August when Kieran Gould, who had beaten Teddy O'Driscoll in the Munster final at Grange, was opposed by Brian Kinchin who won the Ulster title after impressive wins over Mark McSorley and Martin Mullan. The outcome of the National final was never in doubt over the last quarter when Gould built up a good lead to eventually win out over Kinchin by two shots.

The unfortunate Eddie Murphy was to lose two consecutive Munster Under 18 finals when he was again beaten in 1987 despite being strongly favoured to take the

Aidan McVeigh, then Secretary to Northern Branch An Bol Chumann, presenting the 1987 All-Ireland Under 18 Cup to Michael Toal Armagh, with (on right) National Finalist Michael Wall, Midleton, Co. Cork.

title. He went out by a bowl of odds to Michael Wall at Carrignavor. In Ulster the Armagh county minor gaelic football team had made it to the provincial final on 19th July 1987 and lining out at full forward was Michael Toal, Grange, who had also stormed through the road bowls championship with clear wins over the holder Aidan McCreesh and finalist Damien Gribben. Toal had been granted time off training by the football team management to pursue his second Under 18 bowling title having won the National final at that grade over Brendan O'Regan, Drinagh, two years previously. The All-Ireland final was at Tassagh on Sunday 2nd August 1987 and Toal made no mistake in claiming his second National Under 18 honour when he scored the finishing line almost two shots ahead of Midleton bowler Michael Wall.

The Ulster Under 16 final in 1987 had been reported as the best ever seen in that grade of competition. Liam Gribben and Linus O'Hagan had contested a thrilling score in which they disputed the lead with every shot. The title was decided on the last shot when Liam Gribben gained victory by a narrow margin. The beaten finalist, Linus O'Hagan from the Rock club, was regarded as a classic under age bowler who had a unique style of delivery and a quality of play that was often availed of by mentors of the club as a model for emulation. But for gaining employment in the Channel Isles for a period of time he was destined for National honours in bowling at a young age. Linus O'Hagan, when nineteen years old, tragically died in a road traffic accident on 7th September, 1991, some time after his return to Ireland.

The All-Ireland Under 16 final at Whitechurch in July 1987 was won by the Munster champion Richard Murphy, Cork, who beat Liam Gribben, Armagh by two shots.

The Under 18 National final of 1988 which was played at Bauravilla, near

The young Ulster champions and Provincial Finalists of 1987 are pictured with long serving Northern Secretary to An Bol Chumann Na hÉireann, Aidan McVeigh. Included, (from left), are Eddie Carr, Tassagh; Linus O'Hagan, Ballynahone Beg; Michael Rafferty, Madden; and Paul Druse, Armagh.

Skibbereen, was won by the Ulster champion Mark McSorley, Drumcairne, who beat Mick Carroll of Cork by a safe distance on the final throw. A great bowling prospect had emerged in Cork that year in the Under 16 championship when John Creedon, Gaeltacht, ran up a series of convincing wins showing great confidence and exceptional speed. He had beaten north Cork player Martin Kelleher at Crossbarry and in the Munster final was most impressive in his two shot victory over William O'Driscoll, east Cork at the Ovens venue. Stephen Druse, Ballyheridan, had come through in the Ulster championship beating Liam Gribben in the final at Tassagh. It was over the same course that the All-Ireland final was played on Sunday 31st July 1988 but it was the power and assurance of John Creedon that dominated when he gained a clear win of nearly two bowls of odds.

The same John Creedon was even more impressive the following year in the Munster Under 18 championship. He had beaten Philip O'Donovan by over a bowl at Monkstown to reach the provincial final in which he continued his onslaught by beating the accomplished and polished performer Aidan Walsh of Kilmurray by the same distance at Kilumney. By then John Creedon had been unbeaten in championship scores for more than two years. His opponent in the All-Ireland final at Tassagh on Saturday 5th August 1989 was another exciting prospect, John Kelly, who had won the provincial title that year in great contests with Sean O'Hagan, Rock, in the semi-final and Conor Donnelly, Ballynahonebeg, in the final. The National final was to produce the sensational result of that year's championships. The hitherto unbeaten John Creedon won the first shot impressively but John Kelly, Armagh, settled into some powerfully fast and accurate bowling which first saw him go one shot ahead, then two, and in his best bowl of the entire score on the final throw he consolidated the margin to record a shock two shot win. It was John Creedons first defeat in two years of championship bowling and the astonishing victory by John Kelly marked the fifth National title in succession for northern bowlers in the Under 18 grade.

It was a year in which the Ulster champion in the Under 16 category also won the National title. Played at Skibbereen on Sunday 9th July 1989 it was Michael Rafferty, Madden, who had beaten Paul Druse in the provincial final and he held his stirring form into the All-Ireland final when he won by sixty-seven metres on the last shot over the Munster champion, Vincent Kiely, Cork.

The prestigious Under 18 championship had by then really caught the imagination of road bowls followers throughout the country. Not least for the sheer quality of the bowling in successive championships but significantly too for the persistent dominance by northern bowlers in this always exciting grade of competition. The All-Ireland final of 1990 was tailor made to sustain that intense interest. Michael Rafferty of Madden, who had won a National title at Under 14 grade in 1987 and the Under 16 category in 1989, was chasing the same honour at Under 18 level having beaten Eddie Carr in the Ulster semi-final and Liam Gribben in the provincial final in decisive style. His opponent in the National final was no less powerful. Donal O'Riordan, who had won the All-Ireland Under 14 title at Tassagh in 1988, was Munster Under 18 champion of 1990 having beaten Trevor O'Meara in

Liam Gribben, Farmacaffley, Armagh, winner of the original Henry Neary Trophy in 1987, accepting the award from Aidan McVeigh

Donal O'Riordan, Bantry, Co. Cork, who, in 1990, was the first Munster Champion in over five years to win the All-Ireland Under 18 title, receiving the National Trophy from Brendan Roche, then Chairman of Bol Chumann Na hEireann

the provincial final, a young rising star who had defeated the two most fancied players in the grade, John Creedon and William O'Driscoll. In the National final at Bauravilla, Skibbereen on Sunday 8th August 1990, Michael Rafferty went almost two shots down before staging an amazing recovery which brought him to within fifty metres of Donal O'Riordan with only three shots to go. Rafferty then put in a brilliant last shot which scored the finishing line by twenty metres. O'Riordan had it all to do but he eeked everything from it to gain victory by two metres in a most exciting climax. It may have only been two metres but it was so valuable as to gain a National title for Donal O'Riordan and the first All-Ireland Under 18 title for a Munster champion in five years. There was rapid consolation for the beaten Munster finalist Trevor O'Meara when he won the provincial Under 16 title over Vincent Kiely at Carrig no bhFear and that win put him into the National final against Mark McKeown, Navan, who had beaten Eddie Carr, Tassagh, and then Eugene Loughran in the Ulster final. The All-Ireland final was over the Cathedral road, Armagh on Sunday 5th August 1990 and it was a score that Trevor O'Meara led from start to finish. Guided by the legendary Mick Barry, young O'Meara bowled superbly throughout as he built up a distant lead over McKeown to eventually win by two shots.

Undaunted by that experience, Mark McKeown went into the Ulster Under 18 final the following year and had the title at his mercy. It would have been a shock win but he had only sixty metres to cover on the last shot against Michael Rafferty

Mark McKeown, Navan, Armagh, in the 1992 All-Ireland Under 18 Final at Ballingeary, Co. Cork.
Photo : Denis McGarry

Fergal Carr bowling to the backdrop of Tassagh Viaduct in Co. Armagh.
Photo : Philip Wilson/Ulster Gazette

to win the provincial championship. Somehow he made an amazing blunder and all was lost. The Munster championship of 1991 had seen Declan O'Shea bowl his way through some great scores. On his way to the provincial title he outplayed Conor O'Sullivan by two shots at Lyre and then went clear by the same margin against Thomas Connolly before producing a tremendous second half performance in the final at Ballygurteen to beat William O'Driscoll by nearly two bowls. In the All-Ireland final at Armagh on Saturday 3rd August 1991 the young west Cork bowler Declan O'Shea won the first shot but after that he could do little against the brilliant Michael Rafferty who excelled in his performance to go two shots clear and eventually win by that margin.

The 1991 Under 16 championship in Munster was won by Gerard Murray from the Carbery region. He had lost the National Under 14 final in 1989 but was back with much greater bowling power to win the provincial final against Denis Murphy by a bowl of odds at Dunmanway. In Ulster it was a sturdy young player from Newtownhamilton, Michael Rock, who won the provincial title when he beat Seamus McKee on the last shot. It was the twenty- fifth year of the Under 16 National championship and whether Gerard Murray was conscious of that fact or not he turned in a jubilee performance at Ballingeary on Sunday 14th July 1991 to go well clear of Michael Rock who could never regain a challenging position.

There was little doubt that Mark McKeown, Navan, would again reach a National final and that he did in 1992 when he left all his disappointments behind him to storm through the Ulster Under 18 championship with a concluding win over Eddie Carr in the provincial final. But following through in Munster on a similar course of success was his young rival Trevor O'Meara, Waterfall, whom he had met in the Under 16 final two years earlier. O'Meara, a most consistent and determined bowler, had beaten Patrick Murphy at Bottlehill before surging into an early lead in the Munster final at Ahiohill which cushioned him sufficiently against a late rally by Carberry bowler Liam O'Sullivan. But that was a strategy successfully adopted also by Mark McKeown in the All-Ireland final at Ballingeary on Sunday 16th August 1992 when he was the one to go into a substantial early lead and held it securely to win his first National title with a shot to spare.

The traditional bowling area of Fairhill, long associated with the great Tim Delaney, was represented in the All-Ireland Under 16 final of 1992 when Peter Nagle beat Dungarvan player Jason O'Leary in the Munster final at Bridesbridge. But the Madden area of County Armagh, long associated with the bowling greatness of John Rafferty, was also represented in that final at Armagh on 2nd August when Paul Rafferty, already a National Under 14 champion of 1990, was eager and able for another All-Ireland title. He had beaten Seamus McKee, Armagh - whose eleven shot performance that day would have won any other score - with a devastating display of powerful bowling that was on a par with that of most senior players. Not surprisingly the National final was a great contest. Nagle had gone a bowl up only to be overtaken in a great Rafferty revival. There was only twenty metres in it for the last shot but both of them missed the line. Then Rafferty released a tremendous drive that appeared to put it all over and his supporters weren't waiting to vent their

Donnacha O'Brien, (right front), studies the course at the front of the crowd during the 1995 All-Ireland Finals at Cathedral Road, Armagh.

passion. But through it all, and with great calmness and resolve, Nagle amazingly beat the mark and his fans were understandably ecstatic. A final and a finish that will be long remembered.

If ever a player had developed a pattern of getting to a final but losing out in the title score it was Seamus McKee of Armagh who despite his obvious bowling talent was so frequently thwarted in the ultimate contest. That was his experience again in the 1993 Ulster Under 18 final when a large crowd witnessed a surprise result with Malachy Lappin, Keady, coming through to win by a bowl of odds. In the All-Ireland final at Armagh on Sunday 1st August 1993 the Keady player was faced with the daunting task of taking on Donnacha O'Brien, Drinagh, who had impressed immensely throughout the Munster championship. In an excellent contest Malachy Lappin was leading after the first quarter and it went to the last shot with Donnacha O'Brien just getting the better distance on that deciding throw to win the title.

Being young enough to yet again contest the Under 16 championship there was little to stop Paul Rafferty, Madden, from sailing through the 1993 campaign. Austin McKeown, Navan, had put in a tremendous display in the Ulster final but even that wasn't enough against the brilliant bowling of Paul Rafferty who finished with three magnificent shots to seal the issue. The undoubted talent of Donnacha O'Brien was not enough against Michael O'Sullivan in the Munster final at Lyre when a full shot divided them at the finish. In the All-Ireland final at Ballingeary on Saturday 10th July 1993, Michael O'Sullivan was again impressive but a little short of the great display by Paul Rafferty who went into a shot lead early on and grimly held out to claim the title with a fine finish.

It was becoming almost a preconception. Seamus McKee was back in the Ulster Under 18 final of 1994 but amazingly he again found an opponent who was better on the day. This time it was Conor McGuigan, Tullysaran, who sprung the victory and he was most accomplished in doing so. The reigning All-Ireland champion, Donnacha O'Brien had retained his Munster title and was set on doing likewise with the National crown. The final was at Bandon on Sunday 10th July 1994 and it was the composed Conor McGuigan who went a bowl up after six shots only to find Donnacha O'Brien back on level terms soon afterwards. From that to the finish there was little in it; with McGuigan slightly ahead and bowling faultlessly he just held out to win his first All-Ireland title. It was a first also for the proud Tullysaran club which had been in existence for little over a year and yet had the honour of seeing one of its new discoveries claim a National title.

The exciting style and effective play of Austin McKeown, Navan, was seen to good advantage in 1994 when he beat Philip McKeever, Keady, in the semi-final before going on to win the Ulster Under 16 title against Shane Feighan, Tassagh. The Munster title that year was won by Billy McAuliffe, Glanworth, and in the National final at Armagh on Sunday 31st July a very competitive score ensued. First it was McKeown into a useful lead and then McAuliffe was thirty metres in front after halfway. It was over the final stretch that all was decided when three magnificent shots in succession by the strong finishing McKeown left him a bowl up at the line.

It was in the scorching midday sun of Sunday 9th July 1995 that Pat Spillane, north Cork, and Philip McKeever, Keady, fought out the destination of the All-Ireland Under 16 title. McKeever had beaten Brian McKee, Armagh, in the Ulster final and Spillane was the victor in Munster when he won the provincial title at Gloun by a bowl of odds over mid Cork player Kieran Hurley. The final, at Dunderrow, near Kinsale, was dominated for a long way by Spillane who had won the lead on the second shot but a later mistake let McKeever back in. From that point onwards McKeever gained in strength but it was only on the last shot that Spillane was beaten. It was a second National title for Philip McKeever who had won the Under 14 grade two years earlier.

It has often been claimed that one of the most prestigious competitions in the whole range of championships is that involving players in the Under 18 category. That argument lost no credence with the 1995 championship. Donnacha O'Brien, a skilful gaelic footballer who played at full forward for Clanna Gael in Drimoleague, had won the Munster Under 18 bowling title for the third time in succession despite not being eighteen years old until December 1995. It was a clear indication of his remarkable bowling ability over a sustained period.

Donnacha O'Brien, Cork, (left), and Dermot Gribben, Armagh, at the start of the 1995 All-Ireland Under 18 Final at Armagh

Donnacha O'Brien, Cork, bowling for the finishing line in the 1995 All-Ireland Under 18 Final at Cathedral Road, Armagh.

Photo : Harold Ford, Portadown.

Conor McGuigan, Armagh, did the Tullysaran Club proud when he won the 1994 All-Ireland Under 18 Road Bowls title.
Photo : Harold Ford, Portadown

The driving force of Austin McKeown, Armagh, All-Ireland Under 16 champion in 1994.
Photo : Harold Ford, Portadown.

The contest for the Ulster Under 18 title could not have been more exciting. Darren Oliver, Navan, and Dermot Gribben, Farmacaffley, bowled it out in a score that could only be decided on the last shot. Gribben had got away at the outset and strove to protect his lead but Oliver, with the class and power of a future champion, edged closer all the time and was unfortunate to lose out with a perfectly directed final throw. Dermot Gribben had won his first Ulster bowling title but he was in no doubt about the nature of his opposition in the All-Ireland final at Armagh on Sunday 6th August 1995. Donnacha O'Brien was seeking his second National title and Dermot Gribben, himself equally adept at gaelic football, but noticeably improving with every bowling outing, was fit and eager for the challenge. They both opened well and that set the standard for the rest of the score through which each of them bowled superbly in a thrilling contest. Only metres separated the pair over the last quarter until O'Brien seized an opportunity following a Gribben mistake. But Gribben immediately compensated for the error with his best shot of the score and it was then down to the last bowl with O'Brien holding the advantage. Gribben played perfectly and his big following sensed feasible success only for the bowl to marginally but crucially fail to cross the centre ridge and that left O'Brien with a relatively safe effort to clinch the title. That win marked the achievement of two All-Ireland Under 18 titles for Donnacha O'Brien and the final underlined the competitive nature and exciting exploits of that particular category in championship bowling.

The Attraction of Senior Championship Bowling

The supreme honour in championship road bowling in Ireland is the title of All-Ireland Senior Champion and each year, as the leading bowlers in the country strive to gain that distinction, the resultant competition invariably induces a mounting fascination amongst followers of the sport until the culmination ultimately determines the destination of the National crown for another year.

It is an honour that has evaded a number of accomplished senior players over the years. Not least amongst them are Denis O'Donovan, Fishers Cross, Derry Kenny, Clogheen, and Mick O'Driscoll, Cork. Another player to find the National senior title so tantalisingly elusive is Aidan Toal, Grange, who made his concluding bid for honours in 1986 some nineteen years after he had first contested an All-Ireland senior final. He had beaten Martin Boylan, Harry Toal and Patrick Comiskey, to win his third Ulster senior title and was back with another belated chance of winning the National title. He knew it would be his last. At 42 years old such opportunities rarely renew themselves.

In Munster it was the former Intermediate champion of 1978, Declan O'Donovan, Bandon, who had won the senior title. He had beaten Mick O'Driscoll by a bowl at Monkstown before going on to further impress by winning the Munster final at Kilumney against Michael Buckley by more than two bowls of odds.

The All-Ireland final was over the Cathedral road, Armagh, on Sunday 3rd August 1986 and O'Donovan opened with two powerful shots that immediately had Toal going almost a bowl down. However Toal settled into his rhythm and after fourteen shots the margin was fifty metres with O'Donovan holding the advantage. It was at this point Toal made a crucial error with a misjudged slow bowl and with it went his hopes of winning a National senior title as O'Donovan, putting in an excellent performance, went on to win his first and only All-Ireland senior crown.

The following season was a tremendous one for Seamus Sexton, Nadd, and his run through the Munster championship in 1987 underlined the point. He first beat Pat Butler and later Christy O'Driscoll. In the provincial final at the Miles near Clonakilty it was that versatile sportsman Christy Mullins from Bantry who succumbed to the renewed bowling power of Seamus Sexton whose last shot win, whatever about the quality of the overall score, earned him his second Munster senior title and the first in over six years. The Ulster senior championship was played at venues in Tassagh, Keady, Port Mor and Armagh with the 1987 provincial title going to Gerry Boylan, Lislea, who beat Harry Toal in the final over the Tassagh course.

The All-Ireland final at Whitechurch on Sunday 12th July 1987 was for a long way evenly matched but it was Sexton who figured best and when Boylan put in a poor last shot the margin quickly extended to a bowl of odds. Seamus Sexton had

Declan O'Donovan, Cork, on the first shot of the 1986 All-Ireland Senior Final at Armagh

won his first and only All- Ireland senior title and he did so in a season that was his best ever in the sport.

It appeared as though Seamus Sexton might repeat the feat in 1988 when he beat Pat Butler on the last shot at Shannonvale to go into his second successive Munster final. But opposing Sexton was an old rival who had beaten him on their only two previous meetings. Mick O'Driscoll was also into the provincial final having beaten Michael Buckley at Cobh by a bowl of odds. It was one of the best Munster finals ever, for bowling ability, sheer excitement, and elated reactions. It marked the end of a twenty year wait for Michael O'Driscoll of Commons Road, Cork who had displayed the absolute assurance and confidence of a true champion as he led from start to finish in sixteen great shots to win by a bowl of odds. There were unprecedented scenes of jubilation at the Marsh road, Skibbereen, as O'Driscoll was applauded, shoulder high, by ecstatic supporters.

The Ulster championship of 1988 was less exuberant but it did generate significant interest in the emergence of Michael Toal, Grange, as provincial champion in his first year playing at senior level. He had beaten Harry Toal, Armagh in the final at Tassagh during which he produced some exceptionally long drives.

The All-Ireland final at Tassagh on Sunday 31st July 1988 represented two extremes in youth and experience. Michael Toal, just eighteen years old and Michael O'Driscoll more than twenty years in senior bowling. It was the experienced O'Driscoll who got away to the perfect start with record bowling at the outset. Two shots ahead after only three bowls and even further in front at the end of the first quarter the outcome seemed inevitable. Just then an unbelievable drive by Toal had O'Driscoll taking two shots to cover the mark and shortly afterwards there was just a bowl in it with everything still to play for. It was then that Toal really got going as O'Driscoll gradually became less assured. In no time they were level and entering the last quarter Toal went ahead for the first time on the fifteenth bowl with a magnificent shot from the bridge which sent his supporters wild with enthusiasm. Their buoyancy was maintained when Toal increased his lead with two further powerful bowls and there was just no recovery for O'Driscoll who, amazingly, lost by a bowl of odds in a score which he totally dominated for the first half and appeared virtually certain to win at his ease. There was due recognition for the nature of O'Driscolls defeat. "O'Driscoll accepted his defeat with dignity and honour despite having the experience of losing when it seemed almost impossible to do so", said Aidan McVeigh in the *Armagh Observer*. "The most heart-breaking defeat for O'Driscoll in a twenty-seven year senior career" said Seamus O'Tuama in the *Cork Examiner.*

Few had predicted such an outcome even before the early part of the score was to confirm the majority forecasts. Even with Michael Toal's performances in the European championships, Ulster senior play-offs, and underage title wins, speaking multitudes for his ability, he was still not expected to beat a player of Michael O'Driscoll's calibre. It was a stirring success. Michael Toal had become the youngest ever player to win the All-Ireland Senior championship and the first bowler to take the Under 18 and Senior Championship National titles in successive years. In addition he was one of the youngest players to win the Under 18 championship when he took it for the first time at just fifteen years old. This is how the *Cork Examiner* led into a report of the score on Monday 1st August 1988:

> *Nineteen year-old Michael Toal became All-Ireland senior bowling champion in classic style at Tassagh, Co Armagh yesterday. The Armagh man created history by becoming the youngest ever winner of the championship when he defeated Cork's Michael O'Driscoll. Just one year after taking the Under 18 title the young Ulster champion had to wipe out practically a two bowl of odds lead in his march to victory.*

The *Armagh Observer* devoted a full page to the event in the issue of Thursday 4th August 1988. In his report on the final Aidan McVeigh had this to say:

> *In his first attempt at the All-Ireland senior title Michael Toal brought the Hugh Trainor Cup back to Armagh on a day that few road bowls enthusiasts will ever forget. Taking a gigantic step into senior ranks he became the youngest player in history to take the golden prize in bowling. Even more remarkable was the manner in which his victory was achieved as Toal had been in desperate trouble at a very early stage but stormed back with a vengeance seldom seen. A truly magnificent performance.*

It was an achievement that also made the front page of the *Armagh Observer*. Under a banner headline, "Sporting Success" the issue of 4th August 1988 reported:

> *It has been a week of sporting celebrations in Armagh following the two big weekend stories - Pearse Og winning the County Final and young Michael Toal from the Grange capturing the All-Ireland Senior Road Bowls crown. Heartiest congratulations to both. For Ogs it was a fitting reward for a dedicated group of footballers who have brought such honour to themselves, their club, and their native city.*
>
> *Michael Toal's tremendous achievement is also deserving the highest praise. He has become the youngest exponent ever to win the title. Like football, the game of road bowls in also highly popular and its a pity that both finals clashed on the same day. No doubt because of this many people were forced to make a choice and obviously the football final in the Athletic Grounds suffered as a result.*

Following such widespread acclaim for his bowling ability it was little surprise that Michael Toal retained his Ulster title in 1989 with a clear win over Harry Toal who had lost a lot of the speed and authority that marked his bowling of earlier years. In Munster it was Declan O'Donovan, Bandon, who had regained the Munster title following wins against Michael O'Driscoll, Bill Daly and a last shot victory over Seamus Sexton at Inchigeela.

For the All-Ireland final at Bauravilla near Skibbereen on Sunday 9th July 1989 there was no doubting the experience, strength, and bowling ability of O'Donovan. But also acknowledged was the youth, speed, and huge northern support on the side of Toal as they set off in scorching sunshine before a massive crowd of spectators. Toal won the first shot but O'Donovan took the advantage on the second and held it for eleven more beyond that. He was nearly a bowl up at one stage but Toal then drew level and went into a shot lead in the third quarter. O'Donovan came back into serious contention when he got to within forty metres of the leader but Toal pulled ahead again and assured himself of victory with a great second last shot which enabled him to beat the line with his twentieth bowl after a marathon score which stretched over five hours of play. Michael Toal had retained his All-Ireland Senior title and became the first player in over twenty years to do so.

The great Mick Barry had set a unique record of winning three consecutive All-Ireland Senior titles in 1965, '66 and '67 and for a time Michael Toal was on course to emulate that feat. But the prospective opportunity in 1990 was no longer a realistic one when Harry Toal, Armagh, whom many had discounted as a serious contender, caused the shock of the year by putting an end to Michael Toal's senior championship run. He was back in the National senior final for the sixth time and by all accounts his opponent was a formidable one. Little had been seen of Pat Butler in the closing stages of any championship since he took his first National senior title in 1978. It was a very different Pat Butler in 1990. He had beaten Christy O'Driscoll at Whitechurch by over two bowls before taking on Michael Buckley in the Munster final at Ballyshonin. That performance was one of sheer class. Pat Butler, the supreme stylist, whose bowling ability is unquestionable, reigned supreme from beginning to end in a brilliant display which saw him win his second Munster title by three bowls of odds. It was completed with such style, poise and classical bowling that a bemused attendance wondered why it had taken Pat Butler twelve years to get back to an All-Ireland final.

That final was played at Cathedral road, Armagh, on Sunday 5th August 1990 and an added attraction at the start was the renewed rivalry between two former greats in senior bowling, Mick Barry, Cork and Danny McParland, Armagh. It had been more than twenty five years since they first met in championship bowling and each of them thrilled the huge crowd with three exhibition shots that demonstrated the undiminished style and skill of these two great bowl players of the past.

That exhibition may have been something of an inspiration to Harry Toal for when the All- Ireland final got under way he was immediately into a good lead with two powerful opening shots. After six bowls were played there was just three metres between the pair but it was at that point the majestic nature of Pat Butler's bowling became evident. Soon he was a shot in front and with some of the finest bowling seen for many years he eased further ahead to leave Harry Toal rapidly losing ground. In the end the difference was three bowls of odds as Pat Butler finished most impressively to win his second All-Ireland Senior title.

Surprisingly, Pat Butler was not in the running for the 1991 senior championship. The Munster semi-finals that year saw Mick O'Driscoll beat James Buckley at Waterfall whilst Bill Daly defeated John O'Driscoll at Ballyvolane. In the Munster

Having met in Championship Road Bowling for the first time in 1964, Danny McParland, (left), and Mick Barry got together again in 1990 for a series of exhibition shots prior to the All-Ireland Senior Final at Armagh. Fr. Raymond Murray, President of Northern Branch, An Bol Chumann Na hÉireann, supervised the occasion.

final it was Daly who reigned supreme when he won by a bowl of odds over O'Driscoll at Whitechurch. The Ulster championship final created immense interest through the nature of Michael Toals win over the reigning title holder Harry Toal when he covered the course in eighteen brilliant shots to win by two bowls of odds.

Those respective provincial wins set the scene for one of the most attractive All-Ireland senior finals in years when Bill Daly, Cork and Michael Toal, Armagh, were in direct confrontation for the first time in championship bowling. The press previews were lavish in the build-up. With the large heading, "Daly and Toal set for epic senior showdown," the *Cork Examiner* of Friday 12th July 1991, explored the prospects in detail. Bowling correspondent Seamus O'Tuama commented:

> *Next Sunday's Murphy Stout All-Ireland senior bowling final between Bill Daly and Michael Toal at Ballingeary has created more excitement and speculation than any All-Ireland final for years. Munster champion Bill Daly, practically a household name while reigning world champion in the nineteen eighties, faces Michael Toal, twice winner of the title and the youngest All-Ireland senior champion in the history of bowling.*
>
> *Not only is the All-Ireland final at stake, but the captaincy of the Irish team in next year's European championship. And the outcome is likely to shape the battle for supremacy between Munster and Ulster in the coming years.*
>
> *It is Daly's first All-Ireland final appearance since 1985. That unshakable*

> *self-belief which brought him European gold, two world titles, and a senior All-Ireland, was rekindled during the championship. His bowling in the Munster final was better than anything we saw since 1984 and arguably surpassed the bowling on which his reputation was built. His return to the top will be given the ultimate test on Sunday. He will be faced by an opponent who has won many admirers in his short but spectacular career. All of which goes to make this one of the most important All Ireland finals for years.*

The rain fell heavily for the start of the score on Sunday 14th July 1991, at Ballingeary in the Cork Gaeltacht, but even such adverse weather conditions could not detract from the huge appeal of this spectacular All-Ireland bowling final. The road was absolutely thronged for the event which ended in a welter of excitement that will be long remembered. That dramatic conclusion was placed in perspective by Christy Santry in the *Southern Star* of Saturday 20th July 1991 when his detailed report included the comment:

> *Without doubt that uphill stretch of road from Gougane Cross, up through the pass of Keamineagh and beyond the lay-by is as difficult and as trying a stretch of bowling road as there is in the entire county. It was largely responsible for turning this score into one of the most awe-inspiring and exciting finishes that has marked any senior final in recent times.*

The score had been dominated for a long way by Michael Toal after the lead had been shared during the first four shots. With great bowling the Ulster champion stretched his lead to a full shot and this was almost doubled near Gougane Cross at which point the result appeared inevitable. But beyond that point Toal began to falter and Daly seized the opportunity to stage a recovery that brought about a dramatic final quarter. The lead went down to a bowl of odds and just before the finishing line the two marks rested a mere fifteen metres apart. That was the narrow margin as each of them prepared to bowl the final shot that was to determine the destiny of the All-Ireland senior title for 1991. Daly was first to throw and he delivered a tremendous bowl that wound its way high up into the distant climb as his supporters went wild with enthusiasm at the realistic prospect of a dramatic victory. The cheering was loud and prolonged, but as spectators clambered onto vantage points near the finish and Toal took one last look from his mark at the daunting task ahead of him, a tense silence befell the crowd as he prepared his run. The bowl was played perfectly and as it propelled its way uphill the buzz of excitement quickly turned to a crescendo of cheering as Toals supporters first sensed victory and then confirmed it as his effort beat the mark by seventeen metres for a breathtaking success that will rank with his best.

The *Cork Examiner* of Monday 15th July 1991 accorded the event a banner headline and detailed report. This is part of what bowling correspondent Seamus O'Tuama had to say:

> *Michael Toal, Armagh won his third Murphy's Stout All-Ireland senior*

Bill Daly, Cork, in action. Note the bowl in flight at upper centre of picture.
Photo : Denis McGarry

bowling title with a magnificent last shot win over Cork's Bill Daly before a huge crowd at Ballingeary, Co Cork yesterday.

Having dominated most of the score, Toal had his lead cut to just 15 metres for the last shot and then saw Daly place a 200 metre shot in front of him. But Toal responded like a true champion and beat the tip amid tumultuous uproar at majestic Ceim an Fhia.

If this was the second battle of Ceim an Fhia then Toal was a worthy hero. Although he played poorly from the entrance of the pass all this was lost in the flash of brilliance of his final throw.

Daly played a tremendous last shot which not only beat the line but left Toal looking at 200 metres of hard, rising road between him and the laurels. Toal proved his mettle with a fierce bowl in the left hand track and beat the tip by 17 metres.

It was Michael Toal's third National Senior title in four years but, remarkably, neither he or Bill Daly were to feature in the final the following year.

The classic style of Pat Butler was to be seen again in the Munster senior championship of 1992 when he beat Christy Mullins by two shots at Ballinacura and then won his way into the provincial final with a shot win over John O'Driscoll. The other side of the draw had seen Paddy O'Leary, Dungarvan, gain a shock win over Bill Daly on the last shot of their quarter final score at Bottlehill. But O'Leary went out at the semi-final to Neilus Hurley who bowled brilliantly to easily win his place in the Munster final. Hurley was there on merit having bowled with power and passion throughout the championship but it was a daunting task he faced in taking on Pat Butler at Bauravilla, Skibbereen, for the provincial title. It was yet another almost flawless display by Butler who scored the finishing line in sixteen great shots. Hurley had won the first bowl but lost the lead on the second never to regain it as Butler stretched ahead to win by two bowls of odds.

The Ulster championship had its share of surprises in 1992 but the shock result came in the form of Paul Grimley's win over Michael Toal in the provincial final when he got away over the last quarter to win by almost a shot. It may have been unexpected but the win was fully deserved as Grimley, winner of All-Ireland titles at Under 18 and Junior level, bowled the more consistently and finished in a style commensurate with the best senior standard.

The All-Ireland final at Cathedral road Armagh on Sunday 2nd August 1992 was much more closely contested than most people had anticipated. Granted it had been a purple patch for Pat Butler but Paul Grimley from Madden had prepared himself diligently, both publicly and privately, for the big event and to those who were aware of his intense preparations, the quality of his performance on the day came as no surprise. What did amaze the huge attendance was the sheer quality of the bowling and how Paul Grimley dictated the early pace with aplomb and confidence. He had almost gone a bowl up at one stage and even when Butler settled into the classic style of play so characteristic of the man it was Grimley who continued to delight his supporters with tenacious bowling that kept him closely in touch and on course for his first senior title. After thirteen shots they were still virtually level but it was at that point Grimley faltered. A misplaced bowl altered the entire trend of the score and over the remaining four shots he was always straining to regain the initiative. But that assertive position remained elusive as the faultless Butler consolidated his lead to cross the line in eighteen shots, a bowl of odds ahead of Grimley.

This is how BBC Radio Ulster reported the outcome to a background noise of enthusiastic supporters:

> *This is Pat Butler playing his fourth bowl and he is well behind at this stage which is quite a surprise ...... that one has done well for him but Paul Grimley will be equally satisfied that he has retained his lead ...... we're standing on the finishing line now and Pat Butler is just about to play his last shot, his eighteenth shot to cross the line; he has done that; played an effective shot and that means he has equalled the record for the course held by Michael Toal and has won the All-Ireland Senior title ...... has beaten Paul Grimley by a shot ...... Paul made a crucial mistake with his fourteenth bowl and has paid the price for that ...... has fallen behind since then ...... Pat Butler is All-Ireland Senior road bowls champion for 1992 but a very creditable performance by Madden's Paul Grimley in defeat.*

The great Pat Butler was back again in the National senior final of 1993. He had beaten Kieran Gould in the provincial semi-final before taking on John O'Driscoll who had defeated Bill Daly in the other semi-final with each of the Munster finalists

Pat Butler, Cork, about to bowl against Neilus Hurley in the 1992 Munster Senior Final at Bauravilla, Skibbereen, Co. Cork.
Photo : Denis McGarry

gaining victory on the last shot. It was a rather subdued Munster final at Ballyshonin in which John O'Driscoll, who had won the 1986 Intermediate National title over Donald Gribben, failed to fully match the bowling ability of Pat Butler who retained his Munster senior title by a bowl of odds.

The masterly play which marked his performances in 1992 was not fully sustained into the following season by Paul Grimley who went down by three shots in the Ulster final against Michael Toal. That victory by Toal had cleared the way for a most intriguing clash with Pat Butler each of whom had three National senior titles to their credit and neither of whom had ever been beaten in an All-Ireland senior final. The event at Ballingeary on Sunday 11th July 1993 generated widespread interest.

This is part of the extensive preview in the national daily newspaper, *Irish News*, on Wednesday 7th July, 1993:

> *In what is widely regarded by Road Bowling enthusiasts as the single most attractive pairing in the country at the present time, Armagh's Michael Toal takes on reigning champion, Pat Butler, Cork, in the All-Ireland Senior Championship Final this Sunday at Ballingeary in County Cork.*
>
> *Since both men won their respective provincial titles in June the pairing has created a tantalising air of anticipation and the historic but normally quiet Keimineigh Pass, in the heart of the Gaeltacht region of picturesque West Cork, will reverberate to the sound of excited thousands as these two formidable exponents of the game confront each other for the first time in an All-Ireland Senior Final.*
>
> *Undoubtedly this is the most appealing encounter in the Senior Championship in recent years. This event brings together two current masters of the sport in a direct confrontation in which a great deal is at stake. Neither player has ever been beaten in an All-Ireland Senior Final. Pat Butler of Cork is chasing his fourth National senior title having first won it in 1978 and again in 1990 before taking it for the third time last year against Armagh's Paul Grimley. Butler also won the National "King" Tournament last year involving all the top senior players in the country and victory on Sunday would establish him as the supreme bowler of modern times.*
>
> *But Michael Toal of Armagh is in line for that claim also. He too is in pursuit of his fourth All-Ireland Senior title and is the youngest player ever to win the coveted award when, in 1988, the then eighteen year old produced a scintillating display at Tassagh, having just joined the senior ranks for the first time.*
>
> *The towering pass of Keimineigh on the route of this Sunday's score was the site of a minor battle in 1822 made famous in song and story by local poet Maire Bhui Ni Laoire.*
>
> *That same picturesque area near Gougne Barra will this Sunday see the towering figure of Armagh's Michael Toal strive to wrest the title from Cork's Pat Butler for the accolade of supreme bowler in this eagerly awaited clash which promises to be a thrilling score.*

But if ever there was an example of a major fixture failing to live up to all the pre-match speculation this was it. As a contest the event was a real anti-climax due mainly to the difference in class between the two players on the day. Pat Butler was in brilliant form and his overall display was truly magnificent. In contrast Michael Toal was untypically erratic on a day in which very little went right for the Ulster champion. That fact won't concern Pat Butler though who had won his second consecutive All-Ireland senior title - and his third within four years. Toal won the first two shots but was very much overshadowed after that. A marvellous shot by Butler on his third, followed by an incredible effort on the sixth, really opened up the margin and soon there was two bowls of odds between them. Several good efforts by Toal failed to get the anticipated distance and this hapless tendency coupled with occasionally scattered bowls saw him fall into irretrievable arrears. With Butler extending his lead on the shot from Gougane Cross and then placing a perfectly directed bowl into full sight at the next bend Toal was all the time losing ground and at that point was an incredible four shots behind and ready to concede the score.

As Michael Toal confirmed he was conceding and offered congratulations to his magnificent opponent, Pat Butler remarked, "It must have been a nightmare for you Michael," to which the vanquished frankly admitted, "It was even worse than that."

Such is the capricious nature of individual form in championship road bowling. Michael Toal did gain some sporting compensation that year when he won a County Armagh Intermediate championship medal as a midfielder with St Colmcille's Gaelic Football Club, Grange.

The All-Ireland senior final of 1994 again brought into direct encounter, Bill Daly of Cork and Michael Toal of Armagh, for a repeat of that epic National final of three years previously. This time the venue was Bandon, Co Cork on Sunday 10th July and the spacious course was no more than that necessary to accommodate the many thousands wishing to see an intriguing contest in the midst of a once famous bowling stronghold at the gateway to West Cork.

The attendance was a record one and as the tense duel processed its way along the Bandon to Dunmanway road the drama intensified as the finishing line drew nearer. Toal had won the first shot by almost one hundred metres and held the lead until erring with his fourth bowl. The lead changed hands several times as excitement mounted. Daly took a substantial lead but then Toal stormed back only to see his opponent once more gain the initiative. But the best bowling was yet to come. Toal won back the lead with a brilliant eleventh shot but further pressure from Daly on subsequent shots - one of them an unbelievable drive - set him well ahead and the Armagh man's hopes looked forlorn. But after further exchanges the score was again wide open and when Toal reached the finishing straight he was fifteen metres ahead.

Seamus O'Tuama of the *Cork Examiner* takes it up from here:

> *Both men missed the line with their next throws although Toal was just twenty-five metres short of the target. Daly gave him one hundred and thirty-five metres to beat with his last shot. Toal's last bowl always looked a winner and when it*

Michael Toal, Armagh, musters all his strength for this shot in the 1994 All-Ireland Senior Final at Bandon, Co. Cork.
Photo : Denis McGarry

sped past Daly's tip it was greeted by one of the loudest cheers ever to greet an All-Ireland champion.

That same report in the *Cork Examiner* of Monday 11th July 1994 carried the banner headline, "Pulsating win for Toal" and before going into the detail of the score had this introduction:

> *Michael Toal, Armagh, recovered from what looked like certain defeat to beat Bill Daly, Cork, in the last shot of a pulsating Murphys Stout All-Ireland senior bowling final at Bandon yesterday.*
>
> *It was a score packed with drama, which kept the record attendance on their toes to the very last shot. Toal survived a blocked bowl at the halfway stage, a deficit approaching a bowl of odds entering the last quarter, and a dramatic call to win this final. But in the end it was the sweetest of victories for the Armagh man.*

The *Armagh Observer* of Thursday 14th July 1994 also reflected the exciting nature of that epic encounter. Under the headline, "Toals greatest victory", the report went on to describe how the concluding drama commanded "a tense silence in a crowd of more than 10,000", and then a large section of that same crowd erupting in ecstasy "with hats and shirts filling the sunlit air as Toal's power drive beat Daly's last shot".

That win earned for Michael Toal his fourth All-Ireland senior title and also

The bowl soars into the air as James Buckley, Cork, unleashes his opening shot in the 1995 All-Ireland Senior Final at Cathedral Road, Armagh. *Photo : Harold Ford, Portadown*

went a long way towards erasing the memory of his heavy defeat at the hands of Pat Butler in the National final just twelve months earlier.

The senior championship campaign of 1995 was one in which the powerful bowling of James Buckley, Fairhill, was particularly predominant. Ever since he had beaten Eamon Bowen in the first round of the Munster championship at Sally's cross, Buckley was gaining in stature and the nature of his consistent performances throughout the competition set him apart as the most likely contender for the All-Ireland senior title. That revival of his earlier form saw him win the Munster senior final at Lyre, near Clonakilty against Dan O'Halloran and, amazingly, it marked his first provincial senior title.

The path for Michael Toal to the 1995 National senior final was a great deal less complex. He was faced with the undesirable situation of remaining unchallenged for his Ulster title and that, fortunately, is a circumstance unlikely to recur in future years for this or any other player.

The Philip White Tyres/Falken All-Ireland senior final was played over the Cathedral road, Armagh on Sunday 6th August 1995 and attracted a huge crowd in the constant sunshine of that exceptional summer of sweltering heat.

The energy sapping temperatures had little visible effect on the contestants though as they each endeavoured to establish an early dominance in a score that would determine the destiny of the coveted National senior title for 1995. It was James Buckley's first All-Ireland senior final, a fact which in itself was extraordinary given his superb underage record and notable achievements in so many other important senior events. There was no doubting his class though and his current form rendered him favourite to take the title. Michael Toal was playing in his sixth All-Ireland senior final but, remarkably, out of four National title wins, only one of those, his first, had been achieved at a home venue.

Both players opened well, but it was the power and distance of Toal's first shot that created a stir as he immediately went into a forty metre lead. That was quickly reversed by Buckley with a brilliant second shot and after five magnificent drives he was a bowl up. The extent of the lead fluctuated on subsequent shots until Toal again delivered two great bowls and once again they were virtually level. Within five shots of the finishing line a mere ten metres separated the pair and on the bowl down into the bridge it was Buckley who came off best and that set him up for the decisive advantage. Toal had little distance in which to stage any possible recovery and from that to the finish Buckley bowled like a true champion. As he powered over the finishing line to record a two shot win the decisive victory had gained for the Fairhill man his first All-Ireland senior title in a long and successful bowling career that had truly taken off when he won his initial National championship title at Under 16 level in 1982.

In thirty-three years of National senior championship bowling, in which that particular realm of the sport has commanded an imposing perspective, the All-Ireland titles over the period have been shared between sixteen of the leading bowl players in the country.

Denny Murphy, (centre), following his win in the 1974 Munster Veterans Final at Innishannon, also included, (from left) Jerry Murphy, Finalist; Tadhg Twomey, Hilsers, Bandon; Flor Crowley, and semi-finalist Corney Looney, Bandon.

James Buckley, Cork, is carried shoulder high by his supporters after winning the 1995 Final at Armagh to gain his first All-Ireland Senior Road Bowls title.

The Seasoned Performers

The scope for gaining National honours in the sport of road bowls extends to the veteran years and is a championship grade which commands an esteem of its own as practised players pursue an All-Ireland title of special prestige.

The span of championship bowling stretches even beyond that worthy grade to the laudable vintage category which has proven to be a particularly popular annual competition in Munster attracting huge crowds to the closing stages of the tournament. That specific echelon of bowling eminence has not yet acquired the parameters of a National championship as Ulster players tend to retire from active participation in the sport much earlier than their Munster counterparts and have never engaged in competition at that level.

The Veteran championship has proven to be very competitive and indeed for many players the reality of a National title has been as elusive to them then as it was in other grades of bowling over the years. One player who will affectionately remember the Veteran championship is Derry Kenny of Clogheen in Co Cork. It was in that grade of competition he won his first All-Ireland bowling title and that was in 1992. The significance of that great victory can be appreciated when it is remembered that the same Derry Kenny competed in the first ever All- Ireland Senior Final against Danny McParland, over the Moy road, Armagh on Sunday 4th August, 1963. He was one of the finest players ever to grace the bowling roads of Ireland and his first National title on 11th July 1992, was fitting acknowledgement of a man who brought to the game a style of play and skill of performance that was on a par with the very best in the sport.

The first Munster Veterans championship was in 1973 when Denny Murphy, Bandon, beat Paddy Daly in the final at Crookstown. The popular Bandon bowler repeated the feat the following year at Innishannon by beating Templemartin player Jerry Murphy in the final. It was not until 1990 that Ulster entered the championship and that development raised the status of the competition to one of even greater recognition and honour.

The inaugural All-Ireland final in the Veteran grade was played at Bauravilla, Skibbereen, Co Cork on Saturday 7th July 1990. The Ulster Veterans champion was Harry Toal (senior) who had beaten Peter McCreesh, Navan, in the provincial final and he was opposed by John Crowley, Cork, who had defeated Neil O'Sullivan at Granger in the Munster final. Harry Toal had been bowling for more than thirty-five years with a wealth of experience at inter- provincial level but it was the confident, economic bowling of Neil O'Sullivan that dominated as he led throughout to win by well over a bowl of odds.

It was in the 1991 Veterans championship that Derry Kenny showed much of his old flair in a fine win over Denis Collins at Ballinacurra. But he was beaten on the last shot of a provincial semi-final by mid Cork bowler Tom Collins who was joined in the Munster final by Tom Walsh, Carbery, who defeated Mick O'Donoghue by a bowl of odds. Collins won the Munster title at Derinasafa, near Dunmanway and his opponent in the All-Ireland final at Armagh on Sunday 4th August 1991 was Harry Toal (senior) who retained his provincial title when beating Tommy Quinn, Armagh, who lost an early lead as the reigning veterans champion extended his winning odds. But a National title still eluded Harry Toal as Tom Collins commanded the closing stages to win by almost a bowl of odds.

The breakthrough in Ulster eventually came in 1992 for Tommy Quinn whom it will be remembered covered the Knappagh course in twenty-three shots in a senior tournament score against Danny McParland on 13th January 1963. In the provincial Veterans final of 1992 he was a rather fortunate winner on the last shot against Jim Cullen, Ballyheridan. The Munster final that season was at Ballyshonin and it was the year of Derry Kenny who bowled seventeen great shots to lead all the way for a two shot win over Willie Dennis. The All-Ireland final of 1992 was the first three-way contest for the National title with the entry of Connacht champion Willie Carroll from Westport, Co Mayo. It was a thrilling score at Ballingeary on Saturday 11th July as strong favourite Derry Kenny sought his first National championship victory. With some class bowling it was Willie Carroll who surprisingly set the pace and on leading through to the closing stages it took a fast and true shot from Kenny to win it at the last with Tommy Quinn back in third place. It was Derry Kenny's first All-Ireland title in a long bowling career and it didn't come easy.

The All-Ireland finals at Armagh on Sunday 1st August 1993 were previewed in the national daily newspaper, the *Irish News*. This is how the Veterans final was viewed in the issue of Wednesday 25th July 1993:

> *The All-Ireland Veterans championship is also down for decision this weekend and this eagerly awaited event is a three-way contest between the respective champions from Connacht, Munster and Ulster.*
>
> *The Ulster champion is the evergreen phenomenon Harry Toal from Armagh who, amazingly, is still bowling with speed and accuracy after decades of competitive playing. The same Harry Toal featured in inter-provincial scores in the nineteen fifties long before the All-Ireland championships were first organised in 1963. In won't be easy for Toal though. He is faced with formidable opposition in Mayo's Willie Carroll and Cork's veteran stalwart Denis Collins from Clonakilty.*

It's never easy in any All-Ireland championship final but in this one at Cathedral road, Armagh, Harry Toal appeared to be heading for victory and a historic first National title. The *Irish News* of Wednesday 4th August 1993 summed up the outcome:

> *The Veterans final developed into a great tussle which saw Armagh's Harry Toal take command for most of the way only to falter on the penultimate shot. This allowed Denis Collins, Clonakilty, to go clear with Mayo's Willie Carroll finishing a close third in this three- way contest.*

John Crowley, 1990 All-Ireland Veterans Champion with Harry Toal, finalist; Brendan Roche and Aidan McVeigh

At the starting line for the 1995 All-Ireland Veterans Final. Jim Cullen, (left), Armagh; Gerald Burke, Cork; and Willie Carroll, Mayo

The disappointment of yet another defeat at the decisive stage of the championship failed to dampen the enthusiasm of Harry Toal as he accounted for all opposition the following season. Malachy Quigley had beaten Peter Murphy in the provincial semi-final in Ulster and was expected to go further but Harry Toal ended his hopes in the next outing. It was Harry Toal's fourth Ulster Veterans title but still no National honour. In the All-Ireland final at Bandon on Saturday 9th July 1994 he found both opponents too strong as Percy Deane, Dunmanway, recorded a two shot win over the second placed Willie Carroll, Mayo, with Harry Toal a non- challenging third.

A defeat in two Ulster Veterans finals in 1992 and 1993 was a memory satisfactorily erased by Jim Cullen, Ballyheridan, when he produced a faultless display in the provincial final of 1995 to beat former senior player Aidan Toal by a clear margin. The line-up for the All- Ireland final at Cathedral road Armagh on Saturday 5th August, 1995 saw him joined by the redoubtable Willie Carroll, Mayo, and the formidable physique of Cork's Gerald Burke. There was no repeat of the provincial final performance for Jim Cullen as he erred untypically on several shots to allow his opponents away. Gerald Burke was bowling by far the better of the three and it was his power and consistency that assured him of victory with Willie Carroll gaining second place on his final throw.

The All-Ireland Veterans championship is a relatively recent innovation having had its first National final in 1990. There are many bowlers in all the other categories of competition who will one day attain the qualifying status for competing in this event of distinguished prestige - and some of those may still be in pursuit of their first All-Ireland bowling title.

That particular bowling honour is one that eluded Harry Toal, from Armagh City, who died unexpectedly on the 23rd January 1996. His association with the sport has been an enduring one. Harry Toal had been one of the leading bowl players in the early nineteen-fifties when he engaged in several inter-provincial scores over that period. Since then he participated at virtually every level of championship road bowling and contested the All-Ireland Senior final at Ballyshonin, County Cork, against Denis Scully in 1973 and Mick Barry in 1974. He also reached the Intermediate final in 1970, 1972, and 1978, and competed in four of the six Veteran championship finals since 1990.

The unexpected passing of Harry Toal concluded a long history of bowling evolution during which active participation was his prevailing principle right up until his sixty-fifth and final year.

A Presence in all Provinces

The relatively confined areas of the country that are traditionally associated with road bowls is a contributing factor to the uniqueness of the sport. And yet, surprisingly, the game enjoys an active presence in each of the four provinces of Ireland with provincial champions contesting All-Ireland finals in particular categories of competition.

In Ulster the customary districts connected with active road bowling include Newtownhamilton, Keady, Madden, Tassagh, Armagh city, Navan, Rock, Droim Cairn, Grange, Port Mor, Aughatarra, and Tullysaran in County Armagh with Moy, Eglish, and Benburb the allied regions in County Tyrone. The current practice of the sport in Munster is much more widespread and encompasses bowling regions from Youghal in the east of Cork county to Ballingeary in the west; and Skibbereen in the south to Buttervant in the north. There is also a significant presence near Limerick city and in the Dungarvan region of County Waterford. In December 1955 a senior score at Dungarvan, aimed at promoting the game in west Waterford, saw Denny Murphy, Bandon, win the Dungarvan Cup against Con Desmond of Inniscarra.

The Connacht interest in the sport is almost exclusively limited to Westport in County Mayo but is nonetheless a well established preserve in which two clubs, Knockrooskey and Larkill, continue to promote the sport. Both clubs are affiliated under Aughagower Road Bowling region and have built upon a tradition in the area

Filmed during the bitter cold of winter but screened in the summer heat of 19th July 1995, "Wogan's Island," featured Road Bowls and the bowling Bishop John Buckley. Included, (from left), Terry Wogan; Bishop John Buckley; Eamon O'Carroll, founder member of Bol Chumann Na hÉireann and Secretary for twenty years; and Jerry Desmond, Chairman of Bol Chumann and President of the International Bowlplaying Association.
Photo : Denis McGarry

which reflects a history of the game going back almost seventy years. A number of inter-provincial scores involving Armagh and Cork were arranged for the Westport region in the late nineteen fifties but it was not until 1992 that Aughagower bowling region became affiliated to Bol Chumann Na hEireann. Almost a decade before that a reader of a Mayo local newspaper, who was acquainted with the sport in other parts of Ireland, noticed a small advertisement inserted by "Round Tower Bowling Club", which advised of a score at Aughagower near Westport on Tuesday 9th August 1983. He went along out of curiosity and was amazed to find a large number of people present and a good standard of road bowling demonstrated by the players involved.

The venues presently used by the participating clubs in Westport include Larkill road and Ballinrobe road and these are utilised for practice and competition almost every Sunday of the year with additional scores arranged for weekday evenings during the summer period. The bowling activities of the clubs in the region are adequately reported in the weekly provincial newspaper, Mayo News which is based in Westport. Interest is keen within the relatively restricted domain but officials of the bowling region are currently promoting youth involvement in their endeavours to raise the standard and generate future champions in the sport. As it is, they have players participating in several categories of championship bowling including Novice, Junior and Veteran grades. The region has the proud boast that in the first year of affiliation in 1992 they produced the All-Ireland champion in the Novice category when Michael Kennedy became the first Mayo player to win a National title in road bowling.

The present officers of the bowling region are intent on building upon that initial success. The efforts of Peader Tunney, Chairman; James Heraty, Honorary Secretary; and Tom Kennedy, Treasurer; along with the encouragement and support of joint Presidents Charles Hughes and Jim Walsh are directed towards several ambitions for development of the sport in the area. Paramount amongst these is greater youth involvement with the ultimate aim of increasing the number of participating clubs in the region and eventual participation by a player from Mayo and the province of Connacht in the All-Ireland Senior championship. With ongoing sponsorship from North Connacht Farmers Co-operative and Corrib Oil, as well as local hostelries, the combined efforts of committed administrators and prestige funding should ensure a realisation of these ambitions in the years ahead.

The province of Leinster is represented in the realm of road bowling by active clubs in Drogheda, County Louth and Enniscorthy, County Wexford. The Drogheda region first generated a local interest and enthusiasm for the sport in 1989 when supporters Donal Lucey, Joe Reid, Donal Millar, Joe Clarke, Eamon Nugent, Con Fitzsimons, John Hughes, and Moss Gribben, founded the inaugural club in the area. The Drogheda and District Road Bowls Club now has more than one hundred active players and they participate annually in the All-Ireland championships at Novice and Junior levels as well as engaging in domestic competition for most of the year round. The club has been successful in gaining significant sponsorship from Thorsman Ireland Limited whose manufacturing business in electrical installation materials is based in Drogheda, County Louth. The bowling region currently administered by the club comprises players and supporters in the areas of Drogheda, Clogherhead, Tullyallen and Termonfeckin. The venue most commonly used for championship scores is the Boyne road along a picturesque course on the journey from Drogheda to Termonfeckin.

The officers and members of Bol Chumann Droichead Atha have made significant progress since their inaugural participation in 1989 and now have players who compete to a high standard with National championship success confidently predicted for some within the next few bowling seasons. The present officers of the club, Donal Millar, Chairman; Joe Clarke, Honorary Secretary; and Joe Reid, Treasurer, along with Patsy Devlin, Club President; and public relations officer Tommy Leddy, are aiming towards increased participation in National Championships to sustain the impetus established in recent years.

The promotion of road bowls in Wexford is being spearheaded by Dick Boland and Ned Murphy from Clonroach near Enniscorthy and their entry into National championships is imminent.

The introduction of many more areas throughout the country to the competitive excitement of championship road bowling is the ultimate aim of a new coaching video and instruction manual launched by Bol Chumann Na hEireann towards the end of 1995.

In launching the video, "Splitting the Sop: a young person's guide to road bowling", the Minister for Sport in the Republic of Ireland, Bernard Allen, T.D. also announced that he was presenting a trophy for a post-primary schools bowling competition. No stranger to the sport, Bernard Allen spent most Sundays of his youth at scores and once went on the crossbar of his fathers bicycle to a big fixture at Clancool, near Bandon. His uncle Seamie Allen won the Munster senior final against Mick Barry at Tinker's Cross in 1958.

Those associated with the production of the coaching video and instruction manual included Pat O'Sullivan, Rosscarbery; James Caverly, Sharon McGarry, Michael O'Sullivan, Christy Santry, Seamus O'Tuama; national coaches Pat O'Sullivan, Ballygarvan and Sally Greene, Ballincollig; Dr Kathryn O'Donoghue, co-ordinator of the Bowling for Europe project; Bishop John Buckley, Brian Crowley, MEP, Philip Healy, Denis McGarry and video producers, Cork Audio-Visual Education and Realisation Network.

The growing interest in native games such as bowling was a point emphasised by Bishop John Buckley when he offered his support to the project and spoke of the numbers of school students who played the game weekly. That view was mirrored by Minister for Sport, Bernard Allen who strongly advocated that the unique role of indigenous sports in European Union member countries should be nurtured, developed and promoted. Bowling, he said, was truly a healthy, sociable sport but one which required skill, determination, co-ordination, accuracy and concentration; "the sense of challenge involved in mastering such disciplines ensured that bowling would never lose its appeal".

Not losing appeal to the road bowlers of Connacht and Leinster are the

Irish Minister for Sport Bernard Allen, T.D. is pictured with Donald Gribben, (left), and George Smith, Secretary and Chairman respectively of the Northern Branch, An Bol Chumann Na hÉireann.
Photo : Denis McGarry

National championships at Novice and Junior 'C' grades which offers them competition with the champions of Ulster and Munster as well as those from the London bowling region. The London Bol Chumann was founded in 1969 by the late William Jennings, a native of Reenascreena, Rosscarbery, County Cork, along with his brother Barney Jennings and Con Connors from Ballinagree. The sporting activities of players in the London region are suitably explored by Jerome Casey (1994) in his book *"Bowling Down London Way"*.

The first All-Ireland finals in Novice and Junior 'C' grades were played in 1992 and hosted by the Aughagower regional clubs in Westport, County Mayo. It was a most successful organisational and competitive debut for the host region. Michael Kennedy, the Connacht champion had beaten Oliver Kirwan, the Louth and Leinster champion in the semi-final of the Novice championship. The Ulster champion that year was Paul Mackle, Grange, who had beaten Patsy Daly, Eglish, to win the provincial title. But he went out at the semi-final stage to the Munster champion, Eamon Crowley who started strong favourite to win the final but lost out to Michael Kennedy who made history by winning the first All-Ireland title, in any category, for a bowler from Mayo and Connacht. That victory, on 13th September 1992, marks a milestone in the history of road bowling in the west of Ireland.

The All-Ireland Junior 'C' title in 1992 went to the Munster champion, Finbar O'Brien who gave a great display at the Westport venue to beat Willie Carroll, Connacht, and Pat Healy, Leinster.

It was the turn of the Louth region to host their first All-Ireland championship finals in 1993 and these were contested over the Boyne road in Drogheda. The local player Mick Briscoe went out in the Novice semi-final when he and Denis McCarthy, London, were beaten by Mayo bowler Peadar Tunney. The other semi-final in the Novice grade was won by John Lennon, Port Mor over the Munster champion Michael Daly from west Cork. John Lennon had previously won the top grade in the Paul Dobbin Cup, a tournament which annually commemorates the young player and club official at Port Mor who died unexpectedly in August 1987. This was Lennon's first Ulster bowling title and encouraged by a huge following he went one better in the National final at Drogheda when he beat Peadar Tunney by seventy metres in a score of great excitement and some excellent play.

The Ulster and Munster representatives both went out at the semi-final stage of the All-Ireland Junior 'C' championship in 1994 when Pat Sullivan, west Cork, was beaten by John O'Donovan, London, whilst Gregory McSorley, Moy, lost to Willie Carroll, Mayo. The London-Connacht final at Drogheda resulted in a clear win for John O'Donovan with Westport bowler Willie Carroll denied that elusive National title yet again. It was no better for him the following year when he lost a semi-final to the Munster champion, Gerald Brickley, Cork, despite having the advantage of a home venue. The other Junior 'C' semi-final at Westport went to Denis Burke, London, who beat the Ulster champion, Larry Corr, Rock. The All- Ireland final on Sunday 12th September, 1994 was close and exciting and the title went to London bowler Denis Burke who gained the verdict over Gerald Brickley by twenty metres on the final throw.

Johnny Hurley, All-Ireland Novice Champion in 1994 with Jerry Desmond, (left), and Peadar Tunney, Chairman of Bol Chumann Maigheo.

Photo : Frank Dolan

The province of Connacht did have a player through to the National finals in 1994 when Tom Kennedy, Mayo, beat Jerome Casey, London, and Eamon Tuite, Louth, in the Novice semi- final. He was joined in the final by Munster champion Johnny Hurley, Cork, who had beaten the Ulster representative, Seamus O'Neill from Eglish in County Tyrone. The Cork player appeared the stronger bowler of all five semi-finalists and that form held through the final when he dominated where it mattered most to win the All-Ireland Novice title.

The emergence of new and exciting bowling talent was a feature of the 1995 All-Ireland finals at Drogheda. Local man Gary Shevlin, the Louth and Leinster Novice champion, surprised everyone with the style and quality of his play when he produced a marvellous performance to oust Pat O'Neill, London, and Patsy Niland, Mayo, in an exciting semi-final at Boyne road. The other semi-final in that category went to the Munster champion, Michael Hurley, Cork, who finished very strongly to overhaul an early lead established by Fergal McCreesh, Navan, who had impressed greatly in winning the Ulster title a few weeks earlier. The bowling stature of Michael Hurley was further elevated in the All-Ireland Novice final on Sunday 10th September, 1995, when he bowled sixteen great shots over the course at Boyne road to win by a clear margin against Gary Shevlin who lacked some of the speed so evident in his semi- final victory.

The Junior 'C' championship of 1995 lacked nothing in excitement or quality play. That all round sports participant Joe Shortt, Keady, was surprisingly still without a National title in any grade of bowling and his remaining hopes rested with the Drogheda contest in September. But it was not to be this time either as Pa Ryan, Cork, recovered from a virtual hopeless position to regain the lead and secure a last shot win for his place in the final. The other semi-final resulted in a facile win for Pat Thompson, London, against Eamon Tuite, Louth, and Tom O'Malley, Mayo. But even he found a difference in class when it came to the final where he had no answer to the bowling power of Pa Ryan who played with great confidence and speed to win the All-Ireland Junior 'C' title for 1995.

The road bowling champions of each of the four provinces, along with those of the London region, will undoubtedly continue striving to attain the ultimate honours in National titles. But with the current drive to increase the numbers of young participants, and the promotional efforts to extend the sport into areas not hitherto acquainted with the game of road bowls, the distinction of a National title may become progressively more difficult to accomplish.

An Bol Fada for Sporting Prestige

In only two years of staging the tournament a progressive road bowls club at Keady and Tassagh in County Armagh has established An Bol Fada as one of the major National competitions on the bowling calendar.

When the tournament was launched in 1994 the organising committee not only succeeded in gaining substantial sponsorship for the inaugural event but also assured the competition of adequate publicity by issuing a detailed press release well in advance of the big occasion which stimulated interest and generated speculation on the new bowling venture.

The programme is now a consolidated and significant feature of the Easter weekend bowling fixtures in Ireland and has had the consequence of elevating the Joe McVeigh Cup final to a National position of prominence which is in accord with the stature of the great bowler the trophy commemorates. It has done likewise for the Charlemont Hotel Cup which has figured in various categories of National bowling competition for almost thirty years and is now rightfully and firmly ensconced as one of the major prizes on a sporting programme that will undoubtedly gain in momentum as the years unfold. In a wide range of sponsorship the Bol Fada competition also commemorates one of bowlings life-long supporters, the late Pete Grimley of Madden, who exerted a prominent presence on any road over which the sport was played. He was as well known at Munster venues as any other nearer home and it is fitting that one of the major scores on the Bol Fada programme will annually salute the memory of a man so inspirational in sustaining the long tradition of the sport.

The entire eight score programme is fully sponsored in a total prize fund that exceeds £2,000 in addition to the valued trophies awarded to each of the winners in a two day Bol Fada event to which the firm of Arthur Guinness and Son is the main benefactor. The first Bol Fada in 1994 was held over the Keady-Newtownhamilton road but the confines of the venue proved to be inadequate in coping with the attendance and the organisers sensibly switched the 1995 event to the Keady-Castleblayney course which coped admirably with the crowd requirements.

That inaugural Bol Fada in 1994 was attended by the most atrocious weather conditions imaginable and it was the sporting Ted Hickey, Cork, who broke off in the historic opening score which went to Joe Shortt, Keady by almost two bowls of odds. In a score which was dramatic for its changing fortunes, Tassagh's Brian Kinchin and Eddie Carr had a last shot win over West Cork pair Noel O'Brien and Donal Riordan. The third score on the opening day brought the first Munster win when the consistent Paul O'Brien had a comfortable victory over a disappointing Michael Rafferty, Madden. A serious blunder by John Lennon, An Port Mor, in the closing stages of his encounter with Cork's Eddie Daly allowed the Munster man to get away for an easy last shot win.

Joe Shortt, Keady, delivers a shot at Bol Fada on the Castleblayney Road.
Photo : Philip Wilson/Ulster Gazette

In the Under 14 category Philip McKeever, Keady, comfortably beat Cork's Aidan Coppinger whilst the Munster bowler, Padraig Scanlon, took the Under 18 event in a score of missed opportunities against Keady's Malachy Lappin. The doubles score on Sunday also went to Cork with a last shot win for Philip and Tim Pat O'Donovan over the Ulster pair Pat Mallon and Paul Grimley.

However the feature event, for the Joe McVeigh Cup, in that inaugural Bol Fada had involved the two leading senior players in the country. This is part of a preview in the national daily newspaper, the *Irish News* on Wednesday 30th March 1994.

> *The spectacular pairing of senior champions Michael Toal, Armagh, and Pat Butler, Cork, is the enthralling prospect is store this Easter weekend in the Guinness sponsored Bol Fada Tournament at Keady.*
>
> *The Bol Chumann Na hEireann affiliated regional club of Keady-Tassagh has succeeded in clinching the single most attractive pairing in the country at the present time.*
>
> *The exciting nature of this top class encounter is enhanced by the recent record of both players which had each of them vying to establish themselves as supreme bowler of modern times. That accolade presently rests with Cork's Pat Butler. The ultimate decider in this claim to supreme honours was last years All-Ireland senior final in which Butler eclipsed Toal and this supremacy was further established, though less convincingly, in the King of the Roads Tournament some three months later.*
>
> *Until those two defeats Toal was close to reigning supreme having equalled Butler's three All- Ireland senior titles and each of them striving to edge ahead in the honours table. Toal however will relish the fact that now, for the first time, he has the advantage of a home venue in a clash with Butler.*

The content of that particular preview reflected the prevailing expectation within the bowling domain as these two masters of the sport renewed their opposition. Michael Toal had already won the Joe McVeigh Cup in each of the first three years of competition but this time it was Bol Fada and Pat Butler. That was sufficient to make the prospect of winning the Cup yet again all the more fascinating.

The outcome of that encounter is best summed up in this section of a report on the score in the *Irish News* of Wednesday 30th March 1994.

> *The anticipated showpiece in the Keady-Tassagh Easter weekend Bol Fada attracted a huge crowd to the Newtownhamilton road but supporters of Armagh's Michael Toal had to settle for yet another defeat at the hands of Cork's Pat Butler.*
>
> *Neither player lived up to his usual standard and whilst each of them had some marvellous drives they also produced a few uncharacteristically short efforts. In the end it was Butler who had most going for him and he has now clocked up three successive wins over his northern rival.*

An Bol Fada of 1995 had them back in action again. Pat Butler as holder of the

Joe McVeigh Cup and Michael Toal as reigning All-Ireland senior champion who had regained that supreme honour in the meantime. This time the score was over the more spacious Keady-Castleblaney road and the outcome of the event was accorded extensive coverage in the *Armagh Observer* and *Ulster Gazette* of Thursday 20th April 1995.

Butler bowled first after winning the toss and won the first shot but Toal soared into a forty metre lead on the second. The lead was reversed on the fourth bowl and that wavering situation continued as each of them perfected their play through some amazing shots. The bowling over the final quarter was truly superb as they tested each other with a succession of shots that thrilled the crowd. Toal held a lead of thirty metres for the last shot to the line. This is how the *Armagh Observer* concluded a report on the score:

> *With light fading and suspense at the maximum it was all or nothing for both contestants. Butler, renowned for producing a pile-driver on the last one, duly proceeded to do just that and unbelievably opened the corner at Clea Lake Gate. The pressure was now firmly on Toal's shoulders as he and his mentor Donald Gribben found themselves in a repeat of the memorable Bandon final of last year.*

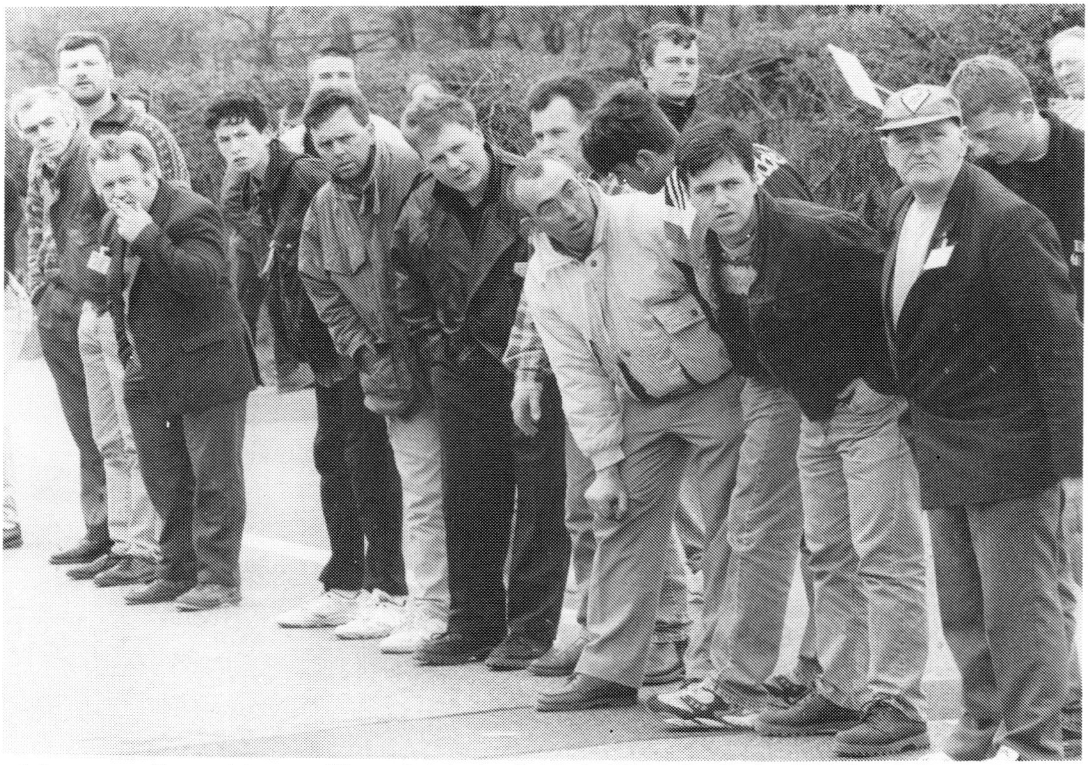

A face among the spectators awaiting a shot during Bol Fada 1995 is Pat Butler, (fifth from left), who lost out the following day in the Joe McVeigh Cup Final

Photo : Philip Wilson/Ulster Gazette

After careful consideration of the play Toal unleashed his bowl and on confirmation that the 1995 McVeigh Bol Fada was his by nearly thirty metres there was euphoria at the lake never seen in Armagh for many years.

It was described then and since as the score of the year, not least for the magnificent bowling by both men, but also for the excellent sportsmanship portrayed by Pat Butler and Michael Toal in a score which had everything that is good for the sport.

The same Bol Fada programme provided additional excitement and drama with seven other important scores on the bill. The Cheers Cabs challenge was won by James McCann, Moy and Joe Shortt, Keady over Paul O'Brien and Tony Carey, Cork. The Leer Premium score was won by Harry Toal, Armagh and Malachy Lappin, Lagan, over Cork's Tim O'Brien and Pat Bohane. The Pete Grimley Cup went to Billy McAuliffe, Cork who beat Austin McKeown, Navan. The father and son duo of P.J. Cooney and Denis Cooney, Cork, beat Brian Kiernan, Madden, and Eamon Cullen, Rock, in the Hughes Bookmakers Derby. The McClelland's Salvage score was won in dramatic fashion by Noel O'Brien and Kieran O'Gorman over Eddie Carr and Brian Kinchin who were literally abashed at a major reversal of the odds over the final shots. The brothers Tim Pat and Philip O'Donovan, Cork, recorded a narrow win of just four metres over Paul Grimley, Madden, and Pat Mallon, Grangemore, in the McGleenan Shield. The Charlemont Hotel Cup final, which was played immediately prior to the major senior event, was won by Conor McGuigan, Tullysaran, who excelled in his score against Donnacha O'Brien, Drinagh, Co Cork.

The sporting atmosphere of the competition and harmonious tone of Saint Oliver Plunkett Accordion Band, Keady, ensures Bol Fada at Easter is an important fixture for road bowls followers anywhere in Ireland.

Team members from Germany, Holland and Ireland at the opening of the International Bowling Festival at Armagh in 1994. Also included are Jerry Desmond, President of the International Bowlplaying Association, and Donald Gribben, Secretary to the Ulster Branch of Bol Chumann Na hÉireann.

Photo : Harold Ford, Portadown.

The European Dimension

The most significant and pervasive development in the history of road bowls in Ireland has been the initiation and perpetuation of International Championships that have created a new and widening perspective to which the sport is rightly and constantly responding.

There is no attempt in this publication to adequately portray the magnitude or detail of such important evolution. That advancement in the sport at such a compelling and prestigious level is one which warrants an exclusive volume to perceptively relate the chronological progression and notable achievements associated with the European dimensions to the game.

The present four year cycle of European Bowling Championships involving Germany, Holland and Ireland provides a focus at International level for players in all categories and offers the ultimate in supreme honours within the sport.

Ever since the first International Bowling Championships were held in Losser, Nederland, in 1969 the events since then have redirected the focal point towards a new and more inspirational stratum. The cultural socialisation deriving from such high profile events has had the subtle effect of persuading some traditional road bowlers in Ireland into a more athletic and fitness orientated approach to these and domestic competitions. The sight of well trained athletes from Germany and Holland meticulously limbering up before taking each shot and then, without breaking their concentration, deliberately removing the sports garments superfluous to their actual playing gear, was in sharp contrast to the traditional approach of many Irish players. For years, if not generations, the bowl player in Ireland was dressed like any other individual and consequently was virtually undistinguishable from the spectators at any score. That particular tradition has been gradually waning as the younger players especially present themselves for competition in a manner and appearance that portrays an image of preparation and fitness.

On the subject of International Bowling Championships, Eithne Vallely (1993) in her cover story, "Jackets on the Grass Verge", in the *Causeway Journal,* states, *"This experience would shake the most resolute upholder of traditional values and many now would like to travel down that path towards development of the game in the areas of increased commercial sponsorship, media coverage, official recognition; towards even moving away from the image of the rolled- up sleeves to the wearing of trendy gear! But perhaps the image of bullet throwers in skin- tight, multi-coloured, luminous lycra doesn't bear thinking about."*

Perhaps not. But recent evidence would suggest that bowlers no longer *"simply detach themselves from the crowd and lay their jacket on the grass verge before throwing the bullet".* Instead they avoid the possibility of starting from a disadvantage by gearing themselves appropriately in terms of outward appearance as well as the necessary mental and physical preparation.

The International games have also provided for a cross-application and inculcation of skills associated with Dutch Moors Bowling, Irish Road Bowling and German Lofting. Teams from each country compete in all three specialities of the sport and the experience derived from the process enhances the individual's ability to compete at the highest level in the category of their choice.

The historic occasion of that first and relatively modest, international bowling event in 1969 is recalled by Christy Santry in the *Southern Star* newspaper of Saturday 30th May 1992, on the day which saw the opening of the ninth European Bowling Championships in Ireland.

> *The June Public Holiday weekend of 1969 symbolises one of the most important milestones in the history of Bol Chumann Na hEireann and indeed in the history of International bowl playing as we have come to know it today. The town of Losser in the northern region of Holland was to present the Irish party with an image of the game of bowl playing that none of them had ever experienced before. As the late founding chairman of Bol Chumann, Flor Crowley, described it in general, as a prelude to the 1977 International, it was an occasion of pageantry and bands, public parades and speech making; something that had never been traditionally associated with the game of bowling on any previous occasion. It was, he said, a scene far removed from road bowling as the Irish party had known it at that time in Dublin Hill, Derinasafa or Ballygarvan.*

When the International Bowl playing Association was founded, the late Flor Crowley became President of the federation and Eamon O'Carroll, who was founding Honorary Secretary to Bol Chumann Na hEireann, also fulfilled that same role with the European body. The Presidency has rotated over the years and is currently held by Jerry Desmond, the present Chairman of Bol Chumann Na hEireann.

In the intervening years since the first International Championships in Losser, Nederland, in 1969, the games have been held in Cork, Ireland (1970); Garding, Schleswig Holstein (1972); Jever, Ostfriesland (1974); Cork, Ireland (1977); Tubbergen, Nederland (1980); Garding, Schleswig Holstein (1984); Norden, Ostfriesland (1988); Cork, Ireland (1992); Tubbergen, Holland (1996).

History was made in Armagh in 1994 when the city was host to the first International Bowling Festival to be held in that particular region. As part of the Armagh Together celebrations the Northern Branch, An Bol Chumann Na hEireann, promoted a magnificent two-day bowling festival on 17th and 18th September 1994 which was sponsored by Philip White Tyres Limited; K'Mac Glass Specialists; and Cross Refrigeration Limited. Teams from Germany, Holland and Ireland competed in lofting and road bowling. A civic reception was accorded the visiting teams promoters, sponsors and all participants at Armagh Council Chambers on the evening prior to the events. The lofting competitions were conducted at Armagh Rugby Club Grounds and the road bowling scores were held over the Cathedral Road, Armagh. The visiting guests were entertained at a presentation function in Drumsill Hotel, Armagh, at which an attractive musical, dancing and cultural display was performed by senior and junior members of Scoil Rince Emain Mhacha.

The total perspective of International Bowling merits a comprehensive exploration of all the European Championships over the years in a publication specifically undertaken for that purpose. No doubt that prospect will some day be realised.

Christy Mullins, Bantry, during the Moors Bowling Championships at Lee Fields, Cork City in 1992.

The excitement and enthusiasm of European Championship Bowling is evident in the 1992 Moors Competition at Lee Fields, Cork City.

Bill Daly Cork, a gold medal winner in European Championship Moors Bowling in 1992

Michaél Toal, Armagh, in the 1992 European Road Bowling Championships at Carrigrohane Straight, Cork City.

Eddie Carr, Tassagh, (second from left), a silver medalist in the 1992 European Road Bowling championships, with John Gribben, then Chairman Northern Branch, An Bol Chumann Na hÉireann; Paddy Comiskey, (left), Treasurer; and Harry Toal, Armagh, a member of the Irish Senior Men's Road Bowling Team.
Photo : Michael Campbell

Two members of the Irish Women's Team, Geraldine McCluskey, Armagh, (left), and Gretta Cormican, Cork, at the 1994 International Bowling Festival at Armagh.
Photo : Harold Ford, Portadown

Dermot Gribben, Armagh, in action during the 1995 All-Ireland Under 18 Final at Cathedral Road, Armagh.
Photo : Harold Ford, Portadown.

A Commitment to Administration

It is a well established fact, but one which merits periodical accentuation, that but for the wisdom and foresight of people like Flor Crowley, Eamon O'Carroll, Hugh O'Neill, and others of like mind, the sport of road bowls as presently constituted and portrayed might be a mere notion rather than a reality.

In the years since the foundation of Bol Chumann Na hEireann in 1954 there has been a succession of dedicated and thoroughly committed officials who have given freely of their time and energy to organising and promoting the sport to optimum effect. Many of these purposeful individuals operate at club level and prefer to devote their energy to that plane of organisation. They form the essential basis and network of the overall sporting body and sustain the foundation and structure of the greater organisation. But for all that it is the Executive membership who implement the philosophy and provide ongoing management of the organisation. The association has been fortunate in its choice of people to lead. Flor Crowley and Eamon O'Carroll are two men with an amazing record of administration in its level of competence and period of duration. Eamon O'Carroll remained committed to the role of Honorary Secretary until 1974 at which time he had devoted twenty years of unswerving dedication to the ideals and operation of the organisation.

A founder member of the association he constantly strove to promote the sport in every possible way and fulfilled his secretarial responsibilities with an enthusiasm and expertise that was an inspiration to others at all levels of organisation and management. A player of considerable competence who figured in many prominent fixtures he attracted a great deal of interest at Dublin Hill in 1960 for a score in the Cork Senior Tournament against Denny Murphy of Bandon. The significant bowling exploits and proficient organisational skills demonstrated by Eamon O'Carroll of Farran over many years were the subject of due recognition in 1993 when he was the worthy recipient of the O'Donovan Dairy Services Hall of Fame Award. Flor Crowley was Chairman of the body right up until his death in 1980 having given a quarter century of service to the sport. During that period the role of Treasurer was ably and meticulously fulfilled over successive years by Hugh O'Neill, Denis McSweeney, and Jerry Keating.

The new Chairman of Bol Chumann Na hEireann in 1980 was Brendan Roche who previous to that period had fulfilled an incredible responsibility in several areas of assignment. He was Treasurer for seven years from 1970 until 1977 and actually doubled as Honorary Secretary for three of those years from 1974 until 1977 before continuing in the secretarial role until 1980. Brendan Roche had been one of the most wholehearted officials in the history of the sporting organisation. Unflinching in his roles at any given time, and these were numerous and varied, he fulfilled his demanding duties with the competence of an expert. Throughout his lengthy period as an Executive officer from 1970 until 1991 Brendan Roche successfully launched many initiatives and constantly motivated significant progress within the association. He conducted a range of diverse duties, all of which were proficiently processed in the best interests of the sport. Until his retirement from the post of Chairman in 1991 Brendan Roche had demonstrated skilful management on every level at which he was required to function.

The role of Honorary Secretary for the ten year period from 1980 until 1990 was very capably administered by Padraig Crowley who fulfilled the demanding part with efficiency and aplomb over that extended term. His successor in the post was Seamus O'Tuama who held it for a two year period from 1990 until 1992. He too met the demands of the position with total dedication and skilful application. In addition to those commitments Seamus O'Tuama provided authentic and authoritative reporting on bowling events through his competent coverage of the sport in the *Cork Examiner.*

The successor to Brendan Roche as Chairman in 1991 was Jerry Desmond who had already served for many years in a leading capacity. He had been Treasurer to Bol Chumann Na hEireann form 1977 until his election as Chairman in 1991. During that time he fulfilled the responsible duty with exacting readiness and has done likewise in the role of Chairman where the demands are intensifying in accord with the widening spectrum of initiatives undertaken by the organisation. A measure of Jerry Desmonds commitment was his acceptance of the position as President of the International Bowlplaying Association which post he has also filled since 1994.

The role of Treasurer in recent years has been scrupulously fulfilled by John O'Donovan who has been in post since 1991. That function is also a growing responsibility but the onerous task is undertaken with equanimity by John O'Donovan who accepts the increasing demands as a measure of progress. In his first year as Treasurer, John O'Donovan, as Managing Director of Dairy Services Limited, sponsored the inaugural Hall of Fame Award for Munster bowlers which went to Mick Barry in 1991 and has since been awarded to Denis O'Donovan (1992); Eamon O'Carroll (1993); Liam O'Keefe (1994); Johnny Creedon (1995).

The formidable responsibility of Honorary Secretary was filled for the two year period from 1992 until 1994 by Christy Santry who is renowned as a distinguished bowling correspondent for the Cork weekly newspaper, *Southern Star*. Christy Santry is a tireless worker for Bol Chumann being involved to a leading extent in virtually every project undertaken by the body. His weekly detailed coverage and objective analysis in the *Southern Star* makes essential reading for all followers of the sport and has helped to mould and influence the positive direction of the game over many years. Since 1994 the position of Honorary Secretary has been held by Tim O'Regan and his deep sense of commitment to the post is evident in the efficiency with which he conducts the business of his office. Tim O'Regan's handling of the additional obligations engendered by the 1996 European Championships was an example of the adept nature of his performance in the duties of that arduous role.

The formation of the Northern Branch of Bol Chumann Na hEireann was in 1963 and resulted in Joe Horan being elected first Chairman to the body with Brian

John O'Donovan

Joe Horan

Dan Mackle

Aidan McVeigh

John Gribben

Paddy Comiskey

Eamon O'Carroll

Brendan Roche

Gerry Donnelly

Toal as Honorary Secretary and Henry Neary as Treasurer. Henry Neary became Chairman the following year and diligently applied himself to the role until his untimely death in 1967. Brian Toal remained as Secretary until the middle of 1968. Joe Horan had given lifelong service to the sport. He was back as Chairman to the Northern Branch in 1970 and continued to fulfill that duty with unremitting application until the end of 1978. Throughout all those years, Joe Horan, who was a renowned cross-country runner and champion pole vaulter, had played and organised the sport of road bowls with a commitment that was so intense as to be constantly challenging. He was a recipient of the Hall of Fame Award in 1981 in recognition of his long and devoted service to the sport. Joe Horan died unexpectedly on 19th May 1983. He was Vice-President of the Association at the time of his death. On the occasion of the first All-Ireland finals in Armagh following the death of Joe Horan, a wreath was laid on his grave at St Patrick's cemetery by Brendan Roche, Chairman of Bol Chumann Na hEireann, accompanied by Northern Branch Chairman John Gribben, in a simple but fitting ceremony attended by relatives and road bowls officials.

The role of Chairman to the Northern Branch was ably filled by Dick Burke from 1967 until 1970 and the duties of Honorary Secretary were efficiently conducted over most of that period by another dedicated official, Joe Duffy. It was also in 1967 that Gerry Donnelly became a member of the Northern Branch Executive and as Treasurer throughout the period from then until 1975 he was a most enthusiastic official who fulfilled many organisational roles beyond the parameters of his monetary responsibilities.

The important role of Treasurer was undertaken by Dan Mackle from 1975 until 1978 during which term that great advocate of the sport, who had been a principled official in the days prior to formal organisation, was meticulous in his function. At the time of his retirement from the post the responsibilities of the office was then shared by joint Treasurers Malachy Quigley and Pat Toal who continued that function until 1981. Dan Mackle, who was an excellent footballer with Armagh Young Ireland's in the nineteen thirties, died on 22nd April 1991. A cup, donated by his family for underage bowling competition, commemorates his lifelong commitment to the sport.

The start of a marathon period for Aidan McVeigh as Honorary Secretary to the Northern Branch of Bol Chumann Na hEireann was in 1975 and he fulfilled that demanding role for no less than eighteen years. It was a period that had many fluctuations in levels of enthusiasm and yet Aidan McVeigh persevered in his role to which he carried the additional responsibility of bowling correspondent for the *Armagh Observer*. In that particular function he was comprehensive in his detail and forthright in his comments as he provided the publicity sustenance for the sport over a great number of years.

It was in 1981 that Paddy Comiskey became Treasurer to the Northern Branch and he remained a most reliable holder of that office until 1993. Paddy Comiskey, who has been another dedicated official and fervent supporter over several decades, was Honorary Secretary to the organisation from 1972 until 1975. His business firm of Comiskey Engineering Limited has been a frequent sponsor of bowling events over the years.

One of the most significant figures in the entire history of road bowls organisation in the north has been John Gribben. His contribution to the sport is immeasurable and his unwavering commitment to the promotion of the game represents a level of input to which the present and future generations will always be indebted. John Gribben was Deputy Chairman as early as 1964 and ever since that period has never been out of a significantly supportive role in the association. He became Chairman of the Northern Branch of Bol Chumann Na hEireann in 1979 and fulfilled that important function in masterly fashion until standing down in 1993. As Managing Director of Armagh Construction Company Limited, he initiated sponsorship of the prestigious Hall of Fame Award in his first year as Chairman in 1979. That inaugural Award went to James Mackle (1979) and since then the recipients of the treasured conferral have been Johnny Darragh (1980); Joe Horan (1981); Pat Lyttle (1982); Joe McVeigh (1983); Basil Shields (1984); John Rafferty (1985); Monsignor Raymond Murray (1986); Paul Feighan (1987); Michael Toal (1988); Andy Mallon (1989); Paddy Comiskey (1990); Jack Ryan (1991); Danny Reilly (1992); Danny McParland (1993); Mick Reilly (1994); Eamon Mallon (1995).

In his fourteen years as Chairman, and many more in a deputy role before that, John Gribben immersed himself in every aspect of the game that had even the slightest potential for positive outcomes. His role was not easy nor was his period in office the most buoyant for the sport. There were times when even the very continuation of the All Ireland Championship series was in jeopardy during the prolongated period when Munster champions were reluctant to travel north. John Gribben exercised his conciliatory management skills to nurture the sport through all those difficult times and restored the organisation and its traditional game to a position of flourishing resurgence before leaving office. All three long serving officers, John Gribben, Aidan McVeigh and Paddy Comiskey retired from their posts in 1993 and later that year were honoured with awards in recognition of their extended term in office. The incoming officers to the Northern Branch, An Bol Chumann Na hEireann, George Smith, Chairman; Donald Gribben, Honorary Secretary; and Sean Gordon, Treasurer, have combined as an effective force in maintaining continuity within the organisation and ensuring efficient co-ordination of the ever increasing and demanding business. The new Executive has been particularly successful in gaining major sponsorship as evidenced in the efficiently managed International Bowling event at Armagh in 1994 and more recently with the announcement of very significant and ongoing financial backing from Philip White Tyres Limited and Falken. Despite the magnitude of transformation the officers of the new Executive, since taking up post in 1993, have been most energetic and progressive in their organisation and promotion of the sport at all levels.

The series of dedicated administrators who, between them, have spanned the period since Bol Chumann Na N Eireann was founded in 1954 have contributed immensely to the evolution of road bowling in Ireland and elsewhere. But each of them would have readily admitted the essential nature of the constant work undertaken by committed members at Club level on whom rests the real foundations of the sport.

BOL CHUMANN NA hEIREANN - MUNSTER OFFICERS

Period	Chairman	Honorary Secretary	Honorary Treasurer
1954 - 1958	Flor Crowley	Eamon O'Carroll	Hugh O'Neill
1958 - 1968	Flor Crowley	Eamon O'Carroll	Denis McSweeney
1968 - 1970	Flor Crowley	Eamon O'Carroll	Jerry Keating
1970 - 1974	Flor Crowley	Eamon O'Carroll	Brendan Roche
1974 - 1977	Flor Crowley	Brendan Roche	Brendan Roche
1977 - 1980	Flor Crowley	Brendan Roche	Jerry Desmond
1980 - 1990	Brendan Roche	Padraig Crowley	Jerry Desmond
1990 - 1991	Brendan Roche	Seamus O'Tuama	Jerry Desmond
1991 - 1992	Jerry Desmond	Seamus O'Tuama	John O'Donovan
1992 - 1994	Jerry Desmond	Christy Santry	John O'Donovan
1994 - 1996	Jerry Desmond	Tim O'Regan	John O'Donovan

BOL CHUMANN NA hEIREANN - ULSTER OFFICERS

1963 - 1964	Joe Horan	Brian Toal	Henry Neary
1964 - 1966	Henry Neary	Brian Toal	Tom McGleenan
1966 - 1967	Henry Neary	Brian Toal	Dan McParland
1967 - 1968	Dick Burke	Brian Toal	Gerry Donnelly
1968 - 1970	Dick Burke	Joe Duffy	Gerry Donnelly
1970 - 1971	Joe Horan	Joe Duffy	Gerry Donnelly
1971 - 1972	Joe Horan	Sean Cullen	Gerry Donnelly
1972 - 1975	Joe Horan	Paddy Comiskey	Gerry Donnelly
1975 - 1978	Joe Horan	Aidan McVeigh	Dan Mackle
1978 - 1979	Joe Horan	Aidan McVeigh	Malachy Quigley / Pat Toal
1979 - 1993	John Gribben	Aidan McVeigh	Paddy Comiskey
1993 - 1996	George Smith	Donald Gribben	Sean Gordon

A Consistent Sponsor

Philip White, Managing Director of Philip White Tyres Limited, with Bol Chumann Officials, following confirmation of the firms intention to sponsor the book, Road Bowling in Ireland. Philip White (second from right) has been a major sponsor for the sport of road bowls over many years. The further financial backing for the book, which provides a comprehensive and accurate account of road bowling over more than half a century, is in addition to a commitment by Philip White Tyres to continue supporting the All-Ireland Bowling Championships as well as a special promotion in 1996 for under age players. Pictured with Philip White are the Executive Officers of the Ulster branch of Bol Chumann na hEireann, (from left) Donald Gribben, Honorary Secretary; George Smith, Chairman; and Sean Gordon, Honorary Treasurer.

Photo: Ian Maginess.

The All-Ireland Champions

BOY'S UNDER 14 CHAMPIONSHIP

YEAR	WINNER	FINALIST	VENUE
1982	Martin Murphy	Terence Rafferty	Ballyshonin
1983	Michael Crowley	Michael Toal	Ballyshonin
1984	Mark McSorley	Brendan Moynihan	Armagh
1985	Peter O'Riordan	Liam Gribben	Whitechurch
1986	Damien Rock	William O'Driscoll	Armagh
1987	Michael Rafferty	Christy Buckley	Whitechurch
1988	Donal O'Riordan	Paul Druse	Tassagh
1989	Raymond Greene	Gerard Murray	Bauravilla
1990	Paul Rafferty	Alan O'Shea	Armagh
1991	Barry Hughes	Peter Nagle	Ballingeary
1992	Peter Nagle	Eoin Carragher	Armagh
1993	Philip McKeever	Raymond O'Dwyer	Ballingeary
1994	Paul O'Rourke	Matthew Grimley	Armagh
1995	Adrian Lappin	Tim Young	Dunderrow

BOY'S UNDER 16 CHAMPIONSHIP

YEAR	WINNER	FINALIST	VENUE
1967	Adrian Mallon	Denis Santry	Armagh
1968	Michael O'Donovan	Thomas Moore	Grenagh
1969	Eamon Bowen	John Cromie	Armagh
1970	Jim O'Driscoll	Patrick Comiskey	Ballyshonin
1971	Patrick Comiskey	Jim Twomey	Armagh
1972	John Carroll	Harry Toal (Jun)	Dublin Hill
1973	Jim O'Driscoll	Malachy Comiskey	Castleblayney
1974	Malachy Comiskey	Andy O'Callaghan	Ballyshonin
1975	Jerry O'Leary	Liam Boylan	Ballyshonin
1976	Willie Collins	Ciaran Toal	Ballyshonin
1977	Liam Boylan	John Hegarty	Ballyshonin
1978	Liam Boylan	John Young	Ballyshonin
1979	Pat Creedon	Philip Rafferty	Blackwatertown
1980	Francis Kiernan	Pat Lawlor	Ballyshonin
1981	Dermot Grimley	Pat Thompson	Armagh

1982	James Buckley	Dominic Donnelly	Ballyshonin
1983	James Buckley	Brian Kiernan	Armagh
1984	Michael Toal	Pat Moynihan	Armagh
1985	Pat McCreesh	Dermot Daly	Whitechurch
1986	Kieran Gould	Brian Kinchin	Armagh
1987	Richard Murphy	Liam Gribben	Whitechurch
1988	John Creedon	Stephen Druse	Tassagh
1989	Michael Rafferty	Vincent Kelly	Bauravilla
1990	Trevor O'Meara	Mark McKeown	Armagh
1991	Gerard Murray	Michael Rock	Ballingeary
1992	Peter Nagle	Paul Rafferty	Armagh
1993	Paul Rafferty	Michael O'Sullivan	Ballingeary
1994	Austin McKeown	Billy McAuliffe	Armagh
1995	Philip McKeever	Pat Spillane	Dunderrow

MEN'S UNDER 18 CHAMPIONSHIP

YEAR	WINNER	FINALIST	VENUE
1971	Jim O'Driscoll	Brendan McIlvenna	Ballyshonin
1972	Paul McQuaid	Dan O'Regan	Armagh
1973	Jim O'Driscoll	Oliver Gribben	Ballyshonin
1974	Harry Toal (Jun)	Jim O'Driscoll	Carrigtwohill
1975	Bill Daly	Stephen Toal	Ballyshonin
1976	John Hurley	Liam Boylan	Ballyshonin
1977	Liam Boylan	Brendan O'Callaghan	Castleblayney
1978	Michael Buckley	Desmond Boylan	Ballyshonin
1979	Pat Bohane	Brian Grimley	Blackwatertown
1980	Dan O'Halloran	Brian Grimley	Ballyshonin
1981	Paul Grimley	Ciaran O'Driscoll	Armagh
1982	Pat Thompson	Philip Rafferty	Ballyshonin
1983	James Buckley	Brian Kiernan	Ballyshonin
1984	James Buckley	Brian Kiernan	Ballyshonin
1985	Michael Toal	Brendan O'Regan	Armagh
1986	Aidan McCreesh	Finbar O'Donovan	Whitechurch
1987	Michael Toal	Michael Wall	Tassagh
1988	Mark McSorley	Mick Carroll	Bauravilla
1989	John Kelly	John Creedon	Tassagh
1990	Donal O'Riordan	Michael Rafferty	Bauravilla
1991	Michael Rafferty	Declan O'Shea	Armagh

1992	Mark McKeown	Trevor O'Meara	Ballingeary
1993	Donnacha O'Brien	Malachy Lappin	Armagh
1994	Conor McGuigan	Donnacha O'Brien	Bandon
1995	Donnacha O'Brien	Dermot Gribben	Armagh

WOMEN'S UNDER 18 CHAMPIONSHIP

YEAR	WINNER	FINALIST	VENUE
1986	Orla Galvin	Michelle McSorley	Armagh
1987	Mary Brady	Bronagh Cullen	Whitechurch
1988	Delia Buckley	Feena Gribben	Tassagh
1989	Geraldine McCluskey	Delia Buckley	Bauravilla
1990	Geraldine McCluskey	Shirley McAuliffe	Armagh
1991	Sharon O'Driscoll	Geraldine McCluskey	Ballingeary
1992	Caitriona Powell	Caitriona O'Rourke	Armagh
1993	Sharon O'Driscoll	Majella Mallon	Ballingeary
1994	Sharon O'Driscoll	Caitriona Powell	Armagh
1995	Kathleen Cooney	Fiona Cullen	Dunderrow

MEN'S JUNIOR 'A' CHAMPIONSHIP

YEAR	WINNER	FINALIST	VENUE
1966	Fachtna O'Donovan	Sean Cullen	Grenagh
1967	Patsy McKenna	Christy Coleman	Knappagh
1968	Mervyn McGregor	Malachy McCreesh	Grenagh
1969	Gerald McKee	Paddy O'Donoghue	Grenagh
1970	Pat Murphy	Colm Grimley	Armagh
1971	Seamus Sexton	Brendan Digby	Ballyshonin
1972	Neilly O'Donoghue	Johnny Mills	Armagh
1973	Joe Twohig	Gerry Boylan	Midleton
1974	Stephen Donnelly	Jack Dan O'Donovan	Ballyshonin
1975	Billy Hurley	Sean Webb	Ballyshonin
1976	Mick Coughlan w/o	Donal Toal	------
1977	Simon Buckley	Paddy McKeown	Castleblaney
1978	Noel O'Brien	Oliver Gribben	Ballyshonin
1979	Joe O'Connor	Paul McVeigh	Blackwatertown

1980	Chris O'Donovan	Martin Kinchin	Ballyshonin
1981	Mick O'Driscoll	Malachy McIlvenna	Armagh
1982	Patsy Coleman	Colm Grimley	Ballyshonin
1983	Paddy O'Leary	James McCann	Ballyshonin
1984	Mick Murphy	Donald Gribben	Ballyshonin
1985	Donie Crowley	Gerald McKee	Armagh
1986	Tom Hayes	Malachy McIlvenna	Whitechurch
1987	Kieran O'Gorman	James McCann	Tassagh
1988	Dan Burke	Martin Boylan	Bauravilla
1989	Noel O'Brien	Fergal McCreesh \ Ted Hegarty	Tassagh
1990	Dan Keneally	Brian Kiernan	Bauravilla
1991	Paul Grimley	Corney Bohane	Armagh
1992	Brian Kinchin	Denis O'Sullivan	Ballingeary
1993	John O'Brien	Paddy O'Neill	Armagh
1994	Philip O'Donovan	Paul Grimley	Bandon
1995	Jim O'Driscoll	Pat Mallon	Armagh

MEN'S JUNIOR 'B' CHAMPIONSHIP

YEAR	WINNER	FINALIST	VENUE
1980	Tom Walsh	Kevin Mackle	Ballyshonin
1981	Anthony O'Neill	Tom McKeever	Armagh
1982	Finbar Doyle	Paul Mills	Ballyshonin
1983	Martin Kinchin	Michael O'Connor	Armagh
1984	Maurice McKenna	Ted Hegarty	Armagh
1985	Tim O'Halloran	Jim Gartland	Whitechurch
1986	John Desmond	Jarlath Devlin	Armagh
1987	John Deasy	Paul McVeigh	Whitechurch
1988	Joe Donnelly	Dan Vaughan	Tassagh
1989	Michael O'Brien	Larry Corr	Bauravilla
1990	John O'Brien	Brendan McIlvenna	Armagh
1991	Michael O'Leary	Shane O'Neill	Armagh
1992	Derry Kenny	Joe Shortt	Armagh
1993	Philip O'Donovan	Nial Smith	Ballingeary
1994	Malachy Lappin	Liam Barry	Armagh
1995	Tim Pat O'Donovan	Johnny Kelly	Dunderrow

MEN'S JUNIOR 'C' CHAMPIONSHIP

YEAR	WINNER	FINALIST	VENUE
1992	Finbar O'Brien	Willie Carroll/Pat Healy	Westport
1993	John O'Donovan	Willie Carroll	Drogheda
1994	Denis Burke	Gerald Brickley	Westport
1995	Pa Ryan	Pat Thompson	Drogheda

MEN'S NOVICE CHAMPIONSHIP

YEAR	WINNER	FINALIST	VENUE
1992	Michael Kennedy	Eamon Crowley	Westport
1993	John Lennon	Peadar Tunney	Drogheda
1994	Johnny Hurley	Tom Kennedy	Westport
1995	Mike Hurley	Gary Shevlin	Drogheda

MEN'S INTERMEDIATE CHAMPIONSHIP

YEAR	WINNER	FINALIST	VENUE
1969	Pat O'Sullivan	Michael Hughes	Ballinadee
1970	Liam Madden	Harry Toal (Sen)	Armagh
1971	Gerald McKee	Mick Sexton	Ballyshonin
1972	Mick O'Driscoll	Harry Toal (Sen)	Blackwatertown
1973	Liam Daly	Al Mallon	Grenagh
1974	Donie Coveney	John Gribben	Carrigtwohill
1975	Donal O'Leary w/o	Harry Toal (Jun)	------
1976	Billy Hurley	Brendan Digby	Ballyshonin
1977	Corney Bohane	Pat Mallon	Castleblayney
1978	Declan O'Donovan	Harry Toal (Sen)	Ballyshonin
1979	Christy O'Driscoll	Al Mallon	Blackwatertown
1980	Pat McCarthy	Sean Webb	Ballyshonin
1981	Tim O'Halloran	Martin Boylan	Armagh
1982	Pat Mallon	John Murphy	Ballyshonin
1983	Pat Murphy	Aidan Toal	Ballyshonin
1984	Neilus Hurley	Martin Boylan	Armagh
1985	Michael O'Driscoll	Patrick Comiskey	Armagh
1986	John O'Driscoll	Donald Gribben	Whitechurch

1987	John Creedon	Pat Mallon	Tassagh
1988	Denis Scully	James McCann	Skibbereen
1989	James Buckley	Harry Toal (Jun)	Tassagh
1990	James O'Sullivan	Paddy O'Neill	Skibbereen
1991	Paddy O'Leary	Harry Toal	Armagh
1992	Tim O'Halloran	Harry Toal	Ballingeary
1993	Michael Gould	Brian Kinchin	Armagh
1994	Paul Rafferty	Andrew O'Leary	Armagh
1995	James O'Sullivan	Brian Kiernan	Dunderrow

WOMEN'S SENIOR CHAMPIONSHIP

YEAR	WINNER	FINALIST	VENUE
1981	Joan Shannon	Bernie Dynes	Armagh
1982	Gretta Hegarty	Rosheen Toal	Ballyshonin
1983	Gretta Hegarty	Rosheen Toal	Armagh
1984	Agnes Hurley	Rosheen Toal	Ballyshonin
1985	Rosheen Toal	Gretta Hegarty	Armagh
1986	Joan Shannon	Rosheen Toal	Whitechurch
1987	Gretta Hegarty	Assumpta Cullen	Tassagh
1988	Joan Savage	Assumpta Cullen	Bauravilla
1989	Gretta Cormican (Hegarty)	Assumpta Cullen	Tassagh
1990	Sandra Dempsey	Rosheen Mackle (Toal)	Bauravilla
1991	Rosheen Mackle	Mary Brady	Armagh
1992	Geraldine McCluskey	Sharon O'Driscoll	Ballingeary
1993	Sharon O'Driscoll	Paula Gillespie	Armagh
1994	Gretta Cormican	Geraldine McCluskey	Bandon
1995	Agnes O'Gorman	Susan Cullen	Armagh

MEN'S SENIOR CHAMPIONSHIP

YEAR	WINNER	FINALIST	VENUE
1963	Danny McParland	Derry Kenny	Armagh-Moy
1964	Danny McParland	Mick Barry	Dublin Hill

1965	Mick Barry	Danny McParland	Armagh-Keady
1966	Mick Barry	Danny McParland	Kilpatrick
1967	Mick Barry	Aidan Toal	Knappagh-Armagh
1968	John Creedon	Danny McParland	Nadd-Cork
1969	Mick Barry	Aidan Toal	Armagh
1970	Mick Barry	Danny McParland	Ballyshonin
1971	Danny McParland	Mick Barry	Eglish-Tyrone
1972	Mick Barry w/o	Danny McParland	------
1973	Denis Scully	Harry Toal (Sen)	Ballyshonin
1974	Mick Barry	Harry Toal (Sen)	Ballyshonin
1975	Mick Barry	John Gribben	Ballyshonin
1976	Danny McParland	Michael O'Driscoll	Ballyshonin
1977	Harry Toal (Jun)	Denis Scully	Castleblaney
1978	Pat Butler	Pat Mallon	Ballyshonin
1979	Pat Mallon	John Creedon	Blackwatertown
1980	Gerry Boylan	Dermot O'Sullivan	Ballyshonin
1981	Harry Toal (Jun)	Seamus Sexton	Armagh
1982	Donie Coveney	Harry Toal (Jun)	Ballyshonin
1983	Michael Buckley	Harry Toal (Jun)	Armagh
1984	Bill Daly	Aidan Toal	Ballyshonin
1985	Harry Toal (Jun)	Bill Daly	Whitechurch
1986	Declan O'Donovan	Aidan Toal	Armagh
1987	Seamus Sexton	Gerry Boylan	Whitechurch
1988	Michael Toal	Michael O'Driscoll	Tassagh
1989	Michael Toal	Declan O'Donovan	Bauravilla
1990	Pat Butler	Harry Toal (Jun)	Armagh
1991	Michael Toal	Bill Daly	Ballingeary
1992	Pat Butler	Paul Grimley	Armagh
1993	Pat Butler	Michael Toal	Ballingeary
1994	Michael Toal	Bill Daly	Bandon
1995	James Buckley	Michael Toal	Armagh

MEN'S VETERAN CHAMPIONSHIP

YEAR	WINNER	FINALIST	VENUE
1990	John Crowley	Harry Toal (Sen)	Bauravilla
1991	Tom Collins	Harry Toal (Sen)	Armagh
1992	Derry Kenny	Willie Carroll/Tommy Quinn	Ballingeary
1993	Denis Collins	Harry Toal (Sen)/Willie Carroll	Armagh
1994	Percy Deane	Willie Carroll/Harry Toal	Bandon
1995	Gerald Burke	Willie Carroll/Jim Cullen	Armagh

BIBLIOGRAPHY

BLUETT, ANTHONY. (1994) Things Irish. Mercier Press, Cork.

CASEY, JEROME. (1995) Bowling Down London Way. Betterlith Ltd, Essex.

HICKS, DERMOT. (1973) Road Bowls in Armagh. Armagh History.

MARCUS, DAVID. (1995) Irish Sporting Short Stories. Appletree Press, Belfast.

MURRAY, FR RAYMOND. (1976) The Armagh Bullet Thrower. Armagh History.

TOAL, BRIAN. (1966) Bowling the Armagh Way. Ulster Games Annual, Howard Publications, Belfast.

VALLELY, EITHNE. (1993) Jackets on the Grass Verge. Causeway Vol. 1 No. 1 September 1993. Belfast.

NEWSPAPER SOURCES

Armagh Observer, 1954 - 1961, 1963 - 1995;
Belfast Telegraph, 1994 - 1995;
Cork Examiner, 1970 - 1995;
Evening Echo, 1964, 1967, 1980;
Independent, 1993;
Irish News, 1986, 1988 - 1994;
Irish Press, 1964;
Irish Times, 1982;
Irish World, 1990 - 1991;
Kerryman 1964;
Southern Star, 1964, 1973, 1980, 1984, 1990 - 1992, 1995;
Sunday Times, 1985;
Times, 1992;
Tyrone Democrat, 1967 - 1968;
Ulster Gazette, 1968, 1995.